English Interludes

English Interludes

Mallarmé, Verlaine, Paul Valéry,
Valery Larbaud in England, 1860–1912

Cecily Mackworth

London and Boston
Routledge & Kegan Paul

First published in 1974
by Routledge & Kegan Paul Ltd
Broadway House, 68–74 Carter Lane,
London EC4V 5EL and
9 Park Street,
Boston, Mass. 02108, U.S.A.
Set in Monotype Bembo type
and printed in Great Britain by
W & J Mackay Limited, Chatham
© *Cecily Mackworth 1974*
No part of this book may be reproduced in
any form without permission from the
publisher, except for the quotation of brief
passages in criticism

ISBN 0 7100 7878 1

Contents

Plates

Preface

The four poets discussed in these studies discovered England during the fifty years from 1862 up to the eve of the Great War—that is to say, at a period when great changes were taking place in Anglo-French relationships and especially between the intellectuals of the two countries. Each of these men was marked indelibly in his life and his work by an early contact with England and it is for this reason that I have omitted Rimbaud, who might seem an obvious choice but who came to England at the end, not the beginning, of his career as a poet. On the other hand, I have included Valery Larbaud, who is less widely known in France than Mallarmé, Verlaine or Paul Valéry, and hardly known at all in England. Alone of the four he was a novelist as well as a poet, and he is something of a writer for connoisseurs, but those connoisseurs place him among the greatest of their contemporaries. 'I love Valery Larbaud as I love Catullus or Propertius', said André Maurois; Emile Henriot thought that no one better deserved the Nobel Prize, and Roger Martin du Gard wrote: 'I love his work and do not believe time can threaten it, because Larbaud's originality is fundamental, genuine.' England, even more than Spain or Italy, formed that great Cosmopolitan and few foreign writers have observed her cities and countryside with such close and loving attention.

One chapter deals with the visits to London and Oxford of Mallarmé and Verlaine, when their fame was already established. I have included it because these two visits illustrate, better than any commentary could do, the immense changes that took place in English intellectual attitudes during the last quarter of the century.

My thanks are specially due to Monsieur François Chapon and the staff of the Bibliothèque Doucet, for their unfailing help and kindness; to Professor Barbier of Edinburgh University for so generously sharing some of his vast knowledge of Mallarmé; to Madame Roman-Maspero for details concerning Ettie Yapp; to Mrs Jean Bunker, for kind information about her grandfather, Mr Andrews, for whom Verlaine worked in Stickney; to Madame Agathe Valéry-Rouart, for allowing me access to her archives; to Mademoiselle Monique Kunz, curator, Fonds Valery Larbaud, Vichy; to the late Dr Enid Starkie for suggestions concerning the visits of Mallarmé and Verlaine to Oxford.

1

'Honeyed Poison'

England, seen from across any one of her surrounding seas, has always had a quality of remoteness that has nothing to do with measurable distance. Bewilderment sets in at Southampton, Newhaven, Dover, and deepens with the startling approaches to London. How far the capital is still the fiercely uncompromising citadel of a peculiar, island-reared attitude of mind, is a question of personal sensibilities; how long she will remain so, a matter for conjecture. Poets, in so far as they are romantics, tend to be stunned by differences rather than lulled by resemblances. For Apollinaire, the red-brick banality of the suburbs became 'wounds bleeding in the fog'; Rimbaud watched from his window 'unknown phantoms rolling through dense and eternal coal-dust'; Paul Valéry saw London as 'black, red and white, with flashes of crystal and immense green expanses'. And the London of Henry James, the unyielding London of mid-Victorian days, changed only imperceptibly in spite of all superficial upheavals, as the century crept towards its close. It remained as he knew it, and perhaps remains today:

> too indifferent, too proud, too unaware, too stupid even if one will, to enter any lists that involved her moving from her base. . . . She didn't emulate, so she practised her own arts altogether, and both these ways and their consequences were in the flattest opposition to foreign felicities or foreign standards.

Perhaps it was just this refusal on the part of nineteenth-century London to yield anything of herself, that forced visiting artists, novelists, poets, to react so violently with love or hatred, stimulated sometimes, it seems, almost to frenzy by the evident fact that England and the English did not care whether they were loved or hated. The British were at that time sure of their superiority, certain that Progress was sweeping them onward with the world in their wake, towards a universal well-being, the nature of which was not perhaps very clearly defined, but which existed as a certain and soon-obtainable goal. 'The wheel of time is rolling for an end and . . . the world in all great essentials gets better, gentler, more forebearing and more hopeful as it rolls', wrote Dickens with typical optimism.[1]

Foreigners might, and did, bring back lurid stories about tremendous inequalities of fortune, appalling lack of hygiene in the poorer quarters, drunken men and women sprawling in the gutters ('For such worn-out, overworked creatures there is but one refuge: drunkenness', observed Taine[2]), the insecurity of whole areas where the police themselves refused to venture; they might complain of English hypocrisy, the frightful dullness of Sundays, the Bibles chained on lecterns in every railway station, the parks open only to those 'decently attired', the climate, the drinking laws, the heavy food that upset their stomachs and the general philistinism. It did not matter. They were foreigners, and the general idea of 'lesser breeds without the law', existed long before Kipling expressed it with his usual concision.

There was one kind of foreigner, however, towards whom indifference was tinged with uneasy hostility. These were the French, for Franco-British relations were at a particularly low ebb during the mid-Victorian era. It is amazing now to see how firmly and on how little evidence the British believed in Napoleon III's expansionist schemes. The newspapers were full of the threat to our coasts and worried citizens wrote to *The Times* or the *Daily News*, urging 'earthworks and batteries at chief landing places', 'enlargement of naval reserves', 'completion of the Militia' and other urgent measures. A volunteer corps was indeed formed and in 1861 Louis Blanc noted that,[3]

> It is curious to see the juvenile ardour with which this serious-minded people plays at soldiers in the midst of peace. Lawyers, doctors, shop-keepers, errand boys, and goodness knows what else, stand ready to rush to war and want to learn the best way of killing. . . . The English, though they won't admit it even to themselves, are tormented by a spectre named Invasion. They might almost like us if they did not believe us to be infected, as if with an incurable disease, by a passion for expansion. Why is it that France and England should be more effectively separated by suspicion than by the Channel?

But suspicion was not directed only at French politics. There was also the question of French morals, which threatened a different but equally redoubtable kind of invasion. France was synonymous in middle-class English minds with frivolity, atheism and licentiousness. Paris especially was considered a centre of fascinating vice. 'Paris is more immeasurably wicked than ever', wrote Dickens to his friend

Wilkie Collins on 29 January 1863. '"Long live the devil!" seems to be the motto.' This, it should be remarked, did not prevent him from crossing the Channel on every possible occasion to refresh himself in a bath of this delightful wickedness. More austere characters, or those with less freedom of movement, preferred to ignore the French and all their doings.

Literary society—'rich, plain, proud, polite and admirable' as visiting Emerson called it—tended to reflect and give form to the general trend of bourgeois thinking. Its great figures—Carlyle, Macaulay, Dickens, Tennyson—were also National Examples, respected less for their aesthetic qualities than for the soundness of their views on Protestantism or social progress. Few of the mid-Victorians bothered with contemporary French literature and most of them held it in deep suspicion.[4] The cosmopolitan Brownings did indeed read and discuss George Sand, Balzac and Alexandre Dumas and, as early as 1845, Elizabeth Barrett had written to her friend Miss Mitford that she had read Stendhal's *Le Rouge et le Noir*—a fact which, she added, 'I should not dare to name to a person in the world except you.' Carlyle, who considered all contemporary French writing 'a jingling of formulas', occasionally wrote a ponderous article, on some serious French book, usually because it gave him an excuse to discuss atheism in France or to explain how that unhappy country's unstable social system condemned her to perpetual revolution. As for Tennyson, whose 'strident anti-Gallic cackle' so annoyed Swinburne, he was deeply suspicious of all things French. War, for him, was 'this French God, this child of Hell', and he was quick to denounce any indication that 'the honeyed poison from France' was seeping into English literature.[5] Ford Madox Brown and the Pre-Raphaelite poets and painters were less virulent, but they preferred the decent, industrious Germans, whose example Carlyle so often held up to the country, and even Meredith, who became so frenchified in later life, thought Victor Hugo admirable 'when he forgot to be French'. Only Swinburne, still practically unknown outside a coterie of admiring friends, dared to brave public opinion and write a long, enthusiastic article on *Les Fleurs du Mal* in the *Spectator*. 'It required high intellectual courage', noted Edmund Gosse, who was a young man at the time, 'to champion in an English periodical the merits of any new volume of French verse, not to speak of such a volume as *Les Fleurs du Mal*. England had not yet emerged from its long attack of podsnappery, and there was hardly a critic of authority who dared to advance the claims of French poetry.'[6]

Public events and public policy subsequently modified and sometimes even reversed this attitude as far as sophisticated or intellectual circles were concerned, but it remained for a long time unchanged among the middle classes and the masses. It was against this background that the French poets considered in the following chapters experienced London. The surprising thing is that they all, in greater or less degree, fell in love with the city.

2

The Young Mallarmé

The French Quarter

It must have been partly due to the mutual distrust and even dislike between France and England that Soho in the mid-nineteenth century remained so strangely remote from the rest of London. It was the foreign quarter, following its own customs and living its own life, so little frequented by the English, says a contemporary, that if an Englishman happened to stray into one of the little restaurants in the back streets around Soho Square, all heads would be raised in surprise. A good many Italian and German *émigrés* had arrived there about the middle of the century, mostly to work as cooks and waiters, and there were Greeks, Hungarians, representatives of practically all the European nations, crowding together in gloomy tenements that had once been the dwellings of the nobility. Yet it was the French who formed the largest and most stable community, so that when Cardinal Wiseman was casting about for a site for a church to group the French Catholics of London, he found it natural to choose one in Soho.[1]

This tradition of Soho as the 'French quarter' of London, goes back at least to the fourteenth century, and by 1739, we find a chronicler writing of the parishes of St Martin and St Anne, 'Many Parts of these Parishes so greatly abound with French that it is an easy Matter for a Stranger to imagine himself in France.' He added that at least eight hundred Frenchmen had bought or built themselves houses in the neighbourhood.

A good proportion of these early residents were Huguenot refugees and many of their descendants were still living in the quarter in the nineteenth century. By the 1860s, however, they had been somewhat swamped by other *émigrés*, thrown up on the English shores by successive waves of upheaval and revolution in their own land. The new arrivals were generally republicans, for whom Napoleon III—known in these circles by a variety of unkind nicknames—was the arch-enemy. They were given to writing angry letters to *The Times*, and to founding ephemeral newspapers and semi-secret societies which always broke up rapidly after bitter internecine quarrelling. They disliked England, which they tended to see through the eyes of Ledru-Rollin rather than their own, and they made little attempt to attract sympathy.

In the course of time, some of the French of Soho had set up their own establishments. A few of these had become prosperous and were well known to Londoners, but most of them were modest little places, catering purely for their compatriots. There were numerous shops where French groceries could be bought, agencies 'for the placing of professors of both sexes', and French coffee houses trying to imitate the cafés at home, but resentfully subject to the Lord's Day Observance laws. The hotel-restaurant, La Sablonnière, which advertised itself as 'a French house, where a table d'hôte affords lovers of French cooking and French conversation an opportunity for gratification at a comparatively moderate cost', was the only establishment of this sort to be frequented by a few Englishmen. It had been discovered by the Pre-Raphaelites, who enjoyed flouting public opinion, and Rossetti and Swinburne had dined there on the fatal night of 'Lizzie's' death.[2]

The tradesmen who had built up their own businesses were at the top of the Soho social scale. Then there were innumerable language teachers, governesses, little dressmakers, cooks, actors, music teachers and 'vocalists'. Many of them lived permanently in cheap lodging houses, and the poorest were succoured by the 'French Benevolent Society', which, under the patronage of the ambassador, Comte Flahaut, organised fine charity balls in the elegant quarters around Knightsbridge where there was much coming and going to and from the Tuileries.

Certain back streets of Soho thus curiously resembled those of a small French town, of some northern *chef-lieu* perhaps, where everybody knows everyone else, where housewives hurry along the pavement clutching long loaves and bottles of wine, while their men play endless games of *manille* in the cafés. It was an introverted, incurious life, resentful of the few concessions it was forced to make to Anglo-Saxon habits and, in fact, Henry James's remarks about London might almost have applied in a different, indeed contrary, context, to this little corner of France re-created by her expatriates.

Panton Square[3] lay just off Coventry Street, being bounded on one side by Windmill Street, on the other by Rupert Street. It was typical of the strange contrasts presented by the quarter at that period; only a few steps away there was the turmoil of Leicester Square, with its dubious pleasure haunts, its illegal boxing matches and the extraordinary riff-raff that gave it the reputation of being one of the worst spots in London, 'a gulf of vice where souls are destroyed',[4] so that a group of French Protestants found it necessary to organise a 'Society for the

Protection of the Morals of the French of Leicester Square'.

Here, each evening as dusk began to fall, a whole army of prostitutes, ponces, prize-ring touts, purveyors of children and doubtful virgins, travestis in 'drag', beggars and con-men, jostled opera-hatted swells from the West End, come to take their choice among the expensive women at Kate Hamilton's in Prince's Street or in the Portland Rooms. The cabarets openly advertised 'beds'. The soup kitchen in the Square brought starving wrecks from horrible alleys where the police themselves refused to venture.

The French were numerous and noticeable in the Square, but they were not the quiet, decent citizens of the back streets. Until 1840, the Aliens Office had exercised a strict control over foreigners entering the country, but twenty years later it had been more or less swamped by the flood of immigrants from Europe. Overworked officials contented themselves nowadays with asking the new arrival the reason for his journey and handing him a certificate to be returned to the Customs Office on re-embarking. Thus there drifted to the Square a seething, ever-changing population, composed of deserters from the Army, sailors without ships, refugees from justice, prostitutes shipped over the Channel to profit from the legend of the extraordinary talents shown by 'French girls' (a thriving trade this, which no legal repression had been able to curb), embittered incapables who dreamed of making a fortune without working for it—a miserable, floating population which, because it was conspicuous, confirmed the comfortable belief that vice was a foreign importation.

As for Windmill Street, opening just off the square, it was perhaps the worst spot of all. Here was Laurent's Dancing Academy, where the cheaper type of prostitute paraded; there were the notorious Argyll Rooms; and the Black Bull, noted as one of the most squalid and dangerous taverns in town. Rupert Street was little better, so it must have made a strange impression to step out into Panton Square, wedged between these two turbulent off-shoots of Leicester Square, yet itself as quiet and respectable as any place one could find in London. At one end there was a small garden, planted with rather sickly trees, and most of the narrow, dingy houses let furnished rooms, which were chiefly inhabited by French families. One might easily have supposed oneself to be in some quiet provincial spot in an undefined borderland that was neither quite France nor quite England.

It was here that a very young couple arrived on the evening of 8 November 1862. They were exhausted after a terribly rough crossing from Boulogne in the extraordinary kind of boat, consisting of two hulls joined together, which then and for many years after carried travellers across the Channel. The young man was still almost a boy, small and very slight, with thick, wavy dark hair, large dark eyes and peculiar satyr-like ears—big, long and pointed. He was accompanied by a thin, fair-haired girl, a little older than himself, with a curiously wide, tight-lipped mouth, that suggested suffering, or obstinacy or extreme reserve. Their room at No. 9—a house belonging to a Mr William Grinn—was taken in the name of Monsieur and Madame Mallarmé, and for the next two months they could occasionally be observed slipping out for a walk or watching from an open window. Wrapped up in themselves, they seem to have had no dealings with their neighbours and to have made no friends. They could speak hardly any English and had their own reasons for avoiding their compatriots. They were quiet, decent and withdrawn, and did nothing to attract anyone's attention.

Many years later, on the one and only occasion when he allowed anything concerning his private life to be published, Stéphane Mallarmé wrote to his friend Verlaine: 'Having learned English simply in order to read Poe, I left for England at the age of twenty, chiefly in order to escape, but also to learn to speak the language and teach it in some quiet spot; I had married and this had become urgent.'[5]

Things were not really so simple. The girl who accompanied him was not in fact his wife (and it was probably for this reason that they had chosen a district where landlords would not insist on seeing their 'marriage lines'), and although Mallarmé did indeed learn a certain amount of English during the year he stayed in London, this period had a far more dramatic significance for him than he admitted to Verlaine. The spiritual crisis he went through during those months of exile was in fact quite as acute as that which showy, tumultuous Rimbaud was to experience ten years later, and when it culminated in 'Les Fenêtres', the poem manifested a mental explosion as violent as that which produced parts of Rimbaud's *Les Illuminations*. But no two natures could have been more opposed. Mallarmé, all subtlety and discretion, could never have been drawn into the 'orgiaque misère'[6] of the Rimbaud-Verlaine couple. His own tragedy was to be a silent one, hidden and inescapably solitary, since its only witness was the uncomprehending girl who lived beside him and the single, absent friend to whom he confided his misery in almost daily letters.

A Smell of Cooking

In order to understand all that lay behind the apparently simple statement in the 'autobiographical letter', we must go back to the beginning of the year and to Sens in the department of the Yonne, in central France. Mallarmé called it 'this desert of Sens' and said that it was so gloomy that everything that happened there seemed grey. In reality, it was a charming little town surrounded by ancient ramparts, where fine seventeenth-century houses clustered round a splendid early Gothic cathedral and the river Yonne meandered quietly through the centre. Today Sens has expanded, becoming a thriving industrial city, but the old town has changed little since Mallarmé's father settled there after the death of his first wife and his own rather too hasty remarriage, leaving his two young children in the care of their maternal grandparents in Neuilly.

The Mallarmés came of a long line of those conscientious, unambitious, tradition-bound civil servants who formed the backbone of nineteenth-century France, and it had been taken for granted that Stéphane would follow in their footsteps. He had been a lonely child, and a mildly rebellious one. Monsieur and Madame Desmolins were excellent people, rigidly pious and determined to bring up their charges to be 'worthy of their dear mother', but they do not seem to have understood children, or even tried to do so. Stéphane had been educated from the age of ten in a series of boarding schools where his record had always been undistinguished. His grandmother reported him to be insincere, hard-hearted and over-pleased with himself, but it does not seem to have occurred to her that he might be lonely and unhappy. In fact, he seems to have suffered deeply from lack of affection. Happiness came only in the too brief holidays when he could be with his little sister, Maria, whom he loved tenderly. Then, when he was fifteen, Maria died suddenly after a short illness. It was the great traumatic experience of his life—one of those experiences that can wreck an existence or set it off on a new path where misery is sublimated in creation.

By this time he had become a boarder in the *lycée* at Sens and was getting acquainted with his family in the town, consisting of his now half-paralysed father, a step-mother harassed by poverty and a brood of young step-brothers and sisters. Stéphane detested the thrifty, unimaginative atmosphere in this new home, and consoled himself by scribbling poems in a series of little notebooks that were regularly confiscated by his masters. The poems must have made them even more doubtful of his character, for they betrayed an illicit familiarity with the works of Baudelaire. The first edition of *Les Fleurs du Mal* had indeed appeared in 1857 and had been promptly banned, but not before it had gone the rounds of the *lycées* and set innumerable schoolboys writing darkling sonnets in the manner of 'Une Charogne'.

Altogether, everyone must have been relieved when the boy at last passed his *baccalauréat* and could be articled to the local registrar.

Mallarmé hated the job desperately. It devoured, he wrote to his grandmother, 'not only oneself, but one's time with it'. Sens, his home, the prospect of a lifetime of respectable mediocrity—all this seemed intolerable and above all, lacking in escape avenues, in the unexpected, the larger-than-life, in fact, in the 'étonnement' Baudelaire demanded from life and art.

So he turned again to *Les Fleurs du Mal*. A new edition appeared in 1861, just at the right moment. Then, at about the same time, he seems to have discovered Poe's *Philosophy of Composition*,[7] which was to have so violent an effect on him, and such a lasting influence on his own work. Already, as a schoolboy, he had been fascinated by the translated stories from Poe's *Tales of Mystery and Imagination* that appeared fairly frequently in various literary reviews, and 'The Raven' had struck him—as it did so many contemporary French poets—as a supreme work of art. Now he began to think of translating other poems himself and set about trying to procure them from various friends. To some extent, Poe really did provide a motive for a visit to England, but above all, Mallarmé was confirmed by Poe and Baudelaire in his horror at the prospect of an existence from which all 'étonnement' would be eliminated.

He was obsessed now by a longing for escape, and casting about for a means which would not too greatly dismay his family, he conceived the idea of becoming a teacher of English. Though he had absolutely no inclination towards teaching as such, he thought it might be a door opening out of his prison on to a prospect of freedom. He had noticed that it was a profession which offered a good deal of leisure; an ambitious and talented young man, such as he knew himself to be, might therefore continue his studies and end by obtaining a doctorate. From that point, a ready imagination winged him onward. Already he saw himself a professor at some university, launched on a career which carried with it a good deal of prestige and in which, as he explained to his suspicious and recalcitrant grandmother, he could 'at least be sure of being left in peace'.

The Desmolins hesitated, reminding their ward of delicate health and a tendency to laziness, and finally gave in with such bad grace that he would almost have preferred a refusal. The row broke out again over the question of a stay in England, without which, it now appeared, he could not hope to pass his examination. Back by return post came accusations of duplicity and bad faith. The grandparents suspected the journey to be an excuse for escaping from their supervision. Nor were they altogether wrong, since Stéphane was writing about the same time to his friend Cazalis, 'It is partly to escape from this stifling and sordid atmosphere that I mean to take flight to London next January.'

Meanwhile, two friends were beginning to play an important part in his life. Emmanuel des Essarts was a master at the local *lycée*, five years older than himself and regarded by Stéphane as a tremendous man of the world. Henri Cazalis[8] was a law student, living at the time in Paris. All three were poets; all three were enthralled by Hugo, Gautier, Baudelaire, and imitated them enthusiastically. They believed in each other's genius, shed tears of emotion as they read each other's poems, and exchanged an endless stream of those long, sentimental, bantering and curiously childish letters young men used to write in those days. Both des Essarts and Cazalis contributed to several of the little magazines that abounded in Paris and the provinces, and through them Mallarmé began to publish occasional poems or critical articles in *L'Artiste*, *Papillon*, *Le Senonais* and so on.

Already he was certain of his vocation and even, it seems, precociously aware of the general direction it would take. Already he thought of art as esoteric religion, to a knowledge of which a few initiates might attain by a total dedication of their lives to its service. 'All sacred things are enveloped in mystery,' he wrote in his first published article. 'Religions hide in the shelter of secrets that are unveiled only to the predestined: Art has its own secrets.'[9] Already he knew himself to be one of these 'predestined' initiates who reach glory through the sacrifice of their lives to an ideal. It was an exalting belief, yet it could not entirely satisfy a boy of twenty, especially one as emotionally deprived as himself. By this time, Stéphane was not entirely ignorant of women. There had been, if we are to believe two very early poems,[10] a platonic passion for a young English girl in Neuilly, and from the age of fifteen—Baudelaire *obligens*—he had occasionally frequented prostitutes and even managed to pass a whole night with a certain Emily. None of these experiences seems to have taught him much about love, but it was love he longed for. Lonely and haunted by memories of his dead mother and sister, he dreamed of discovering some creature of superhuman beauty and purity who would be for him mother, sister and lover, united in one impossibly perfect girl. In fact, he needed to incarnate an ideal, and an occasion presented itself in May 1862, when he and des Essarts joined Cazalis for a brief stay in Paris.

Cazalis frequented an international set of respectably bohemian, artistically inclined young people, and one day a number of them set out for a picnic in the forest of Fontainebleau. The party was chaperoned by Madame Gaillard, a rather eccentric lady who kept a literary salon, and by Mrs Yapp, wife of the Paris correspondent of the *Daily Telegraph*. These two were accompanied by their daughters, Nina Gaillard, who was later to become one of the leading muses of literary Paris, and the Yapp sisters, Kate and Harriet,[11] described by a contemporary memorialist as 'the purest type of the beauty of the most beautiful English girls'.[12] Then there was a certain Miss Mary, Henri Regnault, a talented young painter and several other lively, unconventional young men. Stéphane was entranced with them all and enjoyed himself as he had probably never done in his life before. The girls flattered him, the ladies found him charming and begged for verses to commemorate the occasion. The young people raced among the rocks, carefree and uninhibited, enjoying themselves so much that they hardly noticed an obstinately grey sky. It was a memorable day that seems to have made a lasting impression on all those who took part in it. For Stéphane, used to the stuffy restrictions of his petit-bourgeois relatives, it was like a taste of paradise, and he noted that, 'Decidedly, English girls are adorable.'

Cazalis evidently shared this view, for soon after he confided in his friend that he was desperately in love with 'Ettie' Yapp.

From the correspondence which followed, it seems clear that Stéphane himself had been deeply moved by Ettie and had glimpsed in her the ideal he was seeking. Cazalis's letter forced him to make a hasty adjustment of his own feelings. Perhaps it even suited him, at this stage of his emotional development, to worship her from afar, as the property of his dearest friend, rather than make an attempt to claim her for himself as a real woman with all the implications of that reality. It is significant, in any case, that he began from this moment to address Henri as 'Brother', while Ettie became quite naturally 'our sister'.[13]

> She will take her place in my dreams beside Chimène, Beatrice, Juliet, Régine and, better still, in my heart with that poor young ghost who was my sister for thirteen years and the only person I adored until I knew you all. She will be my ideal in life, as my sister is in death [he wrote on the same occasion].

Since Ettie could not be loved, she should be worshipped.

Cazalis was untroubled by such complications. Head over heels in love, he begged all the friends who had been present at the famous picnic to make a 'portrait' of Ettie. Henri Regnault was to do a drawing; the others to celebrate her in verse. Mallarmé set to work, 'trembling, because I want this to be my masterpiece'. Various events, and perhaps his own ambiguous feelings towards Ettie, prevented the completion of the poem until the following year. By that time its subject had changed, yet from the historical evidence, it must have been Ettie whom he first imagined, or remembered, appearing like a radiant vision in the twilight street, half real girl, half a phantom out of the past:[14]

> Et j'ai cru voir la fée au chapeau de clarté
> Qui jadis sur mes beaux sommeils d'enfant gâté
> Passait, laissant toujours de ses mains mal fermées
> Neiger de blancs bouquets d'étoiles parfumées.

For a time at least, Mallarmé cherished this confusion between gay, lively Ettie Yapp and the vanished loves of childhood. Indeed, something of this substitution seems to have always been present in their relationship.

Ettie was unavailable, rendered taboo, so to speak, by Cazalis's love. Stéphane, who rather fancied himself as a Don Juan, felt left out in the cold. 'You are mad, you know, and how I envy you for it!' he wrote to his friend. Something had to happen, and an opportunity arose when he noticed a young German girl who had come to Sens as governess to a wealthy family of the town. He had first glimpsed her walking 'bored and melancholy', by the river. Her mood matched his own and a young foreigner could be more easily approached than the heavily-chaperoned girls of the town. A letter signed simply 'S.M.' declared a purely counterfeit passion. Marie Gerhard responded, took fright, withdrew, and finally allowed herself to be tempted into a meeting. Stéphane's letters became more and more amorous: 'Now my suffering has become hopeless; For the last few days I have been almost mad.' But at the same time he was referring negligently to 'this little German girl I am determined to seduce', and the tears that bespattered the writing paper had been dripped on with water from the washbasin.

Then suddenly, for no reason he himself could discover, the situation changed. Almost from one day to the next, the cynical seducer was forced to recognise that he had fallen into his own trap. Bewildered and alarmed by the force and unexpectedness of his own emotions, he confided as usual in Cazalis and des Essarts:

> I can do nothing else but think of Marie. First she was away in the country and I was like a body without a soul. . . . Now she has returned and my thoughts and heart belong to her so completely that when I take a sheet of paper from my desk, it seems almost sacrilegious to write anything on it which is not about her.

His friends were worried and puzzled. Marie was poor, not in the least pretty and not even very intelligent. She took no interest in art or poetry and seemed to have nothing in common with their friend. They could not understand what he saw in her. Nor, indeed, could Stéphane himself: 'I am attracted to her by something magnetic which has no apparent cause,' he wrote to Cazalis. Then, 'She has a certain look in her eyes that has penetrated my heart once and for all.'

In view of the way in which the relationship developed, one must suppose he had simply discovered another and more accessible substitute for his lost sister. Every line of the romantic outpourings to his friends betrays the unreal nature of his passion. Loneliness, lack of affection, the example of Cazalis and Ettie, had combined to transform a plain, rather stupid young woman into a radiant vision out of an idealised past. Already, he was inhabiting with Marie that island of his imagination in which, twenty-two years later, he was to describe himself as wandering with his sister, discovering under her guidance a 'lucide contour, lacune', and recognising it as the domain of pure poetry.[15]

As to what the real Marie was, or was not, he brushed aside criticisms and warnings, assuring his friends that 'after a couple of years spent with me, she will have become a reflection of myself'.

One could not, in those days, compromise a respectable girl without incurring serious responsibilities. The question of marriage came up inevitably. It is significant that the subject was broached at Fontainebleau, where Stéphane took Marie for an outing. No doubt he hoped to recapture the ecstatic mood of the famous picnic and succeeded sufficiently to make an incautious promise. On his return things must have seemed less simple. He was still a minor and there was no hope of gaining his family's consent. In any case, the three friends prided themselves on their revolutionary opinions and believed that marriage was fatal to genius. Mallarmé was perhaps less emancipated than the others. He wavered, talked about his duty. Des Essarts and Cazalis argued and bullied and finally persuaded him to compromise with a 'trial marriage'. This audacious solution was facilitated by the sudden consent of his family to the long-discussed stay in England. Indeed, the remarkable hurry with which they bundled him off suggests they had got wind of the Marie affair and thought it even more dangerous than the freedom they dreaded for him. It never occurred to them, of course, that he might take Marie with him. As for the young people, they were far too wildly in love to bother with practical questions. As Stéphane explained to Cazalis, 'To have left without taking her with me would have killed her, just as it would have killed me, or rather, it would have been quite simply impossible.' So they arrived in Soho where in spite of the French atmosphere, Stéphane and Marie felt they were setting up 'a real English home'. They warmed themselves at an open fire, sat in leather arm-chairs powdered over with coal dust, and drank ale instead of wine with their supper. A black cat purred by the hearth. Marie knitted or embroidered, while Stéphane read, wrote or worked at his English. There was even a red-armed little maid to bring in the coal and to wonder why there was no bronze statue of Joan of Arc or Buffon on the mantelpiece. All her other French employers had apparently managed to transport across the channel, in the course of a more or less precipitate departure, this ultimate symbol of respectability.[16]

There had been a few catastrophes, it is true. Stéphane, unprepared for the terrible climate, had caught a cold and coughed abominably. Moreover, he had been swindled out of most of his money within twenty-four hours of landing. He had lodged a complaint and been painfully surprised when the magistrates' court had refused to condemn the thief: 'Cheating is allowed here and the court dismissed me, saying I was an ass to have let myself be so deceived,' he reported to Cazalis.

A lawyer had been entrusted by the Desmolins with money for necessities, but there were some difficult days when they found themselves 'poor as Job . . . listening desperately for the postman's double knock that will save our lives'. They were too much in love to care. 'To be poor together is to be rich', Stéphane had declared on leaving France. Like children, they allowed themselves to be tempted on their first outing by a little German clock, bought it for three shillings, and consoled themselves for a meagre diet by listening to its friendly ticking.

There was always something going on in the square: hurdy-gurdies, red-capped monkeys, negroes playing the guitar, 'Lancashire Boys' singing in chorus. There was a Punch and Judy show every day too. Stéphane adored the spectacle, which he rewarded by 'raining down pennies and farthings'. ('What a joy it is', he commented rapturously, 'and what pleasure I take in it!') And there were endless street singers, one of whom persistently sang the 'Marseillaise' outside their window in the hope of stimulating their generosity. Marie objected that the man was just lazy and there were real poor more deserving of their pennies. But to Stéphane the wandering musician was a symbol of freedom, and he wrote to Cazalis:

This man makes music in the streets. It's a job, just like being a lawyer, but it has the advantage of being perfectly useless. Can you imagine any finer life than to wander about thus, offering a gay or a sad tune to the first window in sight, not knowing whether it will open to show the face of an angel or that of an old hag, to play for the sparrows, for the paving stones, for the sickly trees in the square.

London in that season was swathed in fog. It crept through the shutters, bringing 'a special smell you only find here'. When the young couple ventured as far as Hyde Park, they found themselves shrouded in 'a vast circular sphere, impalpable yet real, beyond which we could see the morbid outline of fine, thick trees'.

This illusion of distance, this space between himself and reality, corresponded to Mallarmé's deepest creative instinct. Although he was not yet ready to understand the whole significance this poetic space would assume for him, he responded instantly to the charm of the half-invisible city. Crude lights and harsh reality were veiled and filtered here. Outlines dissolved, nothing was certain, everything became possible. It was the climate proper to his heroes, to hesitant, doubting Hamlet, with whom he was coming to identify himself more and more closely;[17] to Poe, whose 'Ulalume' he had begun to translate that year and whom he already regarded as 'one of the most magnificent beings who has ever honoured this earth'.[18] The third hero of his adolescence had been Baudelaire, whose spleen was irradicably associated with Paris, and it is perhaps significant that it was during this first stay in London that he rejected the poet he had worshipped.[19]

Mallarmé seems, then, to have adapted himself without difficulty to the Victorian version of the English way of life. He was still, during these first days in London, caught up in a sort of spell, nestling in the cosy security of his warm, dim room, rejoicing in Marie's presence, in 'the community that comes of breathing the same air . . . eating the same food, becoming familiar with each other's clothes, writing with the same pen'. For a short time, perhaps for only a few days, he was experiencing perfect happiness, reconstituting the green paradise of childhood loves, reliving the few years when he and the other Marie had played together in perfect security, in the only real home they were ever to know.

The irregular situation of the young couple condemned them to solitude. Stéphane had come armed, in the most conventional manner, with letters of introduction from his grandparents recommending him, as anxious Madame Desmolins assured one of her friends, 'to persons in all the honourable classes of London society, and especially to the rectors of several parishes (Catholic ones, of course) and even to Cardinal Wiseman. . . . We may suppose,' she added doubtfully, 'that such acquaintances will be useful to him, if only he is sensible enough to cultivate them and to earn their protection by his good behaviour.'[20]

Her grandson could not, of course, cultivate any of these useful acquaintances. Nor was there available the sort of literary life he had begun to taste in Paris and seems to have hoped for here. Charming *salons*, such as that of Olympe Audouard to which des Essarts had introduced him, were far away indeed, so was the heady intellectual freedom of the Paris literary scene. Mallarmé was fresh from a land where writers were still steeped in the Romantic tradition, where artists were rebels against society not its mouthpiece, where young men claimed that the concepts of good and evil were irrelevant to art, where even nature, for whom all English writers and painters had such religious respect, was no longer sacred. 'I say that if the poet pursues any moral aim, his poetic force is diminished, and it is not imprudent to wager that the work will be a bad one,' Baudelaire had dared to proclaim. As for the new industrial revolution, which to the English meant progress and the promise of universal happiness, he and his followers saw in it only horror and ugliness, out of which they created a new, morbid kind of beauty, where 'tout, même l'horreur, tourne aux enchantements'.[21] To the literary law-givers who frequented Carlyle's house in Cheyne Walk, the French world of art could only be foreign and hateful, and with the sole, scandalous exception of Swinburne (who was still practically unknown) there was no one to revolt against them. When a few months later Cazalis urged him: 'Try to discover which of the English—or even the American poets are akin to Poe and give off the same powerful, at times even deadly perfume', he could only admit: 'I am terribly alone here. There is no one with whom I can talk of art, of poets, of the Ideal. I don't know a single young poet of any quality in London.'

For the time being, then, his only contact with the outside world was through the Yapps, who had left Paris about the same time as himself and were living temporarily in London. Kate and Ettie, decidedly enterprising young women for the times, had launched into journalism for themselves. They had been acting as Paris correspondents for the *Queen*, contributing lively articles on fashions, life at the Imperial Court and so on, which they signed 'Eliane de Marsy', and letters from friends continued to provide material for very convincing 'Paris letters'. Cazalis was greatly disturbed by this venture, which he feared might turn his beloved Ettie into one of those blue-stockings he considered 'more hideous than a moustached woman'.[22] For the moment, though, he was too much in love to protest. Stéphane acted as go-between for the two lovers, carrying letters and bringing messsages, for, though Mr Yapp liked Cazalis, Mrs Yapp was fiercely opposed to any engagement.

Mrs Yapp seems to have been a rather stern and alarming figure, but the girls were gay and hospitable. Now Mallarmé met the two younger sisters—Florence and little Isabelle, who was still in the nursery. It was presumably from Isabelle he learned his first nursery rhymes with their illogical juxtapositions, so stimulating to the imagination. 'When an exact relationship is created between certain images, a third element detaches itself from them, an element fusible and clear, open to our divination,'[23] he was to explain later, and in 'Cock Robin', 'The Cat and the Fiddle' and so on, he discovered just this element of liberating *suggestion*.[24] So he memorised or copied a number of rhymes, later to be translated and used as examples in his English classes. What his pupils thought of them is not known, but an inspector reported sourly: 'We can only suppose M. Mallarmé to be mentally deranged.'

The Yapps knew a number of well-known writers. Dickens and Thackeray had visited them at various times, so did George Sala, Mr Yapp's colleague on the *Telegraph*, who was then at the height of his fame. There are serious grounds for supposing it was here (rather than through des Essarts as Dr Mondor suggests) that Mallarmé met the Chevalier de Chatelain.[25]

This extraordinary old person was over sixty at the time and had had a remarkably varied career in two countries. In his youth, he had earned a certain celebrity by walking from Paris to Rome in order to study the personality and ideas of Pope Leo XII. Apart from this exploit, much of his early life had been spent in his favourite pursuit of king-baiting. Chatelain was a fervent republican, a friend of Victor Hugo and Louis Blanc, and he devoted a not inconsiderable journalistic talent to the tireless composition of ribald ballads and incendiary newspaper articles in which he relentlessly attacked his *bêtes noires*. After a spell in prison under Louis-Philippe, he had settled in England, where he became a naturalised British subject, devoting himself to a monumental work entitled *Les Beautés de la Poésie anglaise*,[26] containing over a thousand translations of poems ranging from Chaucer to Tennyson. As a passionate admirer of Shakespeare, he was engaged, at the time when he first met Mallarmé, in a mammoth project, the *Shakespeare Memorial*, destined to raise a nation-wide subscription for the erection of a monument to commemorate the poet's three hundredth anniversary. The apathy with which the British public in general and the monarchy in particular, viewed this important event, threw the fiery Chevalier into a frenzy of rage. Queen Victoria was too busy patronising the construction of the Memorial to her beloved Albert to care about

Shakespeare's, and Chatelain's plea for funds went unheeded. This show of royal philistinism provoked a pamphlet as virulent as any with which he had celebrated the misdeeds of Charles X, Louis-Philippe or Napoleon III.

'The celebration of Shakespeare's three hundredth anniversary has been an immense fiasco', he wrote bitterly. 'It has fizzled out for one sole reason, which is that the de facto royalty has refused—no doubt through professional jealousy—to recognise the royalty of genius and has held aloof with all its family.'[27] Queen Victoria did not react and the Chevalier did not even have the satisfaction of martyrdom.

Chatelain had married a woman at least as remarkable as himself. Clara le Chatelain, *née* de Pontigny, was, like her husband, a bilingual writer. From her tirelessly energetic pen poured novels, stories, poems, fairy tales, songs and translations. She was also an indefatigable hostess and, as the *Jersey Express* recalled after her death in 1877:

> her dinners, fancy dress balls, and less formal reunions were quite a feature in London literary life; and the varied acquaintances of the Chevalier, of almost every nationality and shades of religious and political opinion, gave a piquancy to the home circle at Castelnau Lodge[28] which is often found wanting in more pretentious assemblies.

The Chatelains, who believed strongly in the doctrine of *mens sana in corpore sano*, lived according to a minutely regulated routine, and thought nothing of a thirty-mile ramble in the course of a day. Apart from their intellectual and athletic feats, the old couple were celebrated for their mutual devotion and were one of the last recipients of the Dunmow Flitch, with Harrison Ainsworth presiding over the awarding committee.

Mallarmé's relationship with them remains partly mysterious in spite of the discovery of Chatelain's letters.[29] There is only one mention in the published correspondence, and this refers—rather ungratefully in the light of subsequent events—to 'the Chevalier de Chatelain, a bad French poet living in London'. This letter is dated 11 April 1864, and precedes the long, affectionate correspondence which lasted almost to Chatelain's death in 1881. Each sent friends with introductions to the other. Chatelain, worried by his young friend's poverty, sent sums of money, took an interest in his children, mourned when little Anatole died and rallied him over his pessimism ('Anyone would think you were sixty and I only twenty-two. . . . You distress me—so young and so disillusioned. Discover your own youth, my young friend' he wrote after receiving a draft of the sonnet 'Vere Novo').[30] When he drew up his will on 11 May 1878, Mallarmé was one of the main legatees, receiving two bequests of money, one of £120 to be held in trust for his two children; the other of £800—a very substantial sum at the time. He was also to receive a number of literary works (of very doubtful interest, it must be admitted); also, continues the document, 'all my personal correspondence and all my manuscripts and all the personal correspondence and manuscripts of my late dear wife, to the intent that he may publish such of them as he may think desirable', all this 'in token of my gratitude for his devotion to my interests and those of my late dear wife'. 'You are young, vigorous and hard-working', wrote Chatelain informing his friend of his intentions. 'I hope the end of your life will be happy.'[31] The allusion to his 'devotion to my interests' seems to refer to Mallarmé's efforts to find a French publisher for his works and those of Clara. These efforts were apparently unsuccessful, but were none the less appreciated. Mallarmé did not in fact get this quite considerable legacy. The Chevalier was an embittered and quarrelsome old man and the innumerable codicils attached to his will trace the fluctuations of his friendships. However, the correspondence shows no trace of a quarrel or even of a coolness between the two men, and Mallarmé seems to have fallen a victim to the simple pleasure Chatelain, who grew somewhat senile in his old age, took in making and remaking his will. At any rate a codicil dated 28 May 1879 revokes the second clause, depriving him of the five volumes of the *Young Ladies Journal*, the twenty volumes of Reynolds's *Miscellany* and other treasures of Chatelain's library, as well as the more surely welcome £800. He did, however, come into the smaller legacy.

Now among the innumerable journals to which Madame le Chatelain contributed under some fifty pen-names, was the *Queen*. Kate and Ettie Yapp, as we have seen, had begun to contribute to the same journal. All the Yapps were bilingual, as were the Chatelains. Both families were equally at home in France and England. They followed the same profession. It would thus appear normal that they should have known each other, and 'Countess Cornelie de B.' may even have procured the Paris correspondence for her young friends. As for the Chevalier, the fact that he had included two of Poe's poems[32] in his *Beautés de la Poésie anglaise*, would have been enough to arouse Mallarmé's sympathy. It seems strange at first sight that his 'devotion' to Chatelain's interests should have been sufficient to merit such gratitude, and yet have left no trace in his correspondence, but Mallarmé's life was always divided, so to speak, into compartments. People whom he did not consider as authentic artists had little reality for him, although his essential courtesy and kindliness sometimes led them to believe the contrary.

The young Yapps had their own circle of friends and Mallarmé seems to have spent more and more time with them. On 30 November he wrote a gay letter to Cazalis, describing 'a charming little party' at which Ettie had been 'adorably natural' in a high-cut brown dress 'without any exaggerated crinoline', that had shown off her delightful little grecian waist. She had received her guests 'in such a way that she made you feel you had arrived in paradise', while 'the deep goodness that shines in her dark-blue eyes made her look like a seraphim that has been transformed into a Quakeress and can still remember heaven.' The only shadow on the gathering had been the absence of Cazalis, but Ettie had spoken of him in tones that left no doubt as to her feelings. As for Mallarmé, he seems to have thoroughly enjoyed himself.

And what about Marie during all this time? *She* could not be taken to the Yapps or invited to the Chatelains' receptions at Castelnau Lodge. An allusion in the correspondence with Cazalis suggests that Mallarmé, misled by the Yapps' mildly bohemian life in Paris, may have imagined he could confide in them, but he soon realised they were 'English prudes' who would instantly conclude that Marie was a woman of loose morals. She could only stay in her room, listening to the ticking of the little German clock, worrying about money, and feeling herself a burden to Stéphane who could never invite anyone home because of her presence. Her world was bounded by Panton Square. A step to right or to left of the close, comforting little place precipitated her into a terrifying world of filth and brutality, where the day's shopping must be done quickly, before noon, when the prostitutes, the bullies, the thieves and drunkards were still safely asleep. No respectable woman could have ventured into Windmill Street after midday.

Perhaps, too, she was beginning to realise that something was going wrong. As Mallarmé remarked in a letter to Cazalis, she was 'grown-up and sensible'. She did not appreciate Punch and Judy and showed that she thought her lover's enthusiasm childish. She shared, it is true, his pleasure in 'the grace of old, faded things'[33] but her interests were purely domestic and the two had not much to talk about. Nor had anything further been said on the subject of marriage, and she herself was far too discreet to remind Stéphane of a rash half-promise.

Altogether, it is not surprising that, one day, barely a month after their arrival, Stéphane returned from yet another visit to the Yapps' to find her in tears and preparing to leave him.

The two of them wept all night and Stéphane felt he was losing 'half his life . . . the best half'. Yet he does not seem to have made much effort to dissuade her. In fact, the desperate letters he began to pour out to Cazalis after her departure make it clear that, deeply as he missed her and bitterly as his conscience reproached him, he only half wanted her back. Nothing could have been nearer the Hamletian ambiguity he recognised in himself, half-mockingly and half-complacently, than his behaviour during the next few months.

'I am a grotesque, ridiculous clown', he wrote to Cazalis. 'Pay no attention to my letters. One day they'll make Marie out to be a white dove, and the next, they'll blaspheme against her. I shall say yes or no, according to my degree of suffering.'

This suffering was certainly sincere. Perhaps indeed it was all the deeper because it was not the simple, whole-hearted sorrow that normally attends the parting of lovers, but a much more complex feeling that awoke old and agonising wounds in the subconscious mind. The letters written during the following months while he was hesitating and vacillating, betray something more than normal anxiety and remorse. Mallarmé knew that he had hopelessly compromised a respectable girl and that without his protection her life would be ruined. On the other hand, he realised he had made a terrible mistake, that marriage would put an end to his ambition of preparing a doctorate and making a career in the university, that it would condemn him to the mediocre existence of a non-graduate teacher in the provinces, for which he must already have realised himself to be supremely ill-suited.

Yet, in spite of the disillusionments of that month of life in common which Stéphane summed up in the phrase, 'the everyday world smells of cooking', he still felt that Marie was in some way part of himself, and that a separation from him would result in her death. 'She has lost everything, perhaps she will even lose her life. . . . I believe she will die of grief. . . . She is already dead.' This fear reappears constantly, as does the obsessive feeling of guilt at having 'soiled' the virgin girl who had entrusted herself to his care.

The truth is, of course, that Marie was by now entirely identified in his mind with his dead sister. First Ettie, then she, had been the 'Apparition' of the poem begun in Sens and finished in London, and the transition had taken place with a sort of smooth inevitability. Ettie could, and did, remain an ideal, but once Marie had been possessed and known as a reality she could no longer be worshipped as a divinity. From that point on, her presence posed an insoluble problem. Possession brought disillusion, and no doubt a certain resentment as well, simply because Marie was real. No doubt too, it awoke the subconscious terror of incest which psychiatrists tell us ruins so many relationships based on childhood traumas concerning mother or sister. Yet separation evoked an even more terrible menace. It reawoke the irradicable feeling of guilt that so often besets a child after some disaster it feels obscurely it should have, and did not prevent. All the terror and anguish Stéphane had known as a young boy when he 'allowed' little Marie to die, over-whelmed him again when the other Marie left him, perhaps to die by his fault.

Mallarmé thus found himself after Marie's departure in a psycho-logical state which is not entirely uncommon. The more unusual feature of the case was the extent to which he was conscious of what was happening. He seems indeed to have cultivated the identification of the new Marie with the old, understanding perhaps, how fruitful a source of poetic inspiration it would prove. The fantasy was constantly dis-cussed with Cazalis who seems to have found it not only normal but admirable. For both of them, Stéphane's dead sister seems to have been quite as real—or unreal—as his living mistress, and Cazalis found it natural to write after Marie's departure:

Take the same resolution as I have—the resolution to remain widowed.[34] Let us keep our love for those we have lost, povero. In this way, you know, you will feel less alone. Marie, you know, is your sister. She has returned to a life of peace and duty, as the other Marie has returned to heaven. Do not try to call either of them back.

After escorting Marie as far as Boulogne, Mallarmé had returned to London. It would have been too painful to go back to Panton Square and he had found rooms at No. 16 Albert Street, in Knights-bridge. He had recently attained his majority and had a little money at his disposal, so he no longer felt himself to be poor. The new rooms cost the equivalent of 1,200 francs which was fairly expensive for the times. This comparative affluence only increased his remorse, since there was no longer the plea of poverty to excuse his conduct.

The Yapps returned to Paris in March, leaving him lonelier than ever. Although he must have worked at his English, since he did indeed pass his 'certificate of proficiency' in September, there seems to have been little room in his mind for anything except the problem of Marie. Scruples tormented him. 'I quite realise my own unhappiness will pass in time', he wrote to Cazalis. 'And in six months I shall probably have ceased to suffer. . . . No, I shall not be miserable for ever, but Marie will be.'

At night, an uneasy conscience brought dreams of Marie's dead mother, reproaching him for seducing her daughter, then casting her away 'like a bunch of dead flowers'. Waking, there was only the empty room and the friendless streets outside. 'I am alone', he wrote desperately to his friend, 'completely alone with my black cat, and it is horrible.'

Although there is no date on the prose poem entitled 'Plainte d'Automne', there are indications that it was the first of a series of such poems, dated 1864 and inspired no doubt by Baudelaire's *Petits poèmes en prose* and Aloysius Bertrand's *Gaspard de la Nuit*. All the evidence suggests that the first paragraph at least was written during this melancholy spring of 1863 and alludes to the period spent alone in the Knightsbridge lodgings. The opening phrases correspond exactly to the mood of the letters to Cazalis:[35]

> Ever since Marie left me for another star—which of them is it, Orion, Altair, or thou, green Venus?—I have always loved solitude. How many long days have I spent alone with my cat! By alone, I mean without any material being, for my cat is a spirit, a mystic companion. So I can say that I have spent long days alone with my cat, and alone with one of the last authors of the Roman decadence. For since the white being disappeared from my life, I have felt a strange and inexplicable love for all that is summed up in the word 'Fall'.

At the end of April, after endless wavering on both sides, and hurried crossings and recrossings of the Channel, Marie returned to London, this time as Stéphane's fiancée. The young couple settled down in new lodgings in No. 6 Brompton Square. Mallarmé's family was resigned to the inevitable now and his recently widowed stepmother had shown herself more understanding than he would have believed possible. Even Cazalis agreed that he was acting rightly and only des Essarts continued to wave half-heartedly the banner of celibacy.

Once the decision had been taken, Mallarmé's mood seems to have become more serious. The letters to Cazalis are no longer tortured outpourings. Once more he was taking a certain interest in the still strange life around him. The lovers went for a row on the Thames at Richmond, and sentimental Marie gathered forget-me-nots to be included in the evening's letter. When they had tried to moor their boat, the current had swept them on. 'I too drift on the current of the days, and I hardly know how I live', was Stéphane's comment.

Then he attempted to recapture some of his earlier republican and libertarian enthusiasms. On 22 July there was a meeting at St James's Hall in favour of Poland, that 'great spirited and unfortunate people, who were now attempted to be trampled on by the Russian Emperor', as one speaker put it. General Zamoysky was present and a deputation of French working men had crossed the Channel specially to join forces with the English Working Men's Committee led by Mr Ogden, a shoemaker. The meeting passed a resolution: 'Save Poland; unfurl the national flag.' The republican *émigrés* from France were always very much in evidence at this sort of gathering and generally turned up in force when Poland or Hungary put forward their claims to independence. The 'Garibaldian' Mallarmé felt he should have been in sympathy with the crowd, and the following day, when it regathered in Hyde Park to listen to more speeches, he was present. The excitement was as high as it had been the previous evening, but he himself remained unmoved and was obliged to admit that his political passions —never very intense—had quite waned. In fact, he had been chiefly struck by the way the workers in the audience applauded whenever the speaker addressed them as 'gentlemen'. He concluded they were no more worthy of an ideal republic than were the 'hideous and soulless bourgeoisie', and he turned his back on politics for ever.

The letters to Cazalis in the weeks preceding his marriage appear almost contented in their resignation. Stéphane no longer had any illusions concerning his future. 'The smell of cooking' would pervade his life from now on. But this was only the exterior and almost unimportant aspect of accepted renunciation. By marrying Marie, he was relinquishing all hope of creating a reality out of the tenuous dream that had sustained him through adolescence. He was admitting defeat of the most humiliating order. 'Ici-bas est maître.' He had allowed the mundane world to engulf him once and for all.

'If I were to marry Marie for my own happiness,' he admitted to Cazalis on taking the final decision, 'it would be madness. Anyway, is happiness really to be found on this earth? And should we really seek it anywhere except in our dreams? . . . No, I am marrying Marie simply because without me she would not be able to live!'

The marriage was celebrated at Brompton Oratory on 10 August, and it should be recorded at once that Marie made him an excellent and devoted wife and apparently realised his early prophecy that she would soon become 'a reflection of himself'.

It was on 3 June, when the marriage had already been decided but had not yet taken place, that Mallarmé, writing from the lodgings in Brompton Square, enclosed in a letter to Cazalis two poems: 'L'Assaut'[36] and 'Les Fenêtres'. The first, 'tenuous and fragile as a dream', seems to have been inspired by Marie's luxuriant blonde hair and is a charming, though terribly intricate fantasy. The second can be read as the key not only to his personal drama, but to the whole Symbolist attitude, to a way of life and a manner of thinking that was to invade and permeate European poetry for the rest of the century. It is difficult to imagine a work more totally out of tune with the prevailing mood of

English letters. The poem is so important that it should perhaps be quoted here in full:

> Las du triste hôpital, et de l'encens fétide
> Qui monte en la blancheur banale des rideaux
> Vers le grand crucifix ennuyé du mur vide,
> Le moribond sournois y redresse un vieux dos,
>
> Se traîne et va, moins pour chauffer sa pourriture
> Que pour voir du soleil sur les pierres, coller
> Les poils blancs et les os de la maigre figure
> Aux fenêtres qu'un beau rayon clair veut hâler.
>
> Et la bouche, fiévreuse et d'azur bleu vorace,
> Telle, jeune, elle alla respirer son trésor,
> Une peau virginale et de jadis! encrasse
> D'un long baiser amer les tièdes carreaux d'or.
>
> Ivre, il vit, oubliant l'horreur des saintes huiles,
> Les tisanes, l'horloge et le lit infligé,
> La toux; et quand le soir saigne parmi les tuiles,
> Son oeil, à l'horizon de lumière gorgé,
>
> Voit des galères d'or, belles comme des cygnes,
> Sur un fleuve de pourpre et de parfums dormir
> En berçant l'éclair fauve et riche de leurs lignes
> Dans un grand nonchaloir chargé de souvenir!
>
> Ainsi, pris du dégoût de l'homme à l'âme dure
> Vautré dans le bonheur, où ses seuls appétits
> Mangent, et qui s'entête à chercher cette ordure
> Pour l'offrir à la femme allaitant ses petits,
>
> Je fuis et je m'accroche à toutes les croisées
> D'où l'on tourne l'épaule à la vie, et, béni,
> Dans leur verre, lavé d'éternelles rosées,
> Que dore le matin chaste de l'Infini
>
> Je me mire et me vois ange! et je meurs, et j'aime
> —Que la vitre soit l'art, soit la mysticité—
> A renaître, portant mon rêve en diadème,
> Au ciel antérieur où fleurit la Beauté!
>
> Mais, hélas! Ici-bas est maître: sa hantise
> Vient m'écoeurer parfois jusqu'en cet abri sûr,
> Et le vomissement impur de la Bêtise
> Me force à me boucher le nez devant l'azur.

Est-il moyen, ô Moi qui connais l'amertume,
D'enfoncer le cristal par le monstre insulté
Et de m'enfuir, avec mes deux ailes sans plume
—Au risque de tomber pendant l'éternité?

'Les Fenêtres' has often been quoted as an example of the 'life-denying' attitude of the Symbolists, and indeed, Mallarmé added in the accompanying letter the comment that 'Happiness in this mundane world can only be ignoble.' But the poem is much more than the symbolic description of the crisis through which he had just passed. The point is that the dying man can drag himself to the window and then all the horrors of the 'sad hospital' disappear dissolve, in the magnificence of the view without. What the twenty-one-year-old Mallarmé was really doing, was to question the whole concept of reality, to ask himself whether the rags, the misery, the stench of the fetid hospital in which Man must live out his days, are any more real than the 'galères d'or belles comme des cygnes, sur un fleuve de pourpre et de parfums', which offer themselves to him through the twin escape-routes of art and mysticism. From this moment on, Mallarmé's life was to be totally dedicated to the aesthetic expression of these impalpable splendours. Soon, indeed, he came to believe they did not merely belong to the world of imagination, but represented the essential truth about life. This is no doubt what he meant when he told Verlaine that the sole task of the poet is to seek for 'the Orphic explanation of the world'.[37] From that time on he began to search, first for a way by which the basic matter of life could be transformed into perfect beauty; then, in a more austere and abstract spirit, for a way of 'abolishing', 'annihilating' this basic matter itself, so as to obtain from it a new element, 'fusible et clair présent à la divination'[38] which is the pure matter of poetry.

Stéphane Mallarmé, Journalist

On 1 May 1871 the London International Exhibition was opened in the galleries and grounds of the Horticultural Society near the South Kensington Museum.[39] Exhibitions of this sort were becoming increasingly fashionable and the Victorians adored them. They loved to see the vast quantities of ornate furniture, complicated clocks, decorated china, oriental carpets and fine jewellery displayed by the participating nations. Especially they enjoyed the sections showing 'the most recent inventions of science'—the 'feathering propellor', the patent vermin asphyxiator, the model of a patent overhead railway, the calculating machine. All this was well adapted to the spirit of the times—solid, showy and generally suggestive of progress and prosperity. It was specially reassuring to note that France, in spite of the terrible upheaval occasioned by the Franco-Prussian war and the downfall of the imperial régime, had managed a splendid display.

The Yapps had long been connected with various exhibitions of this sort, for Mr Yapp had compiled the descriptive catalogue of the Great Exhibition of 1851 and the Educational Exhibition of 1854, as well as the English version of the catalogue of the Paris Exhibition Universelle in 1867. This year, although the father does not seem to have been concerned with the catalogue, the family were more deeply involved than ever.

They had returned to London after an adventurous and, in many ways, disastrous year in Paris. George Yapp had ceased to act as correspondent of the *Daily Telegraph* before war broke out and had returned to London with Kate, probably on business to do with the approaching Exhibition. Mrs Yapp had remained behind with Ettie, Florence and Isabelle, and for some reason had not been able to leave before the Prussian troops closed round the city. The house in the Place Wagram had been in the direct line of shelling from the German outposts, food had been scarce and, if the Yapps had not been reduced to eating rats like some of the poorest Parisians, they had suffered from the famine like everyone else. There were only a few English journalists left in the city and their reports had to be despatched by balloon, since this was almost the only means by which the beleaguered people could communicate with the outside world. Frenchmen in the provinces, picking up these missives dropped from the sky, had been asked to carry them to the nearest unoccupied town. Brave Ettie had sent lively reports to the *Queen* by this method and 'Eliane de Marsy' had gained a considerable reputation among her readers. But there had been tragedy in the family too. The terrible conditions during the months of the siege had been too much for fragile little Isabelle, and when the Yapps recrossed the channel at last, they were in mourning for the youngest sister.

Kate Yapp had always been a great favourite of Mallarmé's. She had been married for some years now to Ernest Fillonneau, assistant to M. du Sommerard who was in charge of the French section of the Exhibition. Thus, when Mallarmé arrived in London on 9 August as a 'special correspondent' for the Paris press, he could be sure of every facility for covering the Exhibition.

This second appearance of Mallarmé in London, and his unexpected metamorphosis into a journalist, calls for some explanation. He was now, of course, a very different person from the naïve boy who had arrived in Panton Square nine years earlier. Marriage had turned him into a harassed family man, the father of two children, struggling to make both ends meet on the meagre salary of a provincial schoolmaster. But he was also acknowledged as one of the rising young poets, a friend of Catulle Mendès, Villiers de l'Ile Adam, François Coppée, Verlaine, Heredia, all the young, *avant-garde* writers, who had been influenced by Baudelaire and were fretting in a greater or less degree against the neo-classical conventions of the Parnassians or the nostalgic echoes of a dying Romanticism. The first versions of 'Hérodiade' and 'L'Après-midi d'un Faune' had been completed and been received by his friends with admiration or disapproval, but always with a shock of surprise. Then had come the terrible period of depression that had threatened to lead him to madness and perhaps suicide. Instead, it had culminated in 'Igitur', and the construction of a metaphysical system precluding any further transposition of immediate experience.

It is easy to imagine how ill such adventures of the spirit harmonised with the teaching of English verbs to unwilling little boys. Mallarmé had no talent for this profession, was quite incapable of keeping his classes in order and seems to have had no illusions as to his own proficiency in the language, since he wrote to Catulle Mendès about this time, 'The only English words I know are those contained in the volume of Poe, and I pronounce them well, so as not to spoil the rhythm. By using the dictionary and guessing, I think I might make a good translator.' In fact, teaching was torture to him—'the only thing I ever heard him complain about', says Paul Valéry. Yet he laboured conscientiously, using methods of his own which scandalised hidebound inspectors and sent disastrous reports circulating through the Ministry of Education. Then, in the fallacious hope of balancing the family budget, he had begun work on a textbook, *Les Mots anglais*,[40] of which T. S. Eliot has said unkindly that, 'an examination of this curious treatise and the strange phrases it gives under the impression that they are familiar English proverbs, should dispel any rumour of Mallarmé's English scholarship.'[41] Nevertheless, the little book reveals a good deal about his own poetical methods and gives a clue to some of the 'obscurity' with which he has so often been reproached. This obscurity had already done him a good deal of harm in his career, and had roused the horror of at least one school inspector, who discovered and denounced him as the author of 'certain insane verses'.

In this summer of 1871, Mallarmé was not yet quite resigned to this dreary monotony of a teacher's life. It still seemed to him that, with his knowledge of English, there must be some alternative way of making a living. Various suggestions were put forward by friends. Journalism?

A post in a library? Translations? Mallarmé considered them all and finally decided to follow the example of Catulle Mendès and try his hand at reporting. He had remained in touch with friends in London (chiefly with the Chatelains, since the Yapps had been living mostly in Paris) who had sent him English newspapers and kept him supplied with news of literary events. A stay there, he felt, would provide useful contacts, especially with publishers who might commission him to make some translations, but he seems, too, to have had a strong longing to revisit the city. It held bitter memories for him, yet, as sometimes happens with regard to places where one has been very unhappy in youth, he thought of it with nostalgia, and described it in later days as 'very captivating'.[42]

He must have known, too, how greatly the literary situation had changed during the intervening years. The Pre-Raphaelites were accepted now; Rossetti was a power in the world of art; they were no longer a slightly suspect *avant-garde*, but recognised as men of talent, even of genius, and earning the substantial rewards that England offered in those days to her leading artists. A new generation had grown up meanwhile to represent the revolutionary element in English letters, and renewed contacts between Paris and London had revealed the names of young men who believed in Art for Art's sake and whose attitude contrasted strongly with the moral and social preoccupations of their immediate elders.

There was indeed far more interchange between French and English writers than there had been for a long time previously. Even among the general public there was now more interest in, and sympathy for, France. The departure of Napoleon III, the stirring events of 1870, had caused many people to revise their attitude towards the old enemy. Tentative political friendship had led to a greater sympathy for the French attitude towards art. In this respect, Swinburne's influence had been predominant. The tiny little man, with his shock of red hair, his immoderate habits and the vague aura of scandal that surrounded him, had rocketed suddenly to fame after the publication of *Poems and Ballads*. His name was in all the newspapers, his portraits filled the shop windows and stories of his eccentricities delighted and scandalised a public that was growing a little tired of insipid goodness. Young men walked the streets arm in arm, chanting his verses.[43] Ruskin, who had recently managed to intimidate the whole of intellectual society into accepting his judgments almost as if they were inspired from on High, had called *Atalanta* 'the grandest thing ever done by a youth, though he is a demoniac youth'. John Morley launched in the *Saturday Review* an attack of such virulence that it would have landed its author in court under modern libel laws; the *Contemporary Review* thundered about the rise of 'a new, fleshly school of poetry'; and Dr Symonds called the author an 'impure windbag'. Swinburne enjoyed the controversy as much as the praise, and indeed his image was being built up, almost by chance, exactly as he liked to see himself. And Swinburne, of course, was passionately pro-French. His 'Ode on the Proclamation of the French Republic' had thrilled innumerable readers. French literature had suddenly become stimulating, exciting. Translations of Parnassian verse appeared in most of the reviews; French plays were performed in London theatres. People wanted to know what was happening in France. They might deplore what they learned, but at least it interested them.

In this climate, there was every chance that a young poet of acknowledged promise would be well received. Mallarmé hesitated as usual, unable to decide between different alternatives and finally allowed himself to be persuaded by a friend he had met in Avignon, where he had been teaching for a time.

William Bonaparte Wyse was one of those eccentric men of letters, fairly common in nineteenth-century Britain, who were rich enough to pursue their own course, enthusiastically following odd by-ways of literature and despising, or affecting to despise, their more successful colleagues. He was an Irishman of distinguished family, whose mother was a granddaughter of Lucien Bonaparte, and his whole life had been a succession of violent literary love affairs. He had been swept off his feet by Southey, Coleridge, Shelley and Byron, then by Lamartine, then by the Greeks and Romans. These passions spent, he had been even more deeply thrilled by Rabelais and had come to France in order to read him in his natural surroundings. Wandering down to Avignon, he had discovered the existence of Provençal poetry, had fallen in love again and decided to study the language and write in it himself. This he managed to do, and even published several volumes of verse in Provençal, though he was never capable of pronouncing a single intelligible word.

Wyse was naturally in touch with the Société du Félibrige, which often met in Mistral's house at Maillane and grouped the few poets writing in Provençal. They were amused and intrigued by the voluble Irishman whom they discovered to be 'a demon of gaiety, who surpassed even the Meridionals'.[44] Mallarmé was teaching at this time in Avignon, and he too had come into contact with the Félibriges. Their companionship was just what he needed, for like many intensely introspective people, he benefited from the society of more exuberant, extrovert types. Soon he was on very friendly terms with Fréderic

Mistral, Jean Brunet, Roumanille and specially Théodore Aubanel. Through them he met Bonaparte Wyse.

The two men took to each other at once. Wyse had the essential quality Mallarmé looked for in a friend: he lived for poetry. He was erudite too, and had a taste for magic, astrology, demonology and strange out-of-the-way scraps of knowledge. All this must have appealed to the younger man, who was groping at this time towards his conception of the poet-alchemist and becoming more and more convinced that 'there exists a secret parity between the ancient methods and that spell-binding which is poetry'.[45] Although there are no records of their conversations, one may suppose that at least some of Mallarmé's knowledge of the 'herbes, atlas et rituel'[46] of the ancient alchemists, was due to Wyse.

We do know that they discussed William Beckford. The eccentric owner of Fonthill could not fail to appeal to the Irishman, whom one suspects of seeing himself somewhat in the image of a nineteenth-century Beckford. It was at this time that Mallarmé began to work on his preface to Beckford's *Vathek*. It was probably Chatelain who encouraged him to revive a work practically unknown in France at the time, and it may well have been on account of Wyse's interest in the subject that he sent his new friend with a letter of introduction to the Chatelains. In any case, it was Wyse who finally persuaded Mallarmé to undertake the journey to England, by inviting him to stay at his house in Bradford-on-Avon. Mallarmé seems to have been extremely anxious to accept this invitation, but there remained the problem of paying for the journey. The Exhibition, and his connection with Fillonneau through the Yapps, provided a solution. Through Catulle Mendès he was able to obtain commissions to cover the event for no less than four journals, while it was probably Mr Yapp, who showed himself, says Mallarmé, 'exquisitely kind', who persuaded George Sala, his ex-colleague on the *Telegraph* and the most famous journalist of his day to allow the visitor to stay in the house he rented at No. 1 Alexander Square, off Brompton Road (at that time Fulham Road).[47]

He found the Yapp family installed at No. 27 Northumberland Place, near Kensington Gardens. They were as welcoming as ever, but the atmosphere was very different from the gay, nonchalant existence of 1862. Florence's distress at her little sister's death had resulted in a nervous breakdown from which she was struggling to recover; Ettie, too, had been exhausted by the terrible months in Paris and she mourned unceasingly for little Isabelle, cherishing her sadness, she wrote to her devoted friend Gaston Maspero, 'because it is all that remains to me of my child'.[48] Her health was bad and she was beginning to take on 'that indefinable air of a girl who has remained unmarried'.[49] Yet she was still full of courage, working hard, writing, translating, sending lively descriptions of her daily life to Maspero in Paris, telling him of the great dinner in honour of the Exhibition, attended by the Queen herself, and at which Ernest Fillonneau had been present, and urging him to read *Poems and Ballads* 'by our own great, mad poet Swinburne. I find them so beautiful I want you to know them.'[50] But Mallarmé knew she had been finally abandoned by Cazalis and Mrs Yapp took him aside to murmur that his friend had ruined her poor child's life.

A few days later, the Yapps were recalled unexpectedly to Paris and this was the last time Mallarmé was to see Ettie in England. So this is perhaps the moment to describe the final stage of this charming friendship which inspired at least two of his finest sonnets.

Gaston Maspero, the brilliant young Egyptologist, had been hopelessly in love with Ettie for some time, and it was to him she turned when the bitterness of the broken romance with Cazalis began to soften and pass. The couple were married in December of this same year, 1871, and settled down in Paris. Maspero adored his young wife and was heart-broken when she died in November 1873, after the birth of their second child. Mallarmé had been informed immediately, and wrote to Maspero in deep distress on the evening of the same day: 'Can it be possible! How can we believe her dead, this exquisite young woman who seemed destined in every way, and above all by her loving-kindness, to use that sort of radiance that shone in her, for the consolation of others. . . .' And a revealing postscript added, 'I consider this loss as so personal a sorrow, that I have forgotten to speak for Madame Mallarmé, who is inconsolable.'

The story of this friendship does not quite end with Ettie's death. Maspero apparently met Madame Blavatsky in Paris, or perhaps elsewhere, at about this time when he was in a state of inconsolable sorrow. According to the Maspero family, it was at her instigation that he began to attend spiritualistic seances in the hope of getting into touch with his dead wife. A curious photograph, evidently faked, shows 'proof' of his success.[51] A cloud of ectoplasm issues from the body of an elderly medium while Ettie's face, hovering above her, seems to have been conjured up from the drawing made by Henri Regnault after the picnic at Fontainebleau.

Now Maspero had confided in Mallarmé when he was making these experiments, and in the light of these confidences the sonnet dedicated 'Pour votre chère Morte, son ami' takes on a far more precise meaning than that which has generally been attributed to it.

The Young Mallarmé

The poem is dated 2 November 1877—and was thus composed, or sent, on the fourth anniversary of Ettie's death. Mallarmé imagines the ghost of his lost friend admonishing the widower grieving by his dying fireside:

> Sur les bois oubliés quand passe l'hiver sombre
> Tu te plains, ô captif solitaire du seuil,
> Que ce sépulcre à deux qui fera notre orgueil
> Hélas! du manque seul des lourds bouquets s'encombre.
>
> Sans écouter Minuit qui jeta son vain nombre,
> Une veille t'exalte à ne pas fermer l'oeil
> Avant que dans les bras de l'ancien fauteuil
> Le suprême tison n'ait éclairé mon Ombre.
>
> Qui veut souvent avoir la Visite ne doit
> Par trop de fleurs charger la pierre que mon doigt
> Soulève avec l'ennui d'une force défunte.
>
> Ame au si clair foyer tremblante de m'asseoir,
> Pour revivre il suffit qu'à tes lèvres j'emprunte
> Le souffle de mon nom murmuré tout un soir.

The words 'la Visite', taken in conjunction with the photograph, are evidently an allusion to these spirit manifestations, though there is no indication as to whether Mallarmé himself believed in the results obtained, or whether he was merely showing sympathy and concern for Maspero and possibly trying to dissuade him from thoughts of suicide.

Now, with the Yapps gone, he found himself once more alone in London, with no one to provide free meals, and funds sinking rapidly. The house in Alexander Square was conveniently near the Exhibition and he spent his first few days in London conscientiously tramping through its endless galleries. It was hard work for a man in poor health and he found it a strain to have to keep an eye on the clock as he wrote. 'I have put off writing this note from one day to another,' he confided to his publisher Lemerre, on 13 August. 'First I have to carve up this monster of an exhibition, then share out the bits between my reviews and send them each a first helping. My morning visit to the galleries and my struggle with posting-time must be my excuse.' Lemerre and he had discussed the possibility of a French translation of the catalogue, but it turned out—as they might have foreseen—to be much too late to undertake a work of this sort. 'The French who want to see the Exhibition have already been here', he noted, disappointedly.

It was the first of a number of disillusionments and from the immediately practical point of view, this London journey, on which he had based such high hopes, turned into something of a fiasco. Two journals never even acknowledged the articles dispatched from France and a third—*Le Français*—refused to publish them. Finally, three rather flowery 'Letters', approximating fairly closely to the journalistic style of the time, appeared in *Le National* under the signature L. S. Price, while the rest of the 'carve-up' was lost for ever.

Nor was this the only disappointment. It seems that the visit to Wyse never took place, though the two men met in London, where, Mallarmé wrote, 'Wyse has only a few days to spare me.' They seem to have gone together on a mysterious expedition to Chislehurst, where Napoleon III was living in exile with his family. A letter to Catulle and Judith Mendès, dated 15 August, carries the postscript, 'I am just leaving for Chislehurst to congratulate my sovereign on his feast-day.' This remark appears all the more puzzling when one remembers that Mallarmé, like nearly all the French intellectuals, loathed the ex-Emperor and had been delighted by his departure from France. 15 August was not this Napoleon's birthday, nor the feast of his patron saint, when sympathisers might have been expected to congratulate him. It was, however, the birthday of the first Napoleon, and one may suppose Mallarmé to have accompanied Wyse to Chislehurst on a pilgrimage in honour of his great-grand-uncle. Or could it have been Wyse himself whom Mallarmé was setting out to visit at Chislehurst? 'My sovereign' might thus be a jocular reference to Wyse's pride in his descent from the Bonaparte line.

In any case, he seems to have been desperately short of money. Marie, hardly recovered from the birth of her son, worried terribly. 'I am horrified at the thought of you there without money and deprived of even the ordinary necessities of life,' she wrote on 25 August, and on 2 September, 'I am more worried than ever today, my poor dear, and to think I can't even help you! ... How I suffer at not being able to send you what you need; but I myself have only a few francs in my purse.'[52]

But Mallarmé had good reason for remaining in London. Wyse had proved himself unreliable and soon began to show himself gossipy and spiteful[53] but he played an important role in his young friend's life, since it was he who introduced him to John Payne and opened the door to a warm, rewarding and life-long friendship.

Payne had been born in the same year as Mallarmé. He was an excessively shy man, perhaps because he had had a particularly unhappy childhood, due largely to the active dislike with which his father had viewed every form of art and the zeal with which he tried to suppress his son's poetic tendencies. Young John had always been, in his father's view, morbidly precocious. At the age of ten he had translated a number of odes from Horace; between fourteen and nineteen, he had made verse translations of the whole of Dante's *Inferno*, the second part of Goethe's *Faust* and *Hermann und Dorothea*, Lessing's *Nathan der Weise*, Calderón's *El màgico prodigioso*, numberless poems from ancient and modern French, Italian, Spanish, Portuguese, Turkish, Persian and Arabic, all of which languages he had taught himself—apart from Greek, Latin and French learned at school. In the spare time that remained from his work as a solicitor's clerk, he wrote poetry and critical articles and read voraciously in a dozen languages. Naturally, he had felt out of place in the harsh, materialistic world of home and school.

Although Payne was given to fits of gloomy reticence, he could, when launched on one of his favourite subjects, be extraordinarily vivacious and talkative. He knew a great many people, frequented Madox Brown's literary soirées, Dr Marston's Sunday evenings and the Rossettis' house in Chelsea. A visitor who met him at the Rossettis' was struck by 'his foreign appearance and electric ardour and power of expression, which seemed almost to give shocks to the subdued atmosphere of that literary abode.'[54] The 'foreignness' was in fact rather carefully cultivated. Payne adored France and felt himself better appreciated and more at home in the literary society of Paris than in London. He worshipped Villon and Rabelais, translated Banville and the Parnassians, idolised Wagner[55] and did all he could to break through the insular crust of mid-Victorian prejudice by introducing the poets and the ideas he loved to English readers.

Although John Payne was an excellent translator, he was never more than a minor poet and never attained much recognition in England. However, he was a poet, in the sense in which Mallarmé understood the term and his poetry corresponded in many ways to the mood of Mallarmé's early work. Mallarmé had evoked a Saint Cecilia, 'musicienne du silence',[56] whose sublime music called for no material harp or lute; he had discovered in 'l'ombre musicienne aux symboliques charmes'[57] his own poetic climate. Payne, on the other side of the Channel, had been striving to give expression to 'the viewless things', to 'unseen mists'; he had invited readers of his first collection of verse[58] to enter 'this shadow land of mine'. Like Mallarmé, he took the aristocratic view of art and believed that no concessions should be made to the masses. Where Mallarmé had deplored that 'les premiers venus entrent de plein-pied dans un chef-d'oeuvre',[59] Payne regretted that Tennyson 'with all his great qualities ... owed his popularity mainly to the way in which he pandered to the weaknesses of the intellectually lower classes and to his cunning fashion of adorning and idealising the grossest gospel of disguised materialism and crass optimism.'

Mallarmé, who had once spent such bitterly lonely months in London, was so overjoyed to discover these affinities that he never realised (or perhaps never admitted to himself) the profound differences that lay beneath such similarities. Sensitive, beauty-loving Payne lacked the heroic quality that was developing beneath the shrinking hesitancy with which Mallarmé faced everyday life. He would never make the absolute renunciation through which Mallarmé had discovered the joys that lay beyond the windows of the 'triste hôpital' and perhaps his nature was too pessimistic to understand that they might exist. For the present, though, Mallarmé felt he had found a sort of second self, an echo of his own deepest aspirations. 'You know what a remarkable poet is Payne', he wrote a few months later.[60] 'He is one of ourselves, for he has been making simultaneous discoveries with the poets of our age, inventing the enthusiasms and preferences that we cherish most closely. He knows French literature better than any of us.'

All day, the two young men wandered through the London streets, talking endlessly. Payne recited 'with an indefinable charm', his favourite poems from the French Romantics. Mallarmé must surely have talked of Poe—who represented for him 'the intellectual God of our age',[61] and whose *Philosophy of Composition* he had taken more seriously than anyone in England or America had done, or ever would do. Evidently he infected Payne with his own enthusiasm, for Payne frequently alluded after this meeting to the debt he owed to Poe and the manner in which his own work had been influenced by 'The Raven' and 'Ulalume'—precisely the two poems Mallarmé loved most. Payne in his turn, talked of Swinburne. He had not cared for *Atalanta in Calydon* and *Poems and Ballads*, because of the 'apparent hardness' he had detected in them, but *Songs before Sunrise* had converted him into the most enthusiastic of partisans. Mallarmé had heard a good deal of talk about Swinburne, but had apparently never read any of his work. However, he took back to France one or even several volumes, probably a present from Payne, who wrote to him a few days later, 'I envy you the pleasure of reading the works of our great poet Swinburne for the first time.'

This first walk in London seems to have re-created for both young men some of the magic charm the Fontainebleau picnic had once exercised on Mallarmé. It was renewed on later visits and Payne commemorated these enchanted evenings in a poem in French:[62]

> Ami, te souviens-tu des longues causeries,
> Nous promenant le soir le long du Serpentin,
> Suivant, les yeux ravis, le rayon argentin,
> Qui, revêtant les tons roses des rêveries,
> S'en allait, lentement, le long des éclaircies?
> Douce, la nuit venait sur l'ombrage serein,
> Et dans l'eau satinée, aux moirages d'étain,
> Les gaseliers [sic] piquaient leurs flammes adoucies.
> Cependant, nous causions, pleins de la fin du jour,
> Du grand et puissant Art, cette noble maîtresse
> Qui sert nos deux coeurs de son fécond amour.
> Sur nos lèvres—refrain qui revenait sans cesse—
> Chantaient les vers aimés, les noms des grands amis;
> Londres pour nous ce soir redevenait Paris.

When they separated, the two poets had become friends for life. Payne was one of the very few men Mallarmé addressed by the title of 'Brother', which he had first accorded to Cazalis. As for Payne, he found in Mallarmé 'an exquisite soul and a heart of gold'.[63] From that time on, each worked tirelessly to further the interests of the other; each became integrated into the other's circle of friends, and for each new opportunities opened out as a new public became familiar with his name.

The Athenaeum

'Create an audience for some of our novelists and contemporary poets! We'll manage to do it', wrote Mallarmé to Emile Zola in November 1875. For some time past he had felt he might act as a sort of liaison agent between the two worlds—still so widely separated—of French and English letters. The idea had been discussed with Catulle Mendès during his first visit to London as a journalist[64] and had no doubt ripened during long talks with John Payne, who visited him in Paris, learned from Marie Mallarmé how to cook *perdreau au chou*, and returned laden with works to introduce to London. The plan took shape early in 1875, when Richard Hengist Horne arrived with an introduction from the Chevalier de Chatelain to visit him in the new apartment in the rue de Rome.

Horne was a friend of John Payne and most of the young English poets, but he was nearer Chatelain in age and had even carried on a long, platonic literary love affair with Elizabeth Barrett before she became Mrs Browning. He sometimes embarrassed his young friends by boyish antics that ill became his years and Mallarmé, who called him in private 'le petit père Horne', knew what pleasure it would give him when he wrote, 'You, who are younger than any of us'.

Horne came to Mallarmé with the recommendation, besides a great deal of mediocre verse and a few novels, of a critical study of Hamlet. He stayed for a time in the rue de Rome and, in the course of long conversations carried out in a mixture of French and English, suggested an anthology of French verse which would introduce the work of the Parnassians to an English public. It never materialised, but out of these discussions another idea took shape.

> Meanwhile [wrote Mallarmé after Horne had returned to England], could we not make something of the following idea, which would help to bind our two literatures even more closely together? Would there be place for a regular weekly letter from Paris (a letter or notes), to be put together in London according to the taste of some magazine, on the literary movement here, and would it pay? I live in a milieu where one knows everything interesting, or just curious, that is going on, and I could send any amount of discoveries or criticisms on the works and authors of the day, and you could make of them a very attractive and precise chronicle of French art and letters.

The idea took root and out of it grew the regular contributions to the *Athenaeum* that began in November 1875 and did much to fulfil the hopes Mallarmé had expressed to Zola. The *Athenaeum* had recently undergone some transformations and had become a lively periodical with a remarkably international outlook. Snippets of news from the most unlikely places informed its readers that 'two Japanese philosophers have been awarded the title of Doctor of Philosophy cum maxima laude', or that 'there are in Siamese only two works yet printed that are of interest to European scholars, namely a grammar and a dictionary. It is all the more satisfactory to learn that the King of Siam himself has commanded the publication of a small encyclopaedia', or, again, it went into the question of 'periodicals in the Magyar tongue'. It paid a good deal of attention to all that was happening in Paris, and Edmond About frequently contributed a letter from that city, recording the main literary and artistic events. Mallarmé had suggested a letter dealing with lesser, but sometimes more curious and interesting aspects of the same subjects. This 'letter' finally took the form of brief notes, entitled 'Gossips' and unsigned, which give us a clue to his own friends and preoccupations. They discussed Zola, Manet (a constant subject of conflict with Henley, who had some influence in the shaping of the *Athenaeum* policy and could not bear Impressionist painting), Albert Coligny's new review, Catulle Mendès, 'some Provençal novelties from Arles and Avignon', and so on. Nor did Mallarmé fail to arrange for insertion in these 'gossips' a little publicity for himself, since we read on 20 November of: 'M. Adolphe Labitte, the well-known bibliophile and librarian of the Bibliothèque Nationale in Paris, at whose hands may be expected shortly the French text of *Vathek* with a preface by M. Stéphane Mallarmé'.

It was through Arthur O'Shaughnessy that Mallarmé became a contributor to the *Athenaeum*. This curious young man, alleged to be a natural son of Lord Lytton, had a good deal of influence in literary circles at this time. He had been a friend of Browning, was a dear comrade of John Payne and saw a lot of Rossetti, William Morris and the other Pre-Raphaelites. A little, neat, lively, dapper person, he was an excellent critic and connoisseur of French literature, and wrote a great deal of rather boneless poetry, in the vague style which was soon to become identified in English minds with Symbolism. He had agreed to translate Mallarmé's 'gossips', and he was one of the men Mallarmé was most eager to meet; another was John Ingram, the foremost English critic of Poe, who later became one of his most intimate friends; there was Edmund Gosse, too, a friend of Bonaparte Wyse; above all, the elusive Swinburne, who had received a copy of the luxurious volume containing his translation of 'The Raven', with illustrations by Manet, and had expressed his admiration for 'these marvellous pages in which the greatest American poet has twice been perfectly translated, thanks to the collaboration of two great artists'.[65] All these lovers of France and French poetry might, Mallarmé thought, be induced to contribute to the review he was planning. It was to be entitled *La République des Lettres*; Catulle Mendès was to be its editor, and he himself was to act as go-between with the English writers whose work was to be a feature of this new publication.[66] At the same time, he was hoping to contact some English reviews and meet some possibly useful publishers.[67]

He arrived in London on 14 August, full of hopes and plans. This time he stayed with John Payne, in his lodgings at 20 North Row, Hyde Park. It was a short visit and it turned out to be as frustrating as his previous ill-prepared descents on London had been. Perhaps he never quite understood that English literary life had not the homogeneous quality of its counterpart in Paris, that one could not drop into a certain café or restaurant and be sure of finding a few poets who would tell one where the others were to be found. In London, there were few meeting places of this sort. The Café Royal had not yet come into fashion with the English intelligentsia, while pubs were still strictly working-class establishments. The Cheshire Cheese in Fleet Street had a literary reputation and was perhaps the nearest thing to the Procope in Paris, but it was little known except to the small coterie who frequented it. One needed introductions to the private houses where men of letters gathered, and even there, things were changing, the old circles breaking up. Nor was August a propitious month. 'There is no one in London just now', he was soon writing sadly to Léon Cladel. 'Nothing but regrets expressed in dozens of letters from all sorts of different places.'

He had been counting a good deal on Gosse—known to be a close friend of Swinburne. Mallarmé had written to him in his best English, immediately after his arrival:

Sir, I am for a few days in London and wish to express you my thanks for having forwarded to Mr Swinburne the copy of the Raven, which my friend Bonaparte Wyse had entrusted to your obligeance. To go and work for a few hours to the British Museum, where I have some books to see, was one of my intends when I came to London: perhaps would you, as being of the house, give me some directions about the ways I must follow to be admitted there.

For both these causes I ask you whether you would be kind enough to tell me where and when I may meet with you in London.

Gosse was away in Cornwall;[68] O'Shaughnessy on holiday;[69] Ingram in Paris; Swinburne on the run from his creditors. Mallarmé found it hard to believe that Swinburne was really unavailable, and Payne traces a rather pathetic picture of him, 'a little, bright brown figure of the Parisian type', often to be seen trotting about Bloomsbury with an elephant folio under his arm, its contents being his translation of Poe's 'Raven' with illustrations by Manet.[70] According to Gosse, he spent much of his time in this way 'trying to find Mr Swinburne by the light of pure instinct'.

Luckily, there remained the British Museum. A good many men of letters—some of them eminent—have been employed at various times in the Reading Room, but in the late 1860s and early 1870s, it was indeed, as Edmund Gosse recalls, 'a nest of singing birds'. Gosse himself had been employed there for some time, as had Coventry Patmore; O'Shaughnessy had been in the Reading Room till 1863, at which date he was transferred to the department of Zoology, where he had worked havoc at first through his notorious absent-mindedness.[71] There was Théo Marzials, an eccentric young poet of Belgian origin, and the assistant conservator was Richard Garnett who had been Antony Panizzi's Chief Assistant at the time when the new domed Reading Room was built to replace the old, cramped quarters. He was a fervent admirer of Shelley, had discovered a number of that poet's unpublished works and had written some interesting studies on the subject.

Mallarmé was welcomed there, for Gosse sent him a letter of introduction to Théo Marzials, 'himself a great sympathiser with your contemporary Parnassians', who would 'put you in the way of obtaining all the help you need'.[72] At the same time, O'Shaughnessy sent an introduction to Richard Garnett, so Mallarmé was given all the necessary facilities for his researches. He was now, and at last, on the point of completing the edition of *Vathek* he had first discussed with Bonaparte Wyse nearly ten years earlier, so he probably wanted to consult Cyrus Redding's *Memoirs of William Beckford*, a rather rare volume, unavailable in France and the only work at that date to deal with this subject.

Strangely enough, Mallarmé never seems to have taken out a reader's ticket. However, there was less formality in those days and Garnett probably invited him into his office and produced, without more ado, the volumes required. Mallarmé was thus able to finish his preface, and on 4 September, O'Shaughnessy could insert a 'gossip' in the *Athenaeum* announcing the publication of *Vathek* in October.[73]

Then the Reading Room closed for its annual cleaning and staff holiday and there was nothing to keep Mallarmé in London. It had been a disappointing visit, but not nearly as unfruitful as it must have seemed at the time. Although it was nearly twenty years before he came again to England, he remained in correspondence with his London friends. They came to see him in Paris, discovered the charm of the modest little apartment in the rue de Rome, where, recalls A. Fontainas,[74]

> On Tuesday evenings when we crowded round Mallarmé to listen, each of us lost the feeling of apartness. The man with his load of banal worries, disappointed in his destiny, nursing unexpressed hopes, secret and unfulfilled ambitions, ceased to feel them important. . . . How can those who have never had the chance to be present at these meetings, imagine that everything can be so transformed by the innocent intellectuality of words?

George Moore, Arthur Symons, Whistler, Havelock Ellis, Oscar Wilde, Aubrey Beardsley and many others used to frequent the famous Tuesday evenings and bring back stories of the extraordinary seduction of the poet's conversation. Over in London, the short 'gossips' in the *Athenaeum* became longer pieces in the *National Observer*, which printed in French articles which even the editor admitted he could not understand.[75] A whole host of friends, which swelled as the years went by, took pride in knowing, and making known, the obscure little Frenchman who lived in semi-poverty and whose work was appreciated only by the restricted number of his countrymen who were ready to follow him into the chilly realms of the Absolute, which he liked to declare was the only area in which he felt himself to be competent.[76] 'In the likeness of the most lovable of men because of his character and charm', wrote Paul Valéry, 'he represented for me the total purity of faith in poetry. Compared with him, all other writers seemed to me to have failed to recognise the sole god, and to have given themselves up to idolatry.'[77]

3

Verlaine's England

The Foolish Virgin

The London Paul Verlaine and Arthur Rimbaud discovered in 1872 was, as we have seen, very different from the city where Mallarmé and Marie had first arrived, like two shy children, ten years earlier. The poverty was as terrible as ever, it is true. It was still the London of Dickens, and the French quarter was as miserable as it had been when Mallarmé lived in Panton Square. 'Today', wrote the Pastor of the French Protestant Church to Queen Victoria on 12 December 1872, 'many-faced misery is as deep, as crushing, among the people to whom I minister as ever it was.' The evolution of public and political opinion, on the other hand, had been rapid. 1870 had come and gone, the British attitude to France had changed; politicians and intellectuals alike took a far more kindly view. Karl Marx observed this evolution from his home in Hampstead, crowded with refugees from the German revolution and from the Commune:

> Here in England [he wrote to Kugelmann[1]] public opinion was ultra-Prussian at the beginning of the war. Now it is just the contrary. In the café-chantants, for example, the German singers with their Wacht am Rhine are booed, while the public joins in the chorus when French performers give the Marseillaise. Apart from the sympathy the masses feel for the Republic, and the distaste of 'respectable' people for the new alliance—so obvious today—between Prussia and Russia . . . the manner in which the war has been waged: requisitions, burning of villages, execution of sharp-shooters, taking of hostages and other recapitulations of the Thirty-Years War, have roused general indignation.

In Soho itself, life was busier, more stimulating. With the swarm of refugees from the Commune, the French quarter had burst its boundaries, spreading northward and even sprouting little annexes in the suburbs. The newcomers had set up their headquarters in several establishments. One met them in the Café de la Sablonnière, traditionally hospitable to Frenchmen and Francophile Englishmen; Barjan's French bookshop in Prince's Street, was another centre, so were the Duke of

York Pub in Gray's Inn Road and a number of restaurants like Victor's in Old Compton Street (*Déjeuner* 1/6; *vin ordinaire* 1/-), the Hotel de Seine in King Street and the Restaurant International recently opened by Monsieur Plantade. In more serious mood, the Communards met at the Cercle d'Etudes Sociales in Francis Street, or attended lectures in a room above the Hibernia Stores on the corner of Old Compton Street or in the centre founded by the refugees of 1851 at the Spread Eagle. Marx's house in Hampstead was a 'refuge of Justice' and French fugitives were always sure of receiving advice and assistance there. Marx and his family, however, soon found them over-turbulent and Karl Meyring tells us they brought 'much annoyance and trouble in their track'.

Tremendous energy went into the founding of innumerable newspapers, which always died prematurely for lack of financial support. Eugène Vermersch was the main figure in this activity and, with Auguste Blanqui, the leading spirit in the colony. He was a tireless journalist and lecturer, a whole-hearted revolutionary who had been condemned to death by MacMahon's tribunals and whose immediate expulsion had been demanded by the *Daily Telegraph* in a column and a half on its front page, as soon as he arrived in England. However, events had moved quickly and a year later he was able to set up his own printing works where he produced his own journals and those of various small socialist groups. The *Imprimerie Anglo-française* had a precarious existence, for there was always some financial backer in disagreement with its policy, so that funds would be suddenly withdrawn after an exchange of acrimonious correspondence. Vermersch had managed, none the less, to produce sixty numbers of a daily newspaper, *Qui Vive*, which had meddled resolutely in English internal affairs and had terrified the more timid *émigrés* by attacking the sacrosanct British royal family. Its tone was decidedly aggressive, but it had been far more interesting than any of the ephemeral French journals previously printed in London. The first number had carried a long critical study of Swinburne's *Songs before Sunrise*; there was a serial recounting the experiences of a political deportee; one could find news of political prisoners in France and of the various workers' movements in England and on the Continent. Then there were useful advertisements: real French caporal tobacco was on sale at Carrera's; someone required a French pastrycook; 'young girls of good family' sought employment as governesses or lady's companions; and there was always a selection of needy 'French gentlemen' looking for pupils.

Qui Vive was indispensable, but like all Vermersch's ventures, it was financially shaky. It expired and was immediately replaced by the *Vermersch-Journal*, which lasted barely three weeks, to be replaced by *L'Union Démocratique*, then by *L'Avenir*, with a new editor, who gave less space to attacking the English bourgeoisie and concentrated on making ferocious fun of the first miraculous cures at Lourdes. It advertised lectures and classes, then tried—and failed—to promote a socialist school for the children of *émigrés*. Vesinier, Landeck and Oudet were producing another daily, *La Fédération*, but were suspected of accepting subsidies from the exiled Emperor. *L'International, La Commune Révolutionnaire*, appeared and disappeared claiming, like all the Communard journals, to be the sole true representative of international socialism.

All these journals evidently gave a faithful picture of the agitated, chimeric climate of the colony in the early 1870s. Among other things, they reveal a good deal of the constant quarrelling and backbiting that went on. Each Communard seems to have had his own idea of what socialism really meant. Blanqui thundered against 'so-called revolutionaries' who refused to accept his intransigent Manifesto, and especially to commit themselves to total atheism. Eudes was suspected of being an apprentice-dictator, Prosper Lissagaray, founder of the Cercle d'Etudes Sociales, was always on the edge of becoming engaged to Eleanor Marx. He had a quarrelsome, aggressive manner, an extraordinary memory and fine qualities of organisation; he believed only in 'the People', hated all the cliques, and was hated by them. Then Vermersch caused more turmoil by accusing Marx of living in luxury on money embezzled from the workers. 'Here, it's a mix-up, a clamour, a confusion, a King Pétaud's Court, that would make a caricaturist double up with laughter', he wrote on 12 August 1872 to M. Vuillaume. [2]

> They've founded clubs, reunions, lodges, circles... study-circles, circles for proletarians, for Communards, for revolutionaries (this last is a secret society; apart from the whole of London, nobody knows about it), a Lodge of the Federation, a Lodge of the Revolution, etc. Naturally, this one excludes that one, who fulminates against the next, who calls the fourth a spy, who says the fifth is a traitor, who asks the sixth to produce accounts. This last having made off with the till, is eating, drinking and enjoying himself and not giving a snap for the five others.

He himself, of course, had contributed as much as anyone to produce this state of affairs, though no one suggested he was other than honest. The atmosphere of suspicion was thickened by the fact that all the refugees knew themselves to be under police supervision. England, indeed, was said to be the most spied-on of all the countries where the ex-revolutionaries forgathered. Reports on their activities were regularly transmitted to France, and everyone knew that these reports were nourished by informers within their own ranks. Who were they? Names flew about, rumour was rife, but no one knew for sure. The Communards, in fact, were following the pattern that political exiles had always followed and would continue to do in the future.

Yet the lives of these refugees was less introverted, less confined, than those of their predecessors had been. The general change in opinion and the horror induced by the massacres at Versailles acted in their favour. Their presence was no longer ignored or resented. The Victorians liked to flavour practical matters with a touch of idealism, and there were plenty of employers ready and anxious to make use of the skilled artisans who were arriving in great numbers. Thus two workmen from the Gobelins manufactory introduced some secret methods to the Old Windsor firm; a couple of artisans from Paris were called in to decorate the sumptuous mansion of Richard Wallace, while painters on porcelain, fan-makers, metal engravers, mechanics, upholsterers, draftsmen, tailors, cooks and shoemakers were positively snapped up by tradesmen anxious to learn the methods and small secrets that produced the admired French luxury goods. The women were in demand as dressmakers, florists, hatmakers and makers of fine lingerie.

The situation of professional men and intellectuals was not so easy. To the conventional bourgeoisie they were still suspect, but there were liberal and intellectual circles where they were welcomed as representatives of a struggle for political freedom that had not been entirely unsuccessful. Most of them made an uncertain living as journalists or French teachers, or took posts *au pair* in English boarding schools. A few had connections that led to important situations. Jules Andrieu later became Governor of Jersey: Camille Barrère French Ambassador to London; Paschal Grousset was admired by Gladstone for his study of Ireland; Brunet tutored the Prince of Wales's sons at Dartmouth. Several lectured at the newly-founded London University or acted as tutors in rich or aristocratic families. They were, on the whole, poor but not without hope and, in general, there was a great deal more contact with the English than earlier generations had known.

Belgium, too, had had her share of refugees in 1871. There was much coming and going between Brussels and London; news was exchanged, rumours ripened and swelled. Tales of the successes of certain compatriots across the Channel were no doubt widely exaggerated. London, from a distance, must have appeared a Mecca where political refugees were welcomed and could pick up a fortune.

Echoes of all this reached Verlaine and Rimbaud, reeling along the dusty Flemish roads or drinking in the taverns of Brussels. They had been wandering for nearly two months now, aimlessly, 'l'âme au sept-iéme ciel ravi'[3] but sparsely nourished by biscuits and copious drafts of wine from the cellars of transient hosts.

Their association had started just a year earlier, in September 1871. Verlaine, twenty-seven years old, author of several books of verse which had been admired by the Parnassians and earned him numerous friends in literary circles, was a rising young man of letters. He had recently married sixteen-year-old Mathilde Mauté de Fleurville and appeared to be settling down, after having sown more than his share of wild oats, to a life of bourgeois domesticity.

The appearance was deceptive and the reformation superficial. Verlaine was, in fact, unstable and easily influenced as a child. From an early age he had shown disquieting signs of a dual personality, and indeed, a perspicacious schoolmate had once made a drawing of him, showing him as 'an astronaut fallen into a sewer'.[4] He adored his mother (who had spoiled and coddled him outrageously) and would never free himself entirely from the religious principles and moral standards she had instilled in him. Yet he had never ceased to be a worry to her, and later there were several occasions when he flew into violent rages, attacking and even wounding her. He was pious and idealistic, yet from his schooldays on he had enjoyed writing obscene verses. Soon there came the longing for absinthe and probably at least one homosexual episode, yet he was now living in apparent harmony with his ultra-bourgeois family-in-law, and the poems of *La Bonne Chanson*, dedicated to his young wife, were tender, pure and even a little sugary.

It was at this point that Rimbaud arrived in Paris, with the manu-script of 'Le Bateau Ivre' as his only luggage. He was nearly seventeen, but looked even younger, though he was big and vigorous, with enormous hands which later filled fastidious Mallarmé with horror. After several fruitless attempts, he had at last broken away from a tyrannical mother and the stifling conformity of his home in the Ardennes. Now he came to seek refuge with a poet he passionately admired. In spite of his cherubic appearance, he was already a force to be reckoned with. He was at the height of his poetic power; he had elaborated a theory of the poet as 'seer' and believed he knew how to attain this state; he was ready to conquer Paris.

It was a shock to find a reformed Verlaine, living a virtuous family life which recalled, though on a higher social and intellectual level, the climate of that bleak house in Charleville over which Madame

Vitalie Rimbaud ruled with an iron hand. As for the Mautés, they saw only an uncouth peasant boy. Literary society, to which kindly Verlaine introduced his protégé, was amused, then annoyed, by the bad manners which became worse when Rimbaud decided it was composed of a collection of pretentious lickspittles. If it stood him as long as it did, it was due to the extraordinary seduction of blazing blue eyes and a marvellous voice, irresistible in spite, or because of, its rough country accent.

Quite soon, the Mautés and Paris had had enough of Rimbaud, and Rimbaud had had enough of them. There remained Verlaine, the fellow-seer, the great poet, imprisoned in the caul of bourgeois conventions. Verlaine needed him, the liberator, just as he himself had need of Verlaine. In spite of the difference in their ages and situation he had soon recognised in the admired older poet, the stuff of a disciple. Here was the unique, essential being with whose collaboration the theories he had been building up in Charleville could be translated into reality. For Rimbaud believed himself to have discovered, or to be on the verge of discovering, the recipe for ultimate happiness:[5]

> J'ai fait la magique étude
> Du bonheur que nul n'élude.

he had written then, but this state of magical joy, which had nothing in common with the banal pleasures the uninitiated call 'happiness', could only be attained through 'the long, immense and systematic derangement of the senses.'[6]

Now this programme, which involved, essentially, the re-creation, or re-invention of love, could only be carried out with the collaboration of a partner-in-alchemy, a sort of golem, created by the wizard, yet possessing an autonomy of his own. The choice of this partner was of the utmost importance; his original matter must be worthy of remodelling; he must be strong enough to take part in such an unprecedented enterprise. Rimbaud led Verlaine through the Paris streets, talking, explaining, persuading. There were stops for long draughts of absinthe, probably for whiffs of hashish—easily procurable in Paris in those days and much in fashion since Baudelaire. Verlaine said, 'I understand you.' Rimbaud believed him. The fact that his friend was married and about to become a father was irrelevant. He was to be offered an initiation that should have provoked a submission as instant and complete as that of the disciples to Christ's invitation: 'Abandon all else and follow me.'

'Truly, in full spiritual sincerity, I had undertaken to restore him to his original state as a son of the Sun.' Such was the promise that Rimbaud had held out and that tore Verlaine, after endless wavering, from his comfortable home, to experience in filth, hunger and squalor, and to construct with his terrible partner, 'une pensée aboutissant à la folie.'[7]

How long did this state of exaltation last? Rimbaud had liberated in Verlaine the demonic (or angelic) forces at whose existence he had guessed, although they had seethed until then largely below the surface. Together, they had experienced 'les passions satisfaites—Insolemment, outre mesure'.[8] Verlaine had been subjugated, hypnotised. Years later, when he was already sick and prematurely aged, he remembered with an acuity that never faded nor diminished, that period of total liberty, of utter abandonment to art and love:[9]

> Tout ce passé brûlant encore
> Dans mes veines et ma cervelle
> Et qui rayonne et qui fulgore
> Sur ma ferveur toujours nouvelle.

Rimbaud, totally dedicated to his insensate enterprise, saw only his companion's acquiescence and an enthusiasm that matched his own. He was very young—too young to grasp the psychological uncertainties that were already torturing Verlaine. How could he have guessed that his friend had written to his deserted wife, barely two days after leaving Paris: 'Do not cry, my poor Mathilde. I am living a bad dream and I shall come back.' Nor could he have realised, or even conceived the possibility that there still existed—for all the revelation offered and accepted—another Verlaine, who believed himself, 'born in reality for calm happiness and affection'.[10] When Verlaine confided towards the end of his life, 'For me, Rimbaud is an ever-living reality, a sun that flames within me and is never dimmed',[11] he was undoubtedly sincere, but he was sincere too, when he confided in Mrs Belloc Lowndes, who remembered how,[12]

> When with me, he always spoke of what had happened twenty years before, and I would listen, moved, to his pitiful accounts of how happy he had been during his brief married life. Always he referred, with painful emotion, to the son he had never seen, or if he had seen him, only as an infant. He talked as if he still hoped his wife would come back to him.

By the time they reached Brussels, Verlaine was in a state of bewildered indecision. Even drink, new company and the gaiety of a big town could not calm the creeping doubts he tried so hard to suppress. Both he and Rimbaud loved the colourful, noisy fairgrounds that abounded in the city. They watched the merry-go-rounds and the swings—probably even tried them out, for these two often behaved like over-excited children—and it was while watching, or experiencing the balancing movement of these swings that Verlaine had recognised the oscillations of his own spirit and written:[13]

> Et mon âme et mon coeur en délires
> Ne sont plus qu'une espèce d'oeil double
> Où tremblote à travers un jour trouble
> L'ariette, hélas! de toutes lyres!
>
> O mourir de cette mort seulette
> Que s'en vont, cher amour qui t'épeures,
> Balançant jeunes et vieilles heures!
> O mourir de cette escarpolette!

Did Rimbaud suspect by now that he had been duped, or had duped himself? He was at any rate restless, 'in a hurry to find the place and the formula',[14] ready for a change. When the refugees they met in the Flemish bars of the rue Haute spoke of golden opportunities in London, he was ready to believe them. As for Verlaine, he could consider himself a Communard for he had held a minor job in the Press department of the Hôtel de Ville during the insurrection. Now he heard news of several old colleagues established in London and rumoured to be doing well. He and Rimbaud were not only in a state of spiritual turmoil, they were also by now practically penniless. The decision was taken; they would try their luck further north. Whatever they may have hoped to find there—a fortune? renewed poetic inspiration?—each must have known in his heart that the essential was already lost. The great enterprise was condemned to failure.

At first, of course, they were swamped with new impressions, preoccupied with practical details of where and how to live. Within twenty-four hours of landing, they had discovered the Langham Street studio of Félix Régamey, artist, Communard and an old friend of Verlaine's. Régamey was pleased to see them and recorded that Verlaine looked grubby but seemed in good spirits.[15] Rimbaud, as often on such occasions, uttered not a word. Régamey was able to give them some good advice, and above all to put them in touch with Eugène Vermersch, of whom they both had high hopes. The Communard leader had just got married and Régamey knew he would soon be leaving his lodgings. He did so in fact a few days later, moving to Kentish Town, where he and his little Dutch seamstress lived in blissful happiness, devoting their leisure hours to the rearing of white mice. ('Just like those Communards!' commented Verlaine.)

The newcomers were thus able to take over his old room at No. 36 Howland Street, near Tottenham Court Road,[16] in a once beautiful Adam building that had fallen into a sad state of disrepair. Most of the tenants were French—there were some tailors, artists and bohemians of all sorts. Verlaine later noticed that one of them had written 'very dirty' with his finger on the filthy window pane of the room next to his own, and that the inscription was still there three months later. It was a miserable place, but certainly no worse than the lodgings they had known in the rue Campagne Première and the rue Monsieur-le-Prince. Within a few days of their arrival, the two had settled down there, and were ready to explore London and all her possibilities.

Their first reaction to the city was one of fascinated horror. 'As flat as a bedbug, if bedbugs were flat', reported Verlaine to his friend Edmond Lepelletier in Paris, 'with little, blackened houses and great "Gothic" or "Venetian" mansions'. The weather, according to the natives, was 'superb' during these early September days, but to him, it looked like 'a setting sun seen through grey *crêpe*'. As for the famous Thames: 'Imagine an immense mud-soup, something like a huge, over-flowing latrine, under authentically babylonian bridges, painted blood-red'. The streets stunned them with their noise, with their omnibuses, carriages, cabs and clanging railway bridges. The crowds, too, were noisy, brutal and incredibly ragged. There was poverty such as they had never seen in the worst quarters of Paris. It was a degrading, pervasive poverty that spread into even the most opulent streets and seemed to go unnoticed or be taken for granted. Rimbaud wept at the misery of this 'bétail de misère'[17] and Verlaine was touched by this compassion, forgetting the cruelty it concealed. They were especially impressed by the flocks of wretched little red-uniformed shoe-blacks who flocked over the pavements, begging for custom. French refugees were always on the alert for examples of British hypocrisy, and Verlaine was soon able to explain to Lepelletier that these children were exploited by a so-called charitable society, 'which naturally forces them to spend their whole Sunday worshipping the Lord'.

Never can there have been more indefatigable sightseers than were Verlaine and Rimbaud during their first days in London. Rimbaud plunging desperately into this alien life, disdained description, was no letter-writer, but Verlaine's racy, slangy pen-pictures show he had the stuff of a journalist in him. His correspondence with Edmond Lepelletier and Emile Blémont reflects an almost delirious rhythm. Within a month, the pair had explored innumerable pubs and cafés, deciding that all were abominable (with a slight exception in favour of La Sablonnière, where Verlaine wrote long letters, begging for news of friends in Paris, and which he found 'a decent little place, which I recommend to visitors'). They had explored the City ('a really interesting quarter, where reigns an incredible activity'). They had been to Madame Tussaud's and the Tower of London. They had seen the Lord Mayor's Show and taken a steamer trip down to Woolwich (chiefly because these pleasure steamers were the only place where one could get a drink on Sunday).

Then, when the London streets were beginning to seem too familiar, they took a ride in what Verlaine calls 'the Towers Subway', and enjoyed a thrill of terror. 'It's an iron tube,' he explained to Lepelletier, 'with gas jets at the height of a man's head, and a floor about a foot wide. Inside, it's hot and stinking, and it trembles like a suspension bridge, and one hears a tremendous roar of water all around.' This was in fact merely the newly opened London tube, which did not, as they had liked to imagine, pass under the Thames, and where they could certainly not have heard the roar of water. Verlaine's imagination had coloured, as usual, everything he had seen.

Culture was not neglected. They went to the National Gallery, where they admired the Italian Primitives and the Bellinis, but thought Turner a great fraud and compared him unfavourably with Monticelli. Nor did they think much of Hogarth. The only English paintings, in fact, which they really approved of, were the Reynolds of the Wallace Collection. Then one day, they were tempted to visit the French Gallery, which was holding its fifth Winter Exhibition. Here, a surprise was in store for them, for there was Fantin Latour's *Coin de Table*, in which, just a year earlier, he had depicted the two of them, together with a group of friends. 'We came unexpectedly face to face with ourselves', commented Verlaine.

Then there were theatres to be visited. They saw a performance of *Macbeth*, an English version of Hervé's *L'Oeil crevé*, played at the Comic Opera in the Strand, and a number of what seem from Verlaine's description, to have been low-class farces. They visited the cabarets to watch the nigger minstrels—a spectacle Verlaine adored— or see horribly thin girls dancing a sort of jig, which they took to be the national dance. On the counter of the Hibernia stores, Verlaine scribbled a poem:[18]

> Dansons la gigue !
>
> J'aimais surtout ses jolis yeux,
> Plus clairs que l'étoile des cieux,
> J'aimais ses yeux malicieux.

Were these the eyes of some pretty English girl, or merely those of

Rimbaud? At any rate, Verlaine took a close look at the women of London, or at least at the prostitutes, whom he described at length to Lepelletier:

> their hair done up in extraordinary buns, velvet bracelets with steel buckles, red shawls. . . . They're all pretty, with cruel expressions and angelic voices. You can't imagine what charm there is in the little phrase 'old cunt', addressed every evening to old gentlemen whose clothes are in better repair than their minds, by delicious misses, dressed in crimson satin skirts, mud-besprinkled, soup-stained and freckled with holes from cigarette ash.

Verlaine seems indeed to have done some independent field-work on this aspect of London life, for on the occasion of a much later visit he was to write back to a tyrannical mistress in Paris: 'Don't worry about the women here. Anyway, as far as they are concerned, London brought me bad luck twenty years ago.'[19]

There were days when the city fascinated them. Everything was unexpected, 'a hundred times more amusing than Italy, Spain or the Rhineland', wrote Verlaine, who had never been to any of these countries. At others, it seemed merely sordid, 'black as ravens, noisy as ducks, eternally drunk . . . a mere collection of little, gossipy villages, all flat and ugly':[20]

> Londres fume et crie. O quelle ville de la Bible!
> Le gaz flambe et nage et les enseignes sont vermeilles.
> Et les maisons dans leur ratatinement terrible
> Epouvantent comme un sénat de petites vieilles.

For two such incorrigible Frenchmen, there was plenty to grumble about. Where, for instance, were the conveniently placed vespasians that were such an essential feature of the Paris landscape? Had the English no natural needs? The cafés were revoltingly dirty and refused to serve alcoholic drinks; English matches would not strike; one could not buy a decent cigar. The list of grievances was interminable and the British Sunday naturally ranked high among them. 'Everything is shut till one o'clock', reported Verlaine. 'Then, from one to three, the doors of a few pubs and eating houses open furtively under the eye of a policeman, who stands, watch in hand, supervising their opening and closing. No theatres, of course, but outdoor sermons and hymn singing wherever one goes.' Then, 'Aoah, very dull!' he adds in his newly-acquired English.

October brought the famous London fog, 'savoureux comme non pas d'autres'.[21] Everyone was coughing, but Verlaine, mindful of his mother's training, put on flannel underclothes, swathed himself in scarves, stuck cotton wool in his ears and drank grog and hot punch. Thus he preserved himself from the colds from which everyone else in London seemed to be suffering. The weather did not, in fact, much trouble this man of the north who disliked the sun and felt more at home under dim, veiled skies which lent mystery to the most banal scene. Yet he had not found what, essentially, he had come to seek. 'So far,' he wrote to Emile Blémont, 'though I have seen a great deal here, I have not discovered the poetry of this country, though I am sure it exists.' Was he, in fact, writing anything at this time? An early letter, dated a couple of weeks after his arrival, mentions 'the interminable docks, which suffice largely for my poetry, which is becoming more and more modern'. The phrase suggests that he composed at least one poem, and probably many more, inspired by these docks that seemed to him 'like Carthage, Tyre and everything, all at once'. It seems strange that this first stay in London, which made such a violent impact on his sensibility, should have yielded so few poems and indeed a letter appeared in *The Times Literary Supplement* on 27 January 1916, signed 'H. F. de V. Norman', stating that 'during the years he spent in London . . . Paul Verlaine wrote many excellent poems which have never been published and the manuscripts of which must exist somewhere in this country.' Verlaine claimed that he had never worked so much, but he seems to have been chiefly occupied in polishing-up verses written in Belgium. Most of the poems directly inspired by London are dated from the autumn of the following year, when he was meditating in prison, or else they are nostalgic recollections composed much later, like 'There', which seems to have been inspired by memories of an evening spent in a pub in the neighbourhood of the Angel:[22]

> 'Angels!' seul coin luisant dans ce Londres du soir,
> Où flambe un peu de gaz et jase quelque foule,
> C'est drôle que, semblable à tel très dur espoir,
> Ton souvenir m'obsède et puissamment enroule
> Autour de mon esprit un regret rouge et noir:
>
> Devantures, chansons, omnibus et les danses
> Dans le demi-brouillard où flue un goût de rhum,
> Décence, toutefois, le souci des cadences,
> Et même dans l'ivresse un certain de décorum,
> Jusqu'à l'heure où la brume et la nuit se font denses.

'There' is perhaps the most 'modern' of Verlaine's London poems—or at least of those that have survived—since it reflects the Impressionist view of life and landscape and forms a sort of link with the canvases Manet was painting back in Paris. Other poems referring to this first experience of England—'Green', for instance, or the untitled poem that begins 'Le piano que baise une main frêle'[23]—seem rather to reflect the qualities he was beginning to discover in this country which had seemed at first so repulsive: 'something very gentle, almost childish, very young, very innocent, with a certain brutality and a gaiety that is amusing and charming'. The conquest of Verlaine by England was already under way.

Yet things were not going well for either of the pair. Funds were running out rapidly and one fine plan after another came to nothing. Verlaine had been confident of earning his living as a journalist and had hardly settled into his lodgings before he was writing to Lepelletier, 'Several serious French journals are being founded here, and I am intriguing to get work on them'. But the only journal that got beyond the talking stage was *L'Avenir*, and it lasted only a month, while those already established were dying off, or too needy to pay their contributors. At one point, we find him assuring his friend in Paris that he was writing for several American journals, but there is no trace of any articles from his pen and he makes no further mention of them. He had planned, too, to undertake the French correspondence of 'a tradesman here, who is a close friend of mine and director of an important firm'. This was presumably Monsieur Istace, a friend of his family, ex-proprietor of a café-concert in Paris and now at the head of the Baccarat Crystal Glass Company in London. This project in turn seems to have come to nothing.

As for Rimbaud, he was ready to teach French if the worst came to the worst, but so were some hundreds of other needy refugees, so the supply greatly exceeded the demand. Otherwise, he refused to be greatly concerned with material things. 'J'ai horreur de tous les métiers', he admitted later, 'Maîtres et ouvriers, tous paysans, ignobles.'[24] He was learning English, far more rapidly than Verlaine, wandering by the docks, sullen and lost in unexplained dreams. It was for Verlaine to provide for the *ménage* and, according to Lepelletier, he used to reproach his friend for laziness and a tendency to avoid the Communard colony.

Their compatriots seem, in fact, to have been strangely unhelpful, perhaps because neither Verlaine nor Rimbaud shared their passion for politics. Verlaine had indeed given Lissagaray three shillings, shortly after his arrival, as a membership fee for the Cercle d'Etudes Sociales but he never attended lectures and laughed at the 'frock-coated revolutionaries' who met in Francis Street. Nor does he seem to have visited Karl Marx, or any of the other serious, Germanic law-givers of international socialism. If he had known that the whole Marx family was as fanatically Shakespearean as himself, he might have taken the trouble to find his way to Hampstead, but he was evidently not aware of this lesser-known aspect of the author of *Das Kapital*.

Perhaps a clue to the strangely isolated life these two led in England, can be found in the sketches left by Cazals,[25] Régamey and Verlaine himself. There they are, slouching along some London street, Verlaine 'robust and lofty' as Carrière later described him, with his high, mongol cheekbones and upturned nose; fair-haired, blue-eyed Rimbaud, tall and gangling still like an overgrown child; both unkempt, perhaps a little unsteady on their feet, hostility to their surroundings marked clear on the two surly countenances; two near down-and-outs, obviously not to be trusted. And indeed, in most of these drawings there lurks a shadowy or schematic policeman, a suspicious eye swivelled in the direction of the shambling pair. The 'eye of the police' was probably more negligent than Verlaine imagined, but the Communards were inclined to be paranoic, and he most of all.

Vermersch, the old companion, once a hero of the boy Rimbaud, was the only one who seems to have shown much solidarity, though Lissagaray and Matuszewicz[26] were prodigal with good advice. A little earlier, Vermersch would doubtless have come to the rescue by printing the new collection of poems Verlaine was preparing. It was to be called *Romances sans Paroles*, and Verlaine had been counting on his help. It was unfortunate that the *Imprimerie Anglo-française* should have gone out of business at just this time, dragging with it in its downfall *L'Avenir* and the only solid foundation for all his hopes.

Vermersch, however, was giving a series of lectures during this autumn and early winter. They were on literary-social subjects: Alfred de Vigny, Théophile Gautier and Blanqui, and were held above the same Hibernia stores where Verlaine had scribbled 'La Gigue' and no doubt other poems. On 1 November he was there to hear Vermersch read an early poem of his own, entitled 'Des Morts'[27] and commemorating the revolutionaries who had died in June 1832 and April 1834. It was a poor example of his talent but it suitably illustrated Vermersch's lecture on Blanqui and was listened to respectfully by an audience composed largely of English and of bourgeois French, 'as little Communard as you can imagine'. On the way out, Verlaine was amused to overhear the comment, 'Those chaps seem just as honest as honest people and they're more amusing.' His poem appeared in the next number of *L'Avenir*, with a laudatory comment that pleased him greatly.

Another ex-Communard who might have been helpful was Jules

Andrieu. He was a serious-minded, middle-aged man, with one blind eye, who had acquired a certain reputation as author of an important *History of the Middle Ages*. He had been a colleague of Verlaine's at the Paris Hôtel de Ville during the Commune, but his role had been far more important and he had been tried in his absence and condemned to death by the Tribunals. The two newcomers had got in touch with him soon after their arrival and it was he who had introduced them to Prosper Lissagaray and the Cercle d'Etudes Sociales. Of all the refugees, Andrieu was perhaps the most potentially useful, for he was acting at this time as tutor to Ford Madox Brown's precocious son Oliver—the 'marvellous child' whose death in 1874 was to throw literary London into mourning. Oliver's genius, both as a writer and a painter, seems questionable today, but he must have been an extraordinarily attractive young man, quite unspoilt by the adulation of his parents and the whole Pre-Raphaelite circle. His tutor, as a man of letters, naturally frequented the receptions at the house in Fitzroy Square. Madox Brown was by now an academician and was reaping the rich rewards England bestowed on her official artists in those days. He was a hospitable man and an endless flow of guests passed through the enormous mansion at No. 37. Most of them were safely established men like Ruskin, Carlyle, Browning, Wilberforce and so on, and they were not, according to Brown's grandson, always pleasant company. 'They ringed in my young horizon', he recounts, 'miching and mowing and telling each other disagreeable stories, each one about all the others when they were out of earshot. Yes, that bitter, enormous, grey-beard assembly of the Great ringed in my child's horizon.'[28]

But not all Madox Brown's visitors were greybeards. Young men and the literary *avant-garde* were admitted as well. John Payne, O'Shaughnessy and Ingram were constant visitors, so was Swinburne, whose eccentricities were always forgiven or overlooked, perhaps on account of his aristocratic connections, or his publicity value.

Rimbaud was the same age as Oliver Madox Brown and shared the same tastes. Verlaine already had a certain reputation as a poet. Howland Street was only a short stroll from Fitzroy Square. Nothing would have been more natural than for Andrieu to introduce his compatriots to the Madox Brown circle. It seems indeed that he was on the point of doing so, for Verlaine wrote on 1 October to Emile Blémont: 'I am shortly to make the acquaintance of Swinburne, and of a poet whose name escapes me, who is as unknown as he is extraordinary.'[29] Verlaine's correspondence shows that at this date he had just re-established contact with Andrieu. Everything points to the conclusion that these two old companions had been discussing the literary scene in London and that Verlaine confidently expected to visit the famous Madox Brown salon.

Yet nothing came of the project. Verlaine's letters contain no further reference to Swinburne, whom every French poet of the modern school was yearning to meet but who was becoming increasingly hard to meet. He was on the run from his creditors and even Mallarmé 'hurrying about Bloomsbury trying to find Mr Swinburne by the sole light of instinct'[30] had never managed to run him to earth. Neither Verlaine nor Rimbaud met him, nor do they ever seem to have crossed the threshold of No. 37.

One can only suppose that gossip concerning the pair had reached Andrieu's ears. Brown, as his son wrote to a friend, was 'very straight-laced'. He tolerated spectacular bouts of drunkenness among his guests, but these did not count as immorality. Any kind of sexual deviation, on the other hand, was unforgivable, and indeed unmentionable, in Victorian England. Whatever peculiar sexual habits the habitués of No. 37 Fitzroy Square may have had—and some of them were very peculiar indeed—these were always prudently concealed from the master of the house, and as far as possible, from each other. Thus Andrieu would hardly have dared to jeopardise an enviable position by playing patron to such a reprehensible couple. Indeed, he was evidently inclined to be 'straight-laced' himself. 'What would Andrieu say if he saw us together again?' objected Rimbaud later, when Verlaine pleaded with him to return to London. The older man was probably something of a moral mentor in the colony, whose members, like most of the early socialists, combined free thought, and even free love, with strict ethical principles.

So hopes began to dwindle and the couple began to face stark reality at last.[31]

> La misère aussi faisait rage
> Par des fois dans le phalanstère:
> On ripostait par le courage,
> La joie et les pommes de terre.

recollected Verlaine in later years, but the joy and the courage were rapidly waning. They had been upheld by faith in the great experiment, in the belief that they were recreating love in a finer, nobler form. Now they found themselves living in sordid poverty, more or less shunned by their compatriots and with their personal relationship already ruined, though neither was ready to admit it.

Verlaine was dreaming more and more of Mathilde, and specially of their infant son. He had been in London barely a week when he learned from Lepelletier that his wife was seeking a legal separation and claiming a substantial pension, while the Mautés had distrained all his belongings, including the manuscript of 'La Chasse spirituelle' which Rimbaud had entrusted to him.[32] Lepelletier's letter brought with it a flood of memories of the short months of happiness he had known at the beginning of his marriage. His next letter enclosed a poem entitled 'Birds in the Night', which he obviously meant Lepelletier to show to Mathilde,

> Vous qui fûtes ma Belle, ma Chérie,
> Encor que de vous vienne ma souffrance,
> N'êtes-vous donc pas toujours ma Patrie,
> Aussi jeune, aussi folle que la France?

Was he sincere? Did he really want to return to the restricted bourgeois existence that had driven him into such frenzies a year earlier? When one studies all the contradictions of his behaviour throughout the years, one is forced to the conclusion that he was always sincere—at that moment. Verlaine was certainly sly, and a terrible liar, but he lied above all to himself and his lies were always founded on a peculiar sort of truth which seemed to him more evident than cold facts. Now that he was separated from Mathilde, she had come to represent for him purity, religion and the high principles his adored mother had taught him as a child. No doubt there were moments when he longed for this state of original purity, feeling he had been driven from it, just as Adam was driven from the Garden of Eden. Then he made desperate, spasmodic efforts to achieve a reconciliation, fulminating against his father-in-law, whom he held responsible for Mathilde's obstinacy.

The Mautés were gossiping about his relationship with Rimbaud, spreading the story, alienating his friends. He was preparing a memorandum, he wrote to Lepelletier, which would annihilate 'this revolting accusation'. In fact, certain poems, a few letters exchanged during brief periods of separation, leave no doubt as to where the truth lay. Several poems from the Paris period are quite unequivocal on the subject, and they are confirmed by the medical report contained in Verlaine's dossier, compiled at the time of his arrest in Brussels. Yet here again, it would be an oversimplification to dismiss his protests as mere lies. He and Rimbaud had dreamed of a love that would be absolutely pure, since it would transcend both good and evil, so his indignation at the degrading interpretation given to the relationship by his enemies was not entirely insincere.

Such an attitude would explain, for instance, a curious incident which occurred about this time. Camille Barrère, who was one of the youngest Communard refugees, has related that he was visited by Verlaine in a great state of agitation, come to complain about the gossip concerning his relationship with Rimbaud. 'They accuse me of being a pederast', he broke out violently. 'But I am not! I am not!'[33]

Though there can be no doubt of the homosexual relationship between the two men, they seem to have felt it was merely one element in the great, alchemic enterprise, through which they had meant to liberate and re-invent love. It may really have seemed to Verlaine that people were interpreting this relationship in a way that degraded it and which he did not deserve. Yet at other times he seems to have longed sincerely for the down-to-earth, everyday love of a husband for his wife. Then he made desperate, spasmodic attempts to achieve a reconciliation, and when Mathilde refused to be convinced, he saw himself as a victim of his father-in-law's machinations and his wife's lack of understanding. So when he complained:[34]

> Et vous voyez bien que j'avez raison
> Quand je vous disais, dans mes moments noirs,
> Que vos yeux, foyers de mes vieux espoirs,
> Ne couvaient plus rien que la trahison.

he probably believed, in all sincerity, that he was speaking the truth and that it was he who had been deserted and abandoned.

Rimbaud observed his companion's pitiful fluctuations with mingled compassion and contempt. He could not console himself with lies, and he knew just where he stood.

'Rimbaud was not writing any more poems in London', Verlaine recalled later, but was working at 'a manuscript whose title I have forgotten, containing strange mysticities and the most penetrating psychological observations.'[35] The manuscript in question was presumably that of Les Illuminations, though it seems strange that Verlaine should have forgotten a title, which he explained in his own preface to the volume, was 'an English word which means coloured plates'.

In any case, Verlaine obviously failed to understand the full meaning of his own phrase, 'Rimbaud was not writing any more poems', and it was not without reason that Rimbaud would shrug his shoulders and sneer when his friend claimed to understand him. Not only had he ceased to write any more poetry, but he must have suspected already that he never would write any more. The poetic prose of Illuminations and Une Saison en Enfer are visions of delirium and despair, with none of the magic significance he saw in certain short poems written back in Charleville. Each of those had been what James Joyce used to call an 'epiphany', a revelation, a sudden manifestation, or fleeting glimpse of the *bonheur que nul n'élude*. Then he had tried to capture, by the methods enumerated in the 'Lettre du Voyant', the entirety of this joy. The experiment had failed and Verlaine, with whom and through whom he had imagined himself attaining a state of superhuman happiness, had failed him too. Before him stretched the cruellest of all visions: the normal destiny of mankind. 'Moi! moi qui me suis dit mage ou ange, dispensé de toute morale, je suis rendu au sol, avec un devoir à chercher, et la réalité rugueuse à étreindre! Paysan!'[36]

So Rimbaud wandered by the docks, dreaming of departure, of escape from this apparently inescapable destiny: 'Ma journée est faite; je quitte l'Europe. L'air marin brûlera mes poumons; les climats perdus me tanneront. Nager, broyer l'herbe, chasser, fumer surtout; boire des liqueurs fortes comme du métal bouillant.'[37]

In those days, the docks at Wapping and Limehouse were bordered with dim, mysterious quarters that contemporary novelists described in lurid terms, generally without having set foot in such a dangerous district. 'Chinatown' really existed then; hashish was easy to procure and when Rimbaud wrote later, 'J'ai avalé une fameuse gorgée de poison',[38] he was probably speaking literally.

With hashish, dream and reality merged into one. Rimbaud believed his own dreams, but there was always a part of himself—the part he so hated—which remained a practical, hard-headed peasant. That part knew that such dreams could not be realised without money, and only Madame Rimbaud, back in Charleville, could provide it.

But Madame Rimbaud was the most tight-fisted of all the hated 'peasants'. Moreover, she had been receiving anonymous letters. Others in the same vein, which Verlaine believed to have been written by his mother-in-law, had been worrying Madame Verlaine in Paris. It is not certain that these two virtuous ladies quite understood what their sons were accused of, but they did realise the two would be better apart. Madame Rimbaud wrote to Verlaine, begging him to send her Arthur home. Verlaine thought this would amount to a confession of guilt, but the situation was becoming serious. Letters to close friends in Paris: Forain, Cabaner, Gros, remained unanswered. Had they turned against him? The Mautés were everywhere, visiting friends and relations, spreading their 'calomnies'. Something had to be done, and it seems to have been by common agreement, though for very different reasons, that Rimbaud left for Charleville just before Christmas, while Verlaine awaited the arrival of his mother. 'Apart from the immense pleasure her presence will give me,' he wrote to Lepelletier, 'it will be very useful from the point of view of "respectability".'

Verlaine seems to have made surprisingly little fuss when Rimbaud returned to France and, in view of subsequent events, we can suppose he never intended the separation to be permanent. The sensible resignation he showed suggests rather that the whole thing was a bluff destined to circumvent the Mautés and restore his own reputation.

A letter, dated December 1872, went off to Lepelletier—one of those decently expressed, reasonable letters that are so different from his usual style and give so strong an impression that they were intended for other eyes. His mother, he informed his friend, was coming to live with him; perhaps they would settle down together in London. They would rent a small house in some modest quarter and live comfortably since 'life is a hundred times cheaper than in Paris, the climate a hundred times healthier, and it is infinitely easier to find work.'

His plans went even further, for the letter continues, 'My life will be happy again, and once I have completely forgotten those horrible people, I shall find peace once more and perhaps, who knows? even remarry. . . . You will say', he adds, 'that I have become a real Anglophile, after having started by vomiting up so many complaints (some of them justified) against this country.'

None of this is easy to believe and some of it was obviously untrue. Yet as always, there was a substratum of truth in Verlaine's most complicated lies. It is hard to believe he really intended to remarry, but he had at last made the acquaintance of a real English family who had welcomed him to their home, given him a glimpse of the calm, orderly life some part of his nature still longed for and even, perhaps set him dreaming for a moment of a lifetime spent in some quiet English suburb, between his mother and an innocent little English wife.

The family evidently had a daughter, referred to as 'Kate'.[39] She was probably one of the pupils with whom Verlaine exchanged French lessons against English conversation. Perhaps he allowed himself to dream of her a little, but he could also hope she would arouse Mathilde's jealousy, and suggest (through Lepelletier, who could be counted on to spread all the news contained in his letters) that he was having a feminine love affair.

Kate, if we are to believe the references in 'A Poor Young Shepherd', was a fragile girl, with a long, pale face. It was she, perhaps, whom he sometimes heard playing the piano in the evenings, 'un air bien vieux, bien faible et bien charmant';[40] she to whom he brought, or imagined himself bringing (for it was not the right season) 'des fleurs, des feuilles et des branches'.[41]

Now, through his new friends, Verlaine was able to draw conclusions concerning the psychology of the natives:

These people [he wrote to Lepelletier] are less kind-hearted than we are, in the sense that they are too nationalistic, too specialised, in mind, heart and spirit. But their speciality is delicious, and there is something very innocent, even in this sort of egoism. Even when they seem ridiculous, they are never odious. Family life, which is stupid in France, because it is weak, is so highly organised here that it tempts even the most bohemian.

He was tempted himself. Christmas came and he shared his friends' enormous meal of roast goose and apple sauce. There was too much of it, even for him, greedy as he notoriously was:[42]

> Londres sombre flambe et fume:
> O la chère qui s'y cuit
> Et la boisson qui s'ensuit!
> C'est Christmas et sa coutume
> De minuit jusqu'à minuit.

The following day (was it the effect of the roast goose?) he felt desperately melancholy. Whatever Kate may have meant for him, she could not console him for Rimbaud's absence. 'Rimbaud (whom you do not know, whom no one but myself really knows) has gone', he wrote to Lepelletier. 'What a horrible void! Nothing else matters.' It was raining. London suddenly seemed unbearably sad. The Christmas season is the worst of all times for the lonely and unhappy and now, watching from his window the unceasing rain pouring down on the grimy roof tops he wrote the verses that begin, 'Il pleure dans mon coeur', that almost too well-known poem, with its apparent simplicity and its underlying precision and exact calculation of effect, that shows Verlaine at his most Verlainian, free at last of the influence of the Parnassians and of Baudelaire, employing his own ruses to express his own essential spleen:[43]

> Il pleure dans mon coeur
> Comme il pleut sur la ville.
> Quelle est cette langueur
> Qui pénètre mon coeur?
>
> O bruit doux de la pluie
> Par terre et sur les toits!
> Pour un coeur qui s'ennuie,
> O le chant de la pluie!

Il pleure sans raison
Dans ce coeur qui s'écoeure.
Quoi! Nulle trahison?. .
Ce deuil est sans raison.

C'est bien la pire peine
De ne savoir pourquoi,
Sans amour et sans haine,
Mon coeur a tant de peine.

All his life, Verlaine was haunted by these attacks of spleen, whose origin always remained tormentingly mysterious, 'un ennui d'on ne sait quoi qui vous afflige', a malady which his conversion could not cure or even alleviate and which he expressed for the first time on this grieving Boxing Day in Howland Street.

A few days later, he was really ill and—being Verlaine—he made the most of it: 'My friend,' he wrote to Blémont, 'I am dying of misery, illness, ennui and loneliness. Rimbaud will forward this letter. Excuse such a short one from a very sick man. Goodbye, perhaps. . . .'

Similar letters were sent to Forain, Lepelletier and Rimbaud and telegrams went off to his mother and his wife.

There was no reaction from Mathilde, but Madame Verlaine *mère* arrived in haste. Two days later, Rimbaud was at his bedside—a tender, solicitous Rimbaud, who nursed his friend devotedly and earned the good opinion of the mother. Surrounded by affection, Verlaine slowly recovered, though the defection of his wife left him more bitter than ever against the Mautés.

His mother returned to France; Rimbaud remained, no doubt against his better judgment. 'Verlaine is like a child left alone in the dark without a light,'[44] he had written to Madame Verlaine and he seems to have stayed out of pity for the friend who clung to him in his sickness. The couple settled down again and life was taken up at the point where it had been broken off.

Verlaine's letters of this period suggest that the advice poured out by the two mothers—Madame Verlaine in person and Madame Rimbaud through the post—had not gone quite unheeded. They were trying, it seems, to be sensible. Rimbaud encouraged his friend to work at the manuscript of *Romances sans Paroles*, which they still hoped, with unquenchable optimism, to see published by the Anglo-French Co-operative Printing Society, phoenic-successor to the *Imprimerie Anglo-française*. They were learning English, he told Emile Blémont, 'like mad'. Verlaine bought a copy of *The Narrative Story of Arthur Gordon Pym of Nantucket* and they used Poe's stories as text-books, as

Mallarmé had done before them, studied collections of popular songs as Mallarmé had studied nursery rhymes, and lost no opportunity of improving their accents by getting into conversation in shops and pubs. The reading of Poe in English evidently brought disillusion, and Verlaine seems to have understood how much of himself Baudelaire had put into the famous translation, for we soon find him complaining to Lepelletier of the 'puerilities' of his old idol, and exclaiming 'How naïve this "clever" chap is!'

The British Museum reading room was not—in spite of all the 'singing birds' on its staff—dedicated to pure aesthetics. Many of the regular readers at this period had very different preoccupations. Karl Marx seldom came now, but his harassed daughter Eleanor was there nearly every day, as were Friedrich Engels, and most of the socialist refugees from France and Germany, as well as the English theoreticians of the New Order. Lissagaray was naturally a frequent visitor and it was probably through him that Verlaine took out a reader's ticket on 23 March, followed two days later by Rimbaud. 'You can get everything there,' wrote Verlaine delightedly to Blémont. A list of books and authors in a little notebook bound in moleskin which Verlaine carried with him for several years, includes Flora Tristan's *Promenades dans Londres*, Shakespeare's Sonnets, *Little Dorrit* and the names of Poe and Tennyson. It seems likely that they refer to books read in the Museum, perhaps under the guidance of kindly Richard Garnett, who was to prove so helpful to Mallarmé a couple of years later. Rimbaud too was working hard at his English. 'Bottom' written about this time, suggests he had been reading *A Midsummer Night's Dream* and he seems to have shared his friend's passion for Shakespeare. But the British Museum had a fine collection of books on occultism and these may have nourished the 'strange mysticities' of *Une Saison en Enfer*.

Verlaine's letters of this period suggest—as they were probably meant to—that the couple spent their time in instructive sight-seeing. 'Every day we make huge excursions into the suburbs and countryside, Kew, Woolwich, etc.', he wrote to Emile Blémont in March. 'As for London, we have explored it long ago. Drury Lane, Whitechapel, Pimlico, Angel, the City, Hyde Park, etc., hold no more mysteries for us. This summer, we shall probably go to Brighton, and perhaps to Scotland and Ireland'. Rimbaud, too, wrote in *Les Illuminations* of these long walks where 'the suburbs fade curiously into the country-side'.[45] But he reveals another side of the picture and shows a haggard Verlaine, tortured by doubts, sleepless, or tormented by nightmares: 'Presque chaque nuit, aussitôt endormi, le pauvre frère se levait, la bouche pourrie, les yeux arrachés—tel qu'il se rêvait!—et me tirait dans la salle en hurlant son songe de chagrin idiot' ('Nearly every night, hardly had he dropped asleep, the poor fellow would rise from his bed, mouth rotting, eye-balls torn from their sockets, just as he had seen himself in his dream, and drag me into the room, yelling about the idiotic misery of his nightmare.')[46]

Rimbaud found Verlaine's misery idiotic, not because he was incapable of pity, but because he believed it to be insincere. He could not understand—or perhaps understood but refused to condone—Verlaine's waverings, the loves and hates that, like his whole attitude to life, were fragmented and often contradictory. Verlaine wanted his mother, wanted Rimbaud, wanted Mathilde; Rimbaud was already wanting his freedom. He was observing the situation with despair, compassion and amusement, sadistically tormenting his companion, then consoling him with the same bewildering lack of logic.[47]

Je nous voyais comme deux bons enfants, libres de se promener dans le Paradis de tristesse. Nous nous accordions. Bien émus, nous travaillions ensemble. Mais, après une pénétrante caresse, il disait: 'Comme ça te paraîtra drôle, quand je n'y serai plus, ce par quoi tu as passé. Quand tu n'auras plus mes bras sous ton cou, ni mon coeur pour t'y reposer, ni cette bouche sur tes yeux. Parce qu'il faudra que je m'en aille, très loin, un jour. Puis il faut que j'en aide d'autres: c'est mon devoir. Quoique ce ne soit guère ragoûtant ... chère âme.' Tout de suite je me pressentais, lui parti, en proie au vertige, précipitée dans l'ombre la plus affreuse: la mort.

(I imagined us as two well-behaved children, free to wander in the Paradise of melancholy. We were united. When we worked together we were both deeply moved, but after some penetrating caress, he would say: 'How strange all you have been through will seem after I am gone; when you will no longer feel my arms beneath your neck, nor have my heart to lay your head on, nor these lips on your eyes. For one day I must go far away. Because there are others I must help, though it's a nasty business, dear heart. Instantly I imagined myself without him, I became giddy, I was plunged into the most awful of all shadows, into death.)

It is Verlaine, the Foolish Virgin, speaking through Rimbaud, who knew well how to enter his mind and speak with his voice, and knew too exactly how to play the subtle game of cat and mouse in which he himself was at once the torturer and the victim.

Verlaine's health was still poor; indeed, he never seems to have recovered completely from the mysterious illness in January. He was sorrowing continually about his wife, the divorce with which he was threatened, the little son he had lost the right to see. Barrère had visited Paris and brought back the news that Mathilde seemed to be 'inclined for a reconciliation'. His friends were urging him to return to Paris and put his affairs in order. He hesitated, found himself unable to take a decision. An active intervention at this moment might have persuaded the Mautés to put a stop to proceedings against him. But they would undoubtedly pose their own conditions, the first of which would be a complete break with Rimbaud. He wavered; Rimbaud presumably joined Lepelletier in urging him to return for a time at least. Finally, it was decided that he should go to Paris, while Rimbaud should return to his mother's farm in Roche. The possibility that the separation would be definitive must have been in both their minds when Verlaine started off for Newhaven, where he was to take the steamer for Dieppe.

The boat left without him. According to his own story, he happened, just before the departure, to overhear a conversation between 'two gentlemen in frock-coats with white moustaches'. What were they saying? Verlaine, reporting the incident to Lepelletier, went into no details, merely remarking that it was due to 'this providential hazard' that he was not languishing in a French prison. As it was, he changed his itinerary, took the Ostend boat with Rimbaud on 4 April and joined his mother in Jehonville.

The two white-moustached gentlemen sound strangely like a convenient excuse, or—in view of Verlaine's paranoic tendencies—their conversation may have been a pure hallucination. Yet the copious police reports on the activities of the French refugees in London do contain a few references to Verlaine, one of which confirms that his departure had not gone unnoticed: 'A certain Verlaine is believed to have left London on the 3rd inst. en route for Paris, allegedly on business concerning his family.'[48] One of Thiers's mysterious agents had been keeping at least an occasional eye on him.

Seven weeks later, on 27 May, the pair were back in London. They had been corresponding, and had met several times. Though Verlaine referred frequently to the political plots and family machinations which foiled all his attempts to reach Paris, he had been working continually at his English and seems to have been merely marking time before he could return to London. He was in poor shape physically, but full of plans: a play in prose, an operetta, 'a ferocious novel, as sadistic as possible, written in a very terse style', a new volume of verse, while awaiting the long-delayed and more and more problematic publication of *Romances sans Paroles*. 'I am bubbling with ideas', he confided now to Lepelletier.

They had moved to new rooms at No. 8 Great College Street[49] in Camden Town. The street consisted at that time of a row of small, eighteenth-century houses, which had once been residential but were being transformed one after the other into lodgings. The Bellocs had their family home in this street and Mrs Belloc Lowndes—the friend of his old age—has described the small, high-ceilinged, beautifully proportioned rooms, and a wall, just opposite her house, which was the oldest in England apart from the Roman Walls. Verlaine found the quarter delightfully gay, and commented that one might almost have been in Brussels.

The 'respectability' campaign had evidently been a success, for contact with the French colony seems to have become closer. Vermersch was living nearby in Prince of Wales Road, Kentish Town, earning a precarious livelihood in freelance journalism. They saw a good deal of him at this time and came to know his Dutch father-in-law, M. de Sommer, who shared his home. Andrieu was another ex-Communard who was going through a difficult time, for the death of Oliver Madox Brown had brought his comfortable job to an end. Lissagaray, endlessly cadging meals off Karl Marx in Hampstead, was lecturing, organising, writing—tireless as ever in the cause of international socialism. 'Good sorts and all in the soup', Verlaine wrote of them to Emile Blémont.

Times were hard and paid work was rare. The only indisputable commodity these refugees were able to offer was their own language, and there was great competition for pupils. Up to this point, Verlaine had managed to exchange lessons, but had never found anyone willing to pay him. So he was delighted and not a little surprised when he was able to announce to Emile Blémont: 'Now I am a tutor.' A series of advertisements in various newspapers had actually produced an answer and he was now giving a two-hour lesson each day at three shillings per lesson: 'enough to pay my rent and tobacco'. In fact, the two friends were presumably living entirely on this sum.

Soon after, there came an offer from a boarding school. Four hours of lessons per day in exchange for meals and a decent salary, and above all the chance of learning English thoroughly at last. It was a tempting proposition, but Verlaine had been reading Dickens, and *Nicholas Nickleby* had made him wary of English schools. Perhaps the head-master would turn out to be another Mr Squeers? He was going to make sure before accepting.

Nothing came of the project and Verlaine was enjoying London too much to like the idea of burying himself in the provinces. 'London is charming now,' he wrote to Blémont on 21 June, and a few days later, he was admitting: 'Return to Paris? I think of it sometimes, but? ... And then, I've acquired a taste for London and the way people live here, although it's rough and childish. Perhaps it is good for one to live for a time among barbarians.' He had quite stopped reading the French newspapers and only enquired casually what was happening in the literary world in Paris. Long days in the British Museum were followed by little tea-parties in the parlours of English friends, on whom he could practise his English. Then there were the lessons to the single, blessed pupil. When he felt in need of distraction, it was easy to beg a free ticket for the Princess Theatre or the St James's Theatre, where Declé's company from Paris and the troop from the Alcazar Theatre in Brussels were giving a series of operettas, which Verlaine adored. He was enthusiastic about *La Princesse Georges* and Lecoque's *Les Cent Vierges*, more reticent about Henri D'Ideville's *L'Homme-Femme* which was showing in London and caused so much talk, and he sat through the entire repertory of Offenbach.

Verlaine never gave the names of any of his English friends and the only one who can be cautiously identified[50] is the poet and critic William Ernest Henley, who was later to play such an important role in English literary life and in Franco-English literary relationships. In 1873, he was only twenty-four years old, a cripple with a huge frame and shrivelled legs, author of the remarkable series of poems entitled 'In Hospital'[51] which every publisher in London had refused because of their unfashionable realism, but were recognised later as a landmark in English poetry. It was at about this time that he came to London, with one foot already amputated, living there in the most bitter poverty before setting off on an appalling journey to Edinburgh, to beg the famous Lister to save his other foot.

Henley was one of the few English men of letters who frequented the Communards at this period, so his political opinions were evidently much further to the Left, or at least less bigoted, than they later became. If Verlaine is to be believed—for his recollections of the past are never very reliable—there must have been several meetings between the two men and they should have got on well together, since Henley took pride in his anti-Puritan attitude and advanced views on morals. He spoke excellent French and Marcel Schwob was amazed, many years later, by the enormous number of obscene expressions he knew in that language. Did he, one wonders, learn some of them from Verlaine? It seems likely, since Verlaine was exceptionally proficient in this respect.

Meanwhile, no doubt because the idea of settling in England for good was taking root in his mind, he was working harder than ever at his English. It was evidently not easy going. For two months now, he had neglected all literary work and devoted his whole time to the study of 'speech and grammar'. As a result, he told Blémont, he could now read Swinburne 'without too much difficulty', but pronunciation was a different matter. To the end of his life his spoken English remained irresistibly comic. He became resigned and good humoured about his failures and was the first to laugh at himself.

One may wonder what Rimbaud thought of all this—of the cosy tea-parties, the plans for a comfortable existence among prim, petit-bourgeois English friends. Was he more exasperated by the reasonable Verlaine of daylight hours, or the Verlaine wracked by nightmares when night fell? By day or by night, drunk or sober, the Foolish Virgin seems to have been getting terribly on his nerves. He had not come to London to settle down to a resigned and poverty-stricken pseudo-marital bliss, and his own problems were of a very different kind. He had discovered neither the 'place' nor the 'formula' and suspected already that he never would discover them. Verlaine reproached him later with 'your disgust at everything . . . your perpetual rage against all things',[52] and now the rage and disgust were too often directed against the partner who had weakened so soon, whom he held partly responsible for the failure of the Great Enterprise. The scenes became more and more violent, breaking out without motive, sparked off by a word or a gesture, or simply by a passing mood. In the past, the sadism that was latent in each of them, had been unleashed for their mutual pleasure. Now the 'tigerish love' in which Verlaine had taken such pride had become feeble, drunken battles:

> Plusieurs nuits, son démon me saisissant, nous nous roulions, je luttais avec lui!—Les nuits, souvent, ivre, il se poste dans des rues où dans des maisons, pour m'épouvanter mortellement.[53]

It was Rimbaud who recorded their life together at this time. He probably wrote most of *Une Saison en Enfer* at Roche, after the final separation, as an act of renunciation, in which he turns his back on the past, on his hopes, on Verlaine and on poetry itself. It contains the long prose-poem 'Délires I' and subtitled 'Vierge folle, Epoux infernal', in which Rimbaud enters with extraordinary acuity into the mind of Verlaine, transmuting him into an infernal version of one of the Foolish Virgins of the Scriptures, who has shown herself unworthy of her Master: 'Ecoutons la confession d'un compagnon d'enfer.' They were indeed living together in Hell.

Through 'La Vierge Folle', we glimpse a subjugated Verlaine, worn with drink and, probably, drugs, his nerves giving out, terrified by childish tricks, forcing Rimbaud by his very passivity into macabre persecutions. What Rimbaud did not realise, or had forgotten in his frustration and anger, was that Verlaine could not be persecuted indefinitely. His friend Delahaye, who knew him through most of his life, noted his 'alternatives of extreme submission with violence in the same proportion'.[54] For months, he had put up with Rimbaud's whims, his sarcasms, his sporadic bursts of mental or physical cruelty. When the revolt came at last, his companion seems to have been utterly bewildered and even horrified. It was touched off by the most trivial of incidents. It was Verlaine, of course, who did the shopping, and probably all the other daily chores. On 3 July, he had gone out to buy the midday meal, choosing a herring, which in those days was about the cheapest food available. Rimbaud, evidently in a nasty mood, was watching from the window when he returned, and called down, 'Ce que tu peux avoir l'air con avec un hareng à la main!'

It was certainly not the first, nor the worst insult that had been hurled at him, but it was the last straw. All the suppressed resentment of the last months rose to the surface in a sudden rage that spurred him to action at last. Without even taking time to pack, leaving clothes, books and manuscripts behind him, he turned round, made for the docks, and took the first boat leaving for Belgium.

He was by no means free of Rimbaud, and their next meeting was to culminate in the tragedy that brought Verlaine to a prison cell in Mons and led to his conversion. But the London episode was over; the great experiment had collapsed in sordid silliness. Looking back, a few months later, while he was purging his prison sentence, he remembered the tumultuous months in London with horror:

> Tout l'affreux passé saute, piaule, miaule et glapit
> Dans le brouillard rose et jaune et sale des *Sohos*
> Avec des *indeeds* et des *all rights* et des *haôs*.

and it seemed to him then that nothing remained of those months but the destructive misery of his memories:[55]

> Ah! vraiment c'est triste, ah! vraiment ça finit trop mal.
> Il n'est pas permis d'être à ce point infortuné.
> Ah! vraiment c'est trop la mort du naïf animal
> Qui voit tout son sang couler sous son regard fané.

England had brought disillusion and despair, yet there remained, indestructible, the revelation of 'something very gentle, almost childish, very young, very innocent'. Gradually, as Verlaine returned to the simple, ardent religion of his childhood, he began to remember this aspect of England and believe he might find definitive peace there. By November, he was writing from Mons to Lepelletier in the usual mixture of French and English: 'Je pioche l'anglais à mort. Of course, since I am to live in London.'

Already, England had become in his imagination what it was always to remain, a place of refuge, a place where he was safe from himself, a return to the womb.

'Myself as a French Master'

Stickney, in Lincolnshire, lies about eight and a half miles north of Boston, in flat, rather marshy country that still remains mainly agricultural. In 1875, it was a large village with a population of about nine hundred. There was an endowed school, founded in 1678, open, according to the founder's bequest 'to all the children of the parish who choose to become free scholars', dispensing instruction in 'English reading, grammar, writing and arithmetic, as well as Latin, Greek and Hebrew if they require such instruction'. The headmaster was at that time Canon Coltman, vicar of the parish and Dean of Lincoln Cathedral, while the acting master was a Mr William Andrews, recently arrived with his wife and family to take possession of the schoolhouse, garden and adjoining paddock, the use of which was deducted from his very modest emoluments of £113 15s od per annum.

It was here that Verlaine arrived on 31 March 1875 to teach French, classics and drawing to the Stickney children, in return for his board and lodging and English conversation with the Andrews family. The arrangement had been made through a scholastic agency in London, where he had hastened, true to his resolution, after being freed from prison. He had spent only a week in the capital and had been careful to avoid his Communard friends. It would have been difficult indeed to make them understand the dramatic transformation undergone by their disreputable colleague.

Eighteen months in prison, the bitter experience of the past, broken health, and above all a religious conversion that was, in fact, a sort of return to his original source—all these had produced a new and no doubt almost unrecognisable Verlaine. Physically, he seemed a great deal older. Although he was only thirty, he was already nearly bald, with the high, polished dome of a forehead that caricaturists were later to exaggerate to vast proportions. Enforced sobriety had calmed the feverish anxiety he had shown in earlier days and the impression he made now was respectable and almost staid.

At the same time, his opinions had evolved in the most disconcerting way. Verlaine did nothing by halves. Having abandoned himself to the Church—'as a child to a fairy tale', George Moore said of him later—he now adopted the most orthodox attitude of nineteenth-century Catholicism on social problems, and accepted them as unquestioningly as he accepted theological dogma. The author of 'Des Morts' had emerged from prison as a royalist, convinced of the merits of an authoritarian regime in Church, State and family. Victorian England provided the most harmonious and successful example of such a regime to be found anywhere in Europe, and the notion of a *Pax Britannica* corresponded perfectly to his new ideals. The only shadow on the landscape was the fact that the Church to whose rules the British people so unquestioningly submitted, was an heretical one. But like most new converts, Verlaine had the missionary spirit, and he landed in England with the optimistic ardour of a new St Augustine:[56]

> O civilisés que civilise
> L'Ordre obéi, le Respect sacré!
> O, dans ce champ si bien préparé,
> Cette moisson de la seule Eglise!

he wrote of this chosen land which, if only it had been Catholic, would have been a paradise indeed.

So Vermersch or Lissagaray would have found it hard to recognise the old Verlaine of Howland Street and College Street, of the Hibernia Stores and the Café de la Sablonnière, and no doubt they would have called him a hypocrite as well as a traitor. Yet this new Verlaine was neither more nor less authentic than the old one. His conversion had merely brought to the surface a personality that had almost, though never entirely, disappeared under the combined influence of absinthe and Rimbaud:[57]

> Mais sans doute, et moi j'inclinerais fort à le croire,
> Dans quelque coin bien discret et sûr de ce coeur même,
> Il avait gardé comme qui dirait la mémoire
> D'avoir été ces petits enfants que Jésus aime.

he wrote later in his autobiographical poem, and the Verlaine who set out for Stickney, neatly clad, with missal and rosary in his pocket, had resuscitated the child who had once lived in loving familiarity with God, and with a Blessed Virgin whose features were surely those of his own mother.

We have Verlaine's own lively description of his arrival in Stickney.[58] He was met by one of his future pupils, a chubby twelve-year-old named Tom West, driving a pony and chaise. Then followed a long drive through the flat fens that were so different from anything he had ever known, till they arrived at last at the neat village with its thatched cottages and prettily laid out gardens. The school building was vaguely Gothic in style, roughly plastered, with outside timberwork painted dark red, and imitation fifteenth century windows. Adjoining it was the master's cottage, where he was to lodge. It was tiny and comfortable, with small sash windows and steps leading up and down between the rooms, and the new arrival noted with admiration the thickly piled rugs and the real antimacassars draped over every chair and armchair.

He had been met at the gate by Mr Andrews himself. The head-master was still a young man, barely thirty years old, and Verlaine was struck by the size of his moustache and his enormous whiskers. He raised his felt hat and said 'Welcome, Moussou', to which Verlaine replied in his best English 'Excuse me, I have got plenty of dust'. Mr Andrews, not to be outdone, proposed, 'Veux-tu laver?'[59] and took his new master to wash in the kitchen, before leading him to the parlour to meet his wife.

In his own account of 'Myself as a French master', Verlaine passes quite lightly over the scene that followed, yet it certainly marked a significant point in his life, for it set the tone for the years that followed, his relationship with the Andrews family, his feeling of almost mystic unity with the countryside around him, and the impression which never left him, even during his most difficult moments, of the constant presence of God.

The Andrews had two children at this time: George, who was then about three and terribly spoiled, and little Lizzie[60] (the child was christened Elizabeth and always known as Lizzie in her family), who was about a year younger and who now lay desperately ill in her cradle in the parlour, while her mother wept helplessly. Verlaine had taken an immediate liking to these simple, wholesome people, with whom, in his new mood, he felt so perfectly in tune. The sight of their distress moved him deeply, but it was difficult to express his sympathy. 'However,' he relates, 'my pantomime was understood and, amid tears with which my own were mingled, my hand was clasped with a warmth that made me welcome from that moment.'[61] Standing by the dying child's cradle, the new master prayed fervently for her recovery and Lizzie did, in fact, take a turn for the better from that moment. By the following morning she was out of danger, and Verlaine remained convinced that this almost miraculous recovery was a direct answer to his prayer. As for the Andrews, if they did not entirely share this view, they believed he had brought luck to their home and from then on they considered him as one of the family.

Next morning, Verlaine was taken by his country-bred hosts to visit the barnyard and the pigsty, and to admire the village green, surrounded by poplars which instantly put this fanatical lover of Shakespeare in mind of a scene from *A Midsummer Night's Dream*. In fact, these first glimpses of the English countryside corresponded perfectly to ideas culled in Shakespeare, though later he complained that it was too conventionally pretty, and at the same time over-civilised and progressive with the new-fangled agricultural methods: steam-propelled flails and artificial manures, which rather spoiled romantic illusions.

The school opened at eight o'clock with prayers, read by Mr Andrews, while the children, carefully segregated according to sex, listened 'very decorously'. Then came the alarming moment when the new master must be introduced to his pupils. Mr Andrews was evidently proud of having acquired an authentic Frenchman for his establishment, and was determined he should be properly appreciated. Either this Puritan was capable of embroidering a little on the truth, or—which is perhaps more likely—the employment agency in London had exaggerated. At any rate, Mr Andrews made a little speech, which Verlaine noted with amusement and was able to reproduce textually for the *Fortnightly Review*:

Monsieur Verlaine, who is a Bachelor of Arts of the University of Paris, is willing to assist me in teaching the French language and the art of drawing. He knows English as well as an Englishman, and most certainly far better than all of you put together, but of course, he cannot pronounce it quite well. I am convinced you will respect and like this gentleman. But should any of you take advantage of his foreign accent to show him the least want of respect, I shall lose no time in correcting the error.

Verlaine adapted himself, as he always had done and always would do, with ease and dignity to new circumstances. He had no need to pretend, no need to force himself. He slipped easily and naturally into his new role and filled it to his own satisfaction and that of the community. The Andrews considered him as a member of their family, the children were sufficiently docile and he had no difficulty in making friends. All through his life, he had found it easy to get on with simple, uncomplicated people, specially with country people, and the solid, slow, kindly East Anglians were just the company he needed in his

present state of mind. As for Farmer Prettyyellow, Farmer Brown,
Farmer Fineham—names that are still familiar in the region—they were
grateful to him for teaching his language to their children and proud
to invite 'Mr Moussou' into their homes. When he needed a little
intellectual stimulation, there was a former curate, Mr Scratton, who
'lisped a little French', Dr Maxwell, 'a good fellow and something of a
free-thinker', and above all, Canon Coltman, the local vicar, who was
also a canon of Lincoln Cathedral, and village magistrate. He was a
venerable old gentleman, with a long white beard, who had travelled
widely and spoke a little French. It was probably he who introduced
Verlaine to the work of his old friend, Lord Tennyson, with whom he
claimed to have been at school and whose father had been vicar of a
nearby parish. He was thus at least partly responsible for the mediaeval-
ism that soon began to mark Verlaine's poetry. The masked knight,
the white-clad lady and so on, are indeed curiously reminiscent of the
Morte d'Arthur, and the Poet Laureate's name appears frequently in his
letters at this period.

Canon Coltman was a lover of poetry, a scholar, a man from whom
the new French master could learn much, and who, as he noted, was
'all kindness and zeal, full of practical and real love for the poor and
sinful'[62]. He was, in fact, more remarkable than Verlaine could realise.
In the 1870s anti-Catholic feeling still ran high in England, the 'papists'
were a race apart and their priests objects of almost superstitious horror.
They appeared in the popular novels of George Borrow and Charles
Kingsley—traitors to their country, emissaries of Rome, given to
turning themselves into hares when surprised at their nefarious work,
or to luring pure young maidens into foreign brothels disguised as
convents. So it is surprising to discover that one of Canon Coltman's
closest friends was Father Sabela, a German priest in charge of the
Catholic chapel in Boston and that he even carried religious tolerance
to the point of contributing generously to the new stained glass windows
in the little church. Verlaine, of course, knew nothing of the under-
currents of religious hatred in a country which, in actual fact, he understood very little. He found the friendship between Canon Coltman and
Father Sabela so natural that he does not even mention it and with the
same ecumenical innocence he attended services at St Luke's when he
could not go to Boston. He found these services dull at first, then grew
to like them, because of the hymns, the music by Handel played on the
organ, and the way the whole congregation shared in the worship.
They made him even more curious of the strange ways of these
Protestants, and the village nonconformists were delighted to see him
one Sunday, strictly attentive as ever, in the red-brick Wesleyan chapel.

He was surrounded, petted and encouraged and his new friends invited him to join in the annual Sunday School outing.

Yet he could not allow himself to forget that he was among heretics. For him, the English seemed like ignorant children, whose very faults and small hypocrisies inspired a certain tenderness. The germ of truth was there, needing perhaps only a little encouragement to flower and bear fruit:[63]

> Tout ce monde est plaisant dans sa raide attitude
> Gardant, bien qu'erroné, le geste de la foi
> Et son protestantisme à la fois veule et rude
> Met quelqu'un tout de même au-dessus de la loi.
>
> Espoir du vrai chrétien, riche vivier de Pierre,
> Poisson prêt au pêcheur qui peut compter dessus,
> Saint-Esprit, Dieu puissant, versez-leur la lumière
> Pour qu'ils apprennent à comprendre enfin Jésus.

A Catholic England, he seems to have felt, would indeed be the earthly paradise.

Verlaine had taken up teaching merely because he could think of nothing better to do and it was the way in which impecunious poets usually earned their living.[64] Soon, however, he became interested in these little country bumpkins who teased him whenever Mr Andrews's back was turned, and seem to have soon become really fond of their new master. Most of them were children of local notables—the doctor's son, the sons of prosperous farmers, destined to follow in their fathers' footsteps and spend their lives in this same region. It is unlikely that they learned much French, and it cannot have been of much use to them if they did. They did enjoy drawing, however, and Verlaine found his classes fascinating. Indeed, he must have been one of the first people to take a serious interest in children's art. At first, it is true, he had been puzzled and even rather shocked by the child's-eye vision of the world thus revealed to him, then, meditating on his pupils' quite unrealistic scribbles, he realised that 'children have a way of seeing peculiar to themselves, exactly like the savage races.'[65] He discovered that they drew for their own amusement, never consciously studying the form or size or even arrangement of the objects they were asked to copy. If one of these objects was turned to the left, he noted, they would place it on the right, and vice versa. An eyebrow would be converted into a wavy brush, eyelashes into tiny stakes, a mouth into a crooked zigzag and a nose into a horizontal zigzag. Now he encouraged the children to draw portraits of each other and their neighbours, to see the human face. He himself drew remarkably well[66] and set the example by scribbling some marvellous likenesses on the blackboard. Canon Coltman, paying an unexpected visit to the classroom one day, was thus confronted with the very recognisable portraits of some of his parishioners and was heard to exclaim, almost in awe, 'What artists these Frenchmen are!' It was in Stickney that Verlaine began a collection of children's art, which he kept for a long time and in which he took great pride.

The days and hours were regulated and passed in peaceful monotony. Lessons from eight to eleven o'clock were followed by a mid-day meal with the Andrews and a sixteen-year-old pupil teacher. Verlaine, who had always been greedy, was distressed at first by the English cooking, the lack of gravy or sauces with his meat, the vegetables boiled in water, the stodgy suet puddings and strangely coloured blancmange. Gradually, however, he came to appreciate some of its aspects, enjoying Mrs Andrews's seed cakes and cinnamon biscuits, and especially her stuffed chine, a regional speciality which he remembered with nostalgia and was never able to taste anywhere else.

By four o'clock, he was free to take long walks in the countryside, or he would wander in the garden, lost in his thoughts or scribbling, as Mrs Andrews noticed without curiosity, in a little notebook, or else he would retire to his room to read the theological works recommended by the prison chaplain and which he now found infinitely more absorbing than any secular books. His library consisted at this time of a Bible, the *Summa* of St Thomas Aquinas, a breviary, the works of St Jeanne Chantal, the *Meditations* of Bossuet, the works of Joseph de Maistre, the philosophical studies of Auguste Nicholas, the three volumes of M.-M. Alocque's *History of the Jesuits*. There were no novels, no poetry. The intellectual regime was to be as austere as the material one.

Mr Andrews was the ideal companion for the sort of man Verlaine had decided to become. He was uncompromisingly upright and strictly religious, but by no means a bore, and not without ambitions. His own education had not gone further than a matriculation certificate from London University and it was presumably for this reason that he had been forced to content himself with such an ill-paid post in a small rural school. However, he was highly intelligent, still young and with no intention of spending the rest of his life in this dead-end job. Verlaine's engagement indeed seems to have been due to the headmaster's ambition to transform the sleepy little school, where few of the subjects in its founder's programme were actually taught, into a fine scholastic establishment, from which he himself would pass on to better things.[67] Thus he had been charmed to discover that his French master was also a competent classical scholar. It was decided at once that they should exchange lessons, and during the long evenings Verlaine taught Mr Andrews Greek and Latin, while Mr Andrews taught Verlaine English and German. It was the first time that Verlaine had studied English methodically and now, under his headmaster's guidance, he began to read through 'all the masterpieces of English literature, from Marlow to Addison and from Fielding to Macaulay'.[68]

'My life is incredibly calm, and I am so glad of it',[69] he reported on 29 April to Delahaye, and to Lepelletier he wrote: 'There are no amusements here and I do not seek any. An immense amount of reading, walks with the pupils (not in a crocodile, you must know) through magnificent meadows full of sheep, etc. Its extraordinary how well I have been feeling, morally and physically, for the last week.'

'Calm' . . . 'peace' . . . these are the words that recur constantly in the letters of this period, and in after years Verlaine used to speak of these months in Stickney as the happiest of his life. Yet the calm was only exterior, an idyllic contrast to inner turmoil. 'I am struggling with a sort of ferocity to beat down the old Me of Brussels and London', he confided in the same letter to Delahaye . . . a difficult task indeed, and Verlaine knew from past experience how little he could trust himself. There had been that shameful episode in Stuttgart, where he had hurried, straight from prison, in the hope of convincing and converting Rimbaud. 'Verlaine arrived here with a rosary clutched in his paw,' Rimbaud had reported cynically to Delahaye. 'Three hours later, we had denied his God and set Our Lord's ninety-eight wounds bleeding again.'

This time he was taking no chances. The first thrill of conversion, that had transformed the prison of Mons into the most delectable of castles,[70] was over now. He was no longer transported by the flood of joy that had temporarily annihilated the material world and filled his cell with the almost tangible presence of Christ and His Mother. Now there remained only a disgust for everything that recalled his old life, and the imperious duty of destroying in himself everything that had brought about his downfall.[71]

> J'avais peiné comme Sisyphe
> Et comme Hercule travaillé
> Contre la chair qui se rebiffe.

For sex, of course, was the first of these malefic elements, and he knew it still threatened him. Nowhere could he have been better protected from this point of view than in nineteenth-century Stickney, where it existed only in its most legitimate form and was certainly never mentioned. The virtuous life of the Andrews family, the unstimulating food, washed down by nothing stronger than China tea, the companionship of children and the aged . . . all these were like barriers between himself and temptation, and Verlaine was profoundly grateful for them. Rimbaud, too, represented the works of the devil, but he was far away, an incessant, restless traveller, 'the man shod with the wind', and Verlaine could make himself believe he was interested only in the state of his friend's soul.

As for drink, Verlaine's attitude to this problem was, and would always remain, special to himself. 'Drink' meant absinthe. The rest— and specially English beer—did not count. In Stickney itself, with its strong nonconformist and teetotal climate, there could be no question of frequenting the *Rose and Crown* or other local pubs. These places were socially unacceptable and there would have been a terrible scandal if a master from the grammar school had been seen entering one of them. Boston was another matter. The eight mile walk to make his regular weekly confession was thirst-inducing and Mrs Andrews noticed several times that 'Moussou' returned curiously gay on Saturday evenings, while on at least one occasion, his pupils met him stumbling across the fields 'most gloriously tipped'.[72] The English middle classes by no means shared the tolerant attitude to drink of aristocratic or intellectual circles, and if the Andrews turned a blind eye to their master's little failing, it was presumably because they believed it to be one of the many incomprehensible habits of foreigners.

There was no absinthe, and thus no sin, but there remained the ever-present temptation of literature. To Emile Blémont, Verlaine admitted he still had 'a weakness for poetry'—secular poetry, that is to say, which he now considered as part of:[73]

Tout cet appareil d'orgueil et de pauvres malices,
Ce qu'on nomme esprit et ce qu'on nomme la Science.

that served only to blind men's eyes to truth. He had decided to write in future only to the glory of God and for the edification of his fellow-men. To Delahaye, he confided plans for a series of psalms, modelled on the psalms of David intoned each Sunday morning by Canon Coltman. Some of the 'Hymns ancient and modern' in use at St Luke's also served as models. Thus the poem beginning: 'Pourquoi triste, ô mon âme—Triste jusqu'à la mort', is practically a translation of the hymn beginning, 'Why restless, why cast down, my soul?'[74] but it also corresponds (and with what surprised delight he must have recognised this correspondence) with the meaningless sorrow that so often oppressed him. As for the last poem in *Sagesse*, beginning, 'C'est la fête du blé, c'est la fête du pain,' it surely refers to the Harvest Thanksgiving, when the villagers brought their finest fruit, flowers and vegetables to heap on the altar, and the congregation sang joyfully: 'Come, ye faithful people, come—Sing the song of harvest home'.

Then there was to be an immensely long poem to Our Lady, entitled 'Le Rosaire', and comprising the whole history of mankind, from Adam and Eve to the present day, and a 'deliberately naïve patriotic novel'. 'Need I add', commented Verlaine after confiding these projects to Delahaye, 'that there will be nothing artistic about them. Oh, how I detest this shadow cast by insincerity.' These plans remained—perhaps fortunately—unrealised.

No one in Stickney knew that he was a man of letters. Mrs Andrews had a vague idea that he sometimes wrote verses. 'But', she wrote long afterwards, 'we had no idea that he was a great poet.'[75] These short poems, scribbled in the garden, or 'on my way home after having taken communion in the catholic church in Boston', or 'in a grassy meadow among grazing cows', or 'wandering in the fields'[76] were for his own pleasure, small weaknesses, concessions to a deplorable disease it was too late to cure. Yet at least one of them shows he had discovered at last that which he had failed to find in London three years earlier: 'the poetry of this country'. 'L'échelonnement des haies' was written soon after his arrival in Lincolnshire, at a moment when, no doubt, the strangeness of his surroundings had rendered him specially receptive and the peaceful gaiety of the scene corresponded, in the Baudelairean sense of the word, with the religious joy in his heart.[77]

> L'échelonnement des haies
> Moutonne à l'infini, mer
> Claire dans le brouillard clair
> Qui sent bon les jeunes baies.
>
> Des arbres et des moulins
> Sont légers sur le vert tendre
> Où vient s'ébattre et s'étendre
> L'agilité des poulains.
>
> Dans ce vague d'un Dimanche
> Voici se jouer aussi
> De grandes brebis aussi
> Douces que leur laine blanche.
>
> Tout à l'heure déferlait
> L'onde, roulée en volutes,
> De cloches comme des flûtes
> Dans le ciel comme du lait.

'L'échelonnement des haies' tells simultaneously of the discovery of the East Anglian countryside and of a fresh, tender peace of mind, just as the rain on the city roofs and the grief in the poet's heart blend in the same sad monotony in 'Il pleure dans mon coeur', and certain memories of the gay, working-class quarters of Brussels translate, in 'Kaleidoscope', the chaotic bewilderment of an experience too overwhelming for so fragile a psychic structure. Dream and reality, poetry and life . . . antitheses that blend and become indistinguishable,[78]

> . . . comme quand on rêve et qu'on s'eveille,
> Et que l'on se rendort et que l'on rêve encor
> De la même féerie et du même décor,
> L'été, dans l'herbe, au bruit moiré d'un vol d'abeille.

The poem, like many others of the period, was enclosed in a letter to Delahaye, with the comment that it was intended 'for myself alone'. This did not prevent the sender from recommending his friend to keep them safely, just in case they were needed, and by September he was urging Blémont to find them a publisher in Paris. The old Verlaine, temporarily stifled and in deep disgrace, was by no means dead. Lurking in some suppressed region of the mind, he was no doubt watching sardonically and asking himself how long this new phase would last.[79]

It was not long before a chance came to test his own strength. The name of Germain Nouveau, poet and painter, was certainly not new to him and indeed, it was too closely associated with that of Rimbaud to leave him indifferent. The previous year, Nouveau and Rimbaud had spent several months together in London. No one knew what their exact relationship had been, but Verlaine cannot have been indifferent to this mysterious episode which may well have repeated some of the aspects of his own adventure. The terrible and invincible attraction of Rimbaud had not waned, but he believed it now to be entirely demoniac and he had no desire to meet the sort of unregenerate friends Rimbaud would be likely to foist on him. Nouveau had been one of the 'Vilains Bonhommes'; he had collaborated with Rimbaud and himself in the *Album Zutique*, published in Paris in 1871 and had shown himself as obscene and blasphematory as themselves. So when Nouveau discovered through Rimbaud that Verlaine was in England and suggested they meet in London, Verlaine was unenthusiastic. 'Quel sorte de Monsieur moral est-ce?' he enquired cautiously of Delahaye. Could he be relied on? Would he not give away the address Verlaine concealed so carefully from 'the leeches'—in other words, Rimbaud (who was trying to borrow money from him) and the Mautés (who were trying to make him pay a pension to Mathilde).

In view of all their common friends and parallel activities, it is hard to believe that Verlaine and Nouveau had really never met. It may have been simply an effect of Verlaine's general evasiveness and taste for covering up simple truths with complicated lies which led him to pretend they were complete strangers. Perhaps he was trying to lure Delahaye into giving away some clue as to his relationship with Rimbaud. In any case he must have known a great deal about Germain Nouveau and the sort of 'monsieur' he could expect to meet. Jean Richepin described Nouveau as 'a weak character, over-excitable, with the nerves of a sensual woman who abandons herself to anyone stronger than herself'. He certainly drank, had probably experimented with drugs, and was altogether part of a past Verlaine remembered with shame and remorse. However, curiosity triumphed and on 7 May he travelled to London to meet the friend of whom he was all the more suspicious since he had been so insistently recommended by Rimbaud.

The poem in which Verlaine describes this meeting, reveals that it started off, as one might expect, with a round of the pubs:[80]

> Ce fut à Londres, ville où l'Anglaise domine,
> Que nous nous sommes vus pour la première fois,
> Et dans King's Cross mêlant ferrailles, pas et voix,
> Reconnus dès l'abord sur notre bonne mine.
>
> Puis, la soif nous creusant à fond comme une mine,
> De nous précipiter, dès libres des convois,
> Vers des bars attractifs comme les vieilles fois,
> Où de longues misses plus blanches que l'hermine
>
> Font couler l'ale et le bitter dans l'étain clair.

The ale and the bitter loosened Verlaine's tongue, and made him more eloquent, more persuasive than ever. The conversation continued in a French restaurant—Vuillet's, just off the Haymarket, which Richepin had recommended to the traveller. And of what else could Verlaine talk but the subject that preoccupied him above all others—his conversion, the strength and peace he had found in the Church, the love for the Blessed Virgin that supplanted and surpassed all other loves. One must remember, too, that Nouveau had only lately emerged from the traumatic experience of a life shared with Rimbaud, an experience which must surely have had a profound effect on so unstable a nature and left it in an especially receptive state. At any rate, Nouveau followed him into a church, and was deeply moved. 'He did not believe yet', says Delahaye, in his preface to *Poésies d'Humilis*,[81] but he owed to his friend 'new and mysteriously powerful sensations'. Just how powerful those sensations were can be judged from a letter written to his uncle, Alfred Silvy, on 26 May. 'I am leaving England for a purely providential reason. I had found a job in a little boarding school in the English countryside, where I had been for two days and should be still if God had not awaited me there. The moral change in me is so great that I am physically a different man'.

So Verlaine returned to Stickney feeling that, if he had not operated a miracle, he had at least sown his seed on unexpectedly fertile ground.

A new problem awaited him at Stickney. 'I am not interested in earning money at present', he had written in April, 'I need nothing for myself now.' He was beginning to realise now that this was not strictly true. The journey to London had been expensive; he had been buying a considerable number of books; and the Boston beer, although it was cheap, was not free. Luckily, the Andrews, Canon Coltman and other friends were there to help him find private pupils. The four daughters of Dr Smith of Sibsey started the ball rolling. They were inattentive pupils and caused him a good deal of trouble. Then the vicar of the same village decided he would like to learn French. He was the Rev. Frank Besant, and perhaps he needed to keep his mind off his troubles, for his wife—the Mrs Annie Besant who was soon to become so famous in theosophist circles—had just left him to follow her Call. Sibsey was rather too far to walk, but an obliging pupil from Stickney, John Souden, with whose family Verlaine was very friendly, used to drive him over and wait till the lesson was over to bring him back. Then came the three daughters of Colonel Grantham of Keal Hall and their little brother. These young ladies adored their new master and used to prepare bouquets of violets to welcome him on arrival.

It seems strange that all these lessons should not have brought in enough to satisfy Verlaine's surely modest needs. However, after his return from the summer holidays, we find him acting as agent to his friend Irenée Decroix, who was working in France as a commercial traveller in wines. The venture was not a success and Verlaine had to report sadly, 'It's no good. The English are practical. They want to taste before they buy.'

Then winter came and the muddy fields lost their charm. Verlaine struggled against the old, stultifying boredom, skated awkwardly on the duck pond, caged his verse in the rigid forms that suited it so ill and sermonised Rimbaud: 'As for me: religious as ever, because it's the only right and sensible thing. All the rest is deception, wickedness, stupidity. . . . How I wish you could be enlightened and reflect on all

this. It makes me sad to see how idiotically you are behaving.' 'Darg-
nières nouvelles,'[82] written at this time in the Ardennese dialect for
which Verlaine used to make fun of his friend, shows a rather un-
charitable glee at the news that Rimbaud, after a long spell of wandering
over the Continent, had been robbed of every penny by a villainous
coachman in Vienna.

As for Germain Nouveau, the promised letters arrived. They showed
him fluctuating, seeking himself, resisting or unable to submit to the
lure of belief. Verlaine, impulsive and impatient as he was, restrained
himself, exhorted with delicacy, waited for the final surrender. His
patience was not rewarded till two years later, when Nouveau's
definitive conversion took place, accompanied by the resolution to
eschew 'everything macabre, hostile and strange', in favour of 'purity,
simplicity and the greatest light of all'. . . .[83]

For some time now, Verlaine had been considering a move to Boston, 'where I should find a little more amusement', he wrote to
Blémont in November. The amusements envisaged must have been
very harmless ones, ranging from long chats in the presbytery with the
Sabela brothers and their sister, to surreptitious pub-crawls with a
certain Italian photographer, a Signor Cella, a member of the fairly
numerous Italian colony in the town. Verlaine had been struggling to
read Dante in the original and had probably been exchanging lessons
with the photographer. They had evidently become exceedingly
friendly and Cella had joined Father Sabela in urging him to make the
move. Once settled, he thought, Germain Nouveau might be persuaded
to join him there. His vacillating new convert was a painter as well as a
poet and Verlaine suggested he might paint some frescoes for St
Mary's. This last scheme never came to anything; the Andrews pleaded
with him to stay and even offered him a small salary; the move was
put off from month to month and he was still in Stickney in February
1876, when his mother at last arrived to join him.

Madame Verlaine had a great deal in common with her son. She
was a gay, charming little woman, immensely sociable, who lived largely
in a dream world peopled solely by noble, angelic and disinterested men
and women. No contact with hard reality—and she had known plenty
of it—could destroy these naïve illusions, nor could her son's worst
escapades destroy her belief in him. One can imagine with what joy
she discovered her Paul in his new role of a sober, devout schoolmaster,
loved and admired by all who knew him. There was no Mathilde, no
Rimbaud, no smell of absinthe on his lips when he kissed her good-
night, no sudden, inexplicable outbreaks of violence. For the first time
in her life, perhaps, she had no need to worry about him.

Madame Verlaine lodged with the hospitable tailor whose wife and family had so often entertained her son. She spoke not a word of English, but this does not seem to have prevented her settling down in Stickney as if she had been there all her life, 'enjoying herself without a care in the world, except to get bread for dinner and supper'.[84] She was friendly with everyone. Mrs Andrews remembered her as 'a sweet old soul' and Canon Coltman admired her piety as she attended morning service at his church, quite unsurprised by the curiously new ritual, and reading her missal throughout the incomprehensible sermons.

Since the pair were so happy in Stickney, it seems strange that they should have moved after only a couple of months from their comfortable lodgings, abandoned all the private pupils, and left for Boston without any serious guarantees for the future. One can only suppose that Madame Verlaine encouraged her son to carry out the vague scheme he had mentioned to the Andrews. Various promises had been held out, chiefly, it seems, by Signor Cella, who assured him he would find plenty of private pupils. There was also a convent and small Catholic school attached to the church. Father Sabela may have promised a post, or lessons. Madame Verlaine, incurably optimistic and strangely imprudent, no doubt saw a glowing future for her miraculously reformed son.

It was late in March or early in April that the couple finally took an affectionate leave of the Andrews and moved with all their possessions to the Whale Inn in Boston.

This establishment was situated at No. 48 Main Ridge and the proprietor at that time was a Mr William Kates. The name was due to the skeleton of a whale which had been thrown up many years earlier on the shore of Skegness and been bought by a previous landlord. It was now installed in the back garden as the chief exhibit in a sort of museum containing local antiquities and a curious rococo grotto, decorated with shells arranged in patterns representing crocodiles, elephants and other animals.[85] Customers who drank at least one pint of beer were allowed a free visit; others were charged a fee of twopence. Verlaine, who had been a steady customer for at least a year, had had the idea of installing a table and two chairs inside the whale's skeleton and serving drinks there. This had been an added attraction and one may suppose he was popular with Mr Kates. Neither he nor his mother seems to have realised that a pub was neither a usual, nor even a respectable place of residence for a language teacher.

Verlaine had loved Boston from the first. It had a fine, predominantly Gothic church, the soaring spire of which reminded him of Rouen. The little Catholic chapel by the Witham (which Verlaine refers to as 'the canal') was adorably simple. The congregation consisted of Irish labourers, Italians and a few other foreigners, as well as members of some old recusant families in the neighbourhood:[86]

> Facing the building [he recounts], on the other side of the canal, stood one of those large, white windmills that are almost unknown among us, and during the service, according to the position of the sun, the shadow of the sails fell lovingly upon the high altar and the officiating priest.

Next door, in the presbytery, lived Father Sabela, his sister and his brother. The latter was studying for the priesthood and turned out, to Verlaine's momentary dismay, to have served with the Prussian artillery at Sedan. He was something of an artist too, and had painted a number of frescoes in his brother's church—the reason, perhaps, why the plans for frescoes by Germain Nouveau had come to nothing. There may have been no available surface left.

There were frequent visits to the presbytery and the Sabela brothers would drop in at the Inn, several times a week, for long chats with the Verlaines. Father Sabela was getting into difficulties with the militant Protestants of Boston, and Verlaine discovered now how strong was the undercurrent of anti-Papist feeling in England. A letter published in the *Boston Guardian* on 20 May actually demanded that Father Sabela should be expelled from the town. 'The Scarlet Woman', the 'Whore of Babylon'—such terms were in common use in those days and the convert who had thrown himself heart and soul into the arms of 'the sole Church' must have been pained by such aggressive bigotry.

The younger Sabela was at first Verlaine's only pupil and even these lessons seem to have been given on an exchange basis, since Verlaine was studying German at the time. Advertisements appeared in the *Boston Guardian* and the *Lincolnshire Herald*: 'Mons. Paul Verlaine, B.L. of the University of Paris, will be glad to give lessons in French, Latin and drawing. First-class references. Address: 48 Main Ridge, Boston', but time wore on, the 'lucrative situation', too glibly promised, never materialised, and Verlaine never had more than three pupils in Boston. Funds were running low; the Verlaines left the Whale Inn for more reassuring lodgings with the Soudens, who had just moved to Boston, but still no pupils came. The experiment had been a failure, and before the mother and son left to spend the summer holidays at home in France, Verlaine had sold his freedom again, this time to a Mr Frederick Remington, to whom he had been warmly recommended by Mr Andrews.

Bournemouth

Bournemouth was at that time a select little watering-place, pretty, quiet and purely residential, priding itself on the fact that there was no trace of trade in the village. Beautiful pine woods, traversed by sandy chines, extended right down to the beach, where there was a small jetty but no port.[87]

> Le long bois de sapins se tord jusqu'au rivage,
> L'étroit bois de sapins, de lauriers et de pins,
> Avec la ville autour déguisée en village:
> Châlets éparpillés rouges dans le feuillage
> Et les blanches villas des stations de bains.

wrote Verlaine, and later he recalled how, from the gorse-covered cliffs, one could see 'the scarcely-perceptible white horses, the shining sails of the fishing boats and the red smoke of the steamers as they were on the point of disappearing or had just gone out of sight'.[88]

The Catholic population was small and it was only in the preceding year that the Jesuit oratory of the Sacred Heart had replaced the small wooden chapel that had previously served their needs. It was probably the presence of the Jesuit community that had encouraged Mr Remington to open St Aloysius, a very select little boarding school charging fees of one hundred guineas per year (a great deal at the time) and destined to receive 'pupils who are unsuited because of their delicate health to the harsher régime of the public schools'. This may have been an euphemistic way of describing boys whom, for some reason or another, the very limited number of Catholic public schools refused to admit. They cannot all have been dunces, however, since one of them at least, the Hon. William Clifford, who got on well with Verlaine, later became a well-known scientist and carried out important research in the field of radiography.

As for Mr Remington, he was a convert, an ex-clergyman of the Anglican church, a large, solemn man, bearded and pince-nezed, with rigid ideas and small aptitude for keeping discipline. He lived with his family at No. 2 Westburn Terrace, one of a pair of semi-detached villas, built in the seaside style in the form of chalets and which were also used as the school premises.[89] Verlaine lodged with the family and received a salary of £60 per year, plus his board and keep, but not his laundry. If one can believe anything in Frank Harris's extremely unreliable account of this period[90] he greatly resented having to pay for his own washing.

There were only twelve boys when Verlaine arrived to take up his post, some of them being Irish and, according to him, 'real little devils'. There was none of the friendly, informal atmosphere of the Stickney grammar school. Here, walks were taken in crocodile and, when spring came, Verlaine, correctly top-hatted, conducted his boys in this formation through the chines and down to the sea for their daily bathe. It is hard to imagine that he bathed himself but, after all, he had learned to play football in Stickney, so perhaps he even made the sacrifice of a quick dip into the chilly water of the Channel. Discipline was sporadic. There was a terrible row when one of the boys spoke of a 'bloody orange', yet smoking was tolerated so long as Mr Remington did not actually see it. He never seems to have intervened to prevent the merciless teasing to which these horrid little boys subjected their foreign master and once, when winter came, some specially devilish child hurled a snowball with a stone in its centre, wounding poor Verlaine on the forehead.

Another English winter! It had a charm of its own and Verlaine wrote in January:[91]

> Il fait un de ces temps ainsi que je les aime,
> Ni brume ni soleil! le soleil deviné,
> Pressenti, du brouillard mourant dansant à même
> Le ciel très haut qui tourne et fuit, rose de crême;
> L'atmosphère est de perle et la mer d'or fané.

But dark, setting in early, brought the old, mortal spleen, and with it, new terrors and regrets: 'solitude du coeur dans le vide de l'âme—Le combat de la mer et des vents d'hiver'.[92] When night fell:[93]

> Le soir se fonce. Il fait glacial. L'estacade
> Frissonne et le ressac a gémi dans son bois
> Chanteur, puis est tombé lourdement en cascade
> Sur un rhythme brutal comme l'ennui maussade
> Qui martelait mes jours coupables d'autrefois.

Verlaine was never to integrate himself into the life of St Aloysius as he had done into that of the Stickney school, but he does not seem to have been unhappy there. There were three learned and pious men serving the 'charming little Jesuitry'. Two were ex-Anglican clergymen—one a Father Anderdon, a nephew of Cardinal Manning, who was giving a series of lectures on Catholic doctrine. Verlaine does not mention them, but one may guess he was there, attentive, in a presumably small audience. He evidently found the rather special nineteenth-century

convert mentality, with its touch of aggressivity and its sometimes naïve enthusiasms, not unsympathetic, and even Mr Remington
turned out more companionable than he had seemed at first. There
were family evenings spent with him and his wife and daughters,
evenings with the Fathers, above all long evenings alone in his little
room with the oil lamp softly lighting the empty pages on the table.
He was preparing the volume that would be published under the title
Sagesse, choosing among the poems written in Stickney, with their
extraordinary diversity of style and mood, rearranging those written
in prison, grouped under the title 'Cellulairement'. No longer was there
any question of renouncing a literary career. *Romances sans Paroles* had
passed almost unperceived, perhaps because of the climate of scandal
which surrounded it and the circumstances of its publication.[94] *Sagesse*,
on the other hand, was the work of a Catholic poet and Verlaine hoped
and expected it would gain him an audience among a large public of
Catholic readers. 'Your verses are quite simply superb', wrote Victor
Hugo after receiving a packet of poems sent off to Jersey. Verlaine
must have dreamed often of the exile in his island beyond the horizon,
for he managed to make himself believe he could see its rocky shores
from the Bournemouth cliffs. Such encouragement from the venerated
old poet cheered Verlaine, but it also made his own exile harder to
bear. He was growing a little tired of England, with its 'anglicanisme
impérieux et rêche'[95] and its little, closed-in Catholic community
that would never—he must have realised it by now—spread its net to
gather in this stiff-necked people. In fact, he was beginning to long for
Paris, where, as he wrote—momentarily off-guard—to Delahaye, 'One
can have a bit of fun.'

Mathilde and Rimbaud were present in Bournemouth as they had
been in Stickney. Delahaye was an indefatigable intermediary with the
Mautés. Through him, Verlaine was able to visit his little son during the
brief Christmas holidays. It was enough to fire his imagination, set him
dreaming that Mathilde would forget the past and return to him. Thus
in 'Un veuf parle', which he probably wrote the following year, reality
and symbol, the visible sea and the sea of his own tears blend in
typically Verlainean style, become indistinguishable one from the
other:[96]

> Je vois un groupe sur la mer.
> Quelle mer? Celle de mes larmes.
> Mes yeux mouillés du vent amer
> Dans cette nuit d'ombre et d'alarmes
> Sont deux étoiles sur la mer.

> C'est une toute jeune femme
> Et son enfant déjà tout grand
> Dans une barque où nul ne rame,
> Sans mât ni voile, en plein courant . . .
> Un jeune garçon, une femme! . . .

Most of the poems for Mathilde were written in England and they have a continuity of their own, a constant climate of nostalgia, broken here and there by sudden outbursts of resentment. 'Birds in the Night', 'Child-Wife', 'Beauté des Femmes', 'Un Veuf parle', and, later still, 'Les chères mains qui furent miennes', all express the same ambiguous, vacillating sentiments, the same self-pity, the same longing for love and incapacity to bestow it in an adult manner. Reconciliation was a dream. Verlaine knew it could never be anything else, and must have known, deep in his heart, that he did not truly wish it to become a reality. He cherished this dream as a child cherishes and fondles a doll, playing that it is alive, and as late as the year 1885, he would write, 'J'ai rêvé d'elle et nous nous pardonnions'.[97] Mourning for lost Mathilde, Verlaine is surely mourning for something lost in himself, and his sudden rages at her treachery are for his own self-betrayal. The Mathilde poems, if we read between the lines, tell us almost everything about Verlaine.

Under contract with Mr Remington, he was to spend six months at St Aloysius, and he seems to have left Bournemouth in April, just after Mr Remington moved his school to a new house at No. 24 Surrey Road.[98] His employer must have been pleased with him, for in July, he was back again. A certain number of boys stayed at the school during holidays—a fact which makes one suppose their parents may have been Empire builders in India or other distant places. Verlaine seems to have been re-engaged in order to supervise these boys and to have accepted Mr Remington's offer, probably without enthusiasm, in return for the promise of a fine reference. His duties could not have been strenuous, and on 2 August we find him writing to Delahaye: 'Je versifie à mort.'

What was he writing? 'La mer est plus belle—Que les cathédrales' definitely belongs to this period. The spell of Tennyson was evidently as strong as ever, for the poem owes all too much to 'Sea Dreams', of which the first lines seem indeed to be a rough translation. The sonnet dedicated to Emile Blémont was probably written at this time. The problem of 'There' is more important. It seems to have been written in Bournemouth and there is good reason to think it belonged to this second period, after Verlaine's stay in Paris with his friend Istace, who had resuscitated his 'café-concert' after the years of exile. Paris had meant the cafés, encounters with old friends, with Forain and others who had last met him in company with Rimbaud. In Stickney, Rimbaud had seemed far away and he had been able to preach, or mock. Back in Paris, he had come face to face with his own past, unable to run away or close his eyes. In 'There', Verlaine allows himself, for the first time since their separation, to recall an incident of their common life in London and to admit at last:

> C'est drôle que, semblable à tel très dur espoir,
> Ton souvenir m'obsède. . . .

But 'There' is also an attempt to throw a bridge between the old life and the new, to relive an old experience in the light of a new one, and back in Bournemouth, safe from temptation, Verlaine was able to conclude:

> Cher recommencement bien humble! Fuite insigne
> De l'heure vers l'azur mûrisseur de fruits d'or!
> 'Angels'! O nom revu, calme et frais comme un cygne!

'There' is a cry of victory, and of thanksgiving and also one of the very few attempts at self-analysis he ever made. He could not, of course, have been expected to realise that he was being over-confident.

Summer came to an end, and Mr Remington kept his promise. Verlaine was able to report on 7 September, 'I have two splendid certificates in my pocket, visa'ed by the local authorities and legalised by the French Consulate in London'. One was presumably from Mr Andrews, the second read:

I hereby certify that Mons. Paul Verlaine was assistant master at my school from September 1876 to Easter 1877,[99] having been recommended to me as a good and efficient master from the grammar school at Stickney in Lincolnshire where he had been previously employed. Mons. Verlaine was engaged to teach French and Latin and to superintend the pupils generally, and I had every reason to be satisfied with the manner in which he fulfilled his duties in these respects. The pupils made considerable progress while under his care, and I would willingly have prolonged the engagement had not Mons. Verlaine been desirous of returning to France.

Witness my hand this seventeenth day of July in the year of Our Lord eighteen hundred and seventy seven.

Fredk. H. Remington B.A. Camb.
quod attestor
G. Brayton Aldridge
Notary Public, Bournemouth.

Verlaine could return to France, his future assured.

Lucien Létinois

It was not assured, of course. Nothing in Verlaine's life ever had been or ever would be. He had believed himself strong enough now to resist temptations in his own country. A post in a religious college in Rethel in the Ardennes had seemed to offer every guarantee. He had been happy in the ecclesiastical atmosphere, beloved, as usual, by masters and pupils. But there were numerous cafés in Rethel, more attractive than the ill-kept English pubs, and no one would be surprised or shocked to find him peacefully installed, sucking at his long Dutch pipe, plunged in some book and sipping at his glass of wine. Nor would it seem unnatural that the wine should be followed by a rum, then by a brandy, by everything, in fact, except the terrible absinthe which he was still careful to avoid. The wine, rum, brandy, etc. sufficed, however, to destroy a precarious stability and the time came when even the tolerant and affectionate priests of Notre-Dame could no longer ignore the lay master's eccentricities. In July 1879, Verlaine's engagement was terminated, with regrets on both sides.

A month later he was back in England, turning to her, as he had done before, when he needed protection from himself. He needed it badly this time, for he was not alone. The young boy who accompanied him was Lucien Létinois, an ex-pupil from Rethel, whom he considered as his adopted son:[100]

> ... puisque mon vrai fils, mes entrailles
> On me le cache en manière de représailles.

The exact nature of Verlaine's relationship with Lucien can only be conjectured. He has left a complete account of it in the series of poems entitled 'Lucien Létinois', incorporated in *Amour*. They give the facts, with a rather suspect frankness, and insist heavily on the Christian purity of his paternal love for Lucien.

It is probable that this relationship did indeed remain technically pure, at least until the end of the year. It must be remembered that Verlaine was not exclusively homosexual, nor during his homosexual periods was he exclusively passive and feminine. His attitude towards

Rimbaud had not been consistently that of the 'Foolish Virgin', submissive to her 'Infernal Spouse'. It was in fact Rimbaud's extreme youth, his innocence and adolescent fragility that had first enraptured him and, in Paris watching over his sleeping companion, he had feared for this vulnerable creature and cried:

O misère de t'aimer, mon frêle amour![101]

There is no doubt that when the seventeen-year-old poet had arrived at the rue Nolet with the manuscript of 'Le Bateau Ivre' under his arm, Verlaine had imagined himself in a protective, almost paternal role. The cartoonist Jean Forain, an exclusive homosexual with whom his name has been coupled, was much younger than himself; Germain Nouveau, his spiritual son, was young and feminine; and much later he was unsuccessfully in love with the painter Cazals, twenty-one years younger than himself. Verlaine's constant and rather surprising success as a schoolmaster was perhaps due, too, to this instinctive love of youth and innocence, and his self-deceiving desire to guide it and win its friendship and confidence.

Now in October 1878, Rimbaud had stayed for a short time at Roche, only twenty kilometres from Rethel. There is every reason to suppose the two men met and that Verlaine found himself confronted with a new Rimbaud in whom there subsisted no trace of the luminous adolescent of 1872. All the numerous sketches made by Verlaine of his friend in London insist on this childish, or boyish aspect, and contrast forcibly with photographs and portraits of the same period.[102] It seems as if Verlaine was striving desperately to retain the vision of Rimbaud as he had first seen him. This was the vision that obsessed him to the end of his days, and the Rimbaud he met in Roche, worn already by hardships, excesses and constant wanderings, was a sort of stranger. Thereafter, he would be a memory, a 'sun', but no longer a reality.

Lucien Létinois was at hand to take his place. He was a tall, gangling, seventeen-year-old rustic from the Ardennes, so he had some points in common with the Rimbaud of 1871. To most people, he seemed large, graceless and stupid. To Verlaine, he seemed 'fin comme une grande jeune fille', with his 'frêles doigts', his 'profil fluet', his 'douceur dive et . . . grace insigne'. Thus his ex-schoolmaster dreamed of reliving the experience with Rimbaud, but this time in a Christian context, without sin or shame.

They set off together for England, not to London, where they stayed only in passing, but to Stickney, the Christian haven. Verlaine had remained in correspondence with the Andrews and knew that his old post had become vacant again. After a short stay with the Soudens in

Boston, Lucien was installed in the Andrews' house in Stickney while Verlaine made his way down to Hampshire to take up a post at the 'Solent Collegiate School', 64 High Street, Lymington.

The school consisted of two large, semi-detached houses, covered with virginia creeper that autumn would soon deepen to a glorious crimson. The old-fashioned little town had a small port, and Verlaine may have sometimes joined the throng of locals who crowded the beach when Lord Tennyson, returning to his home at Faringford, strode majestically to the jetty and embarked on the waiting steamer for the Isle of Wight. All around this town stretched the New Forest and, just as Stickney had struck him as a setting for *A Midsummer Night's Dream*, so the New Forest seemed in his imagination another Forest of Arden. His pupils occasionally managed to snatch a few words with the young ladies of Miss Noakes's girls' school, when the two groups passed each other on the Brockenhurst Road in the course of their daily walk. Verlaine was enchanted to discover that one of his boys had engraved entwined initials on the trunk of one of the great trees 'vain de sa grace hautaine'.[103] Nothing could have been more Shakespearean! 'It was quite romantic!' he recalled years later.[104]

The headmaster of Solent Collegiate School, Mr William Murchison, was an energetic Scotsman who combined his functions with that of town mayor. He was a tremendous talker and he and Verlaine used to spend long evenings smoking their pipes and discussing history, which seems to have been Mr Murchison's hobby. It was presumably from him that Verlaine acquired some agreeable but totally erroneous ideas about the past of this region that appealed to him perhaps even more strongly than Lincolnshire had done:[105]

> O Nouvelle-Forêt! nom de féerie et d'armes!
> Le mousquet a souvent rompu philtres et charmes
> Sous tes rameaux où le rossignol s'effarait.
> O Shakspeare! O Cromwell! O Nouvelle-Forêt!

There were few distractions and few friends, though Verlaine seems to have got on well with Mr Murchison's thirty-odd pupils, three of whom were French. There was the local priest too, Father Patrick O'Connor, but he was a hearty, sporting type of man, captain of the local cricket team, and perhaps not much given to learned or holy conversation such as Verlaine was inclined to expect from his clerical friends. He seems on the whole, to have been strangely absent from his surroundings at this period, wandering about in a Shakespearean haze and living for letters from Stickney:[106]

> ... O ses lettres dans la semaine
> Par la boîte vitrée, et que fou je promène,
> Fou de plaisir, à travers bois, les relisant
> Cent fois ...

Yet these letters that Verlaine read a hundred times, 'delirious with joy', cannot have been altogether reassuring. Lucien was not getting on well in Stickney. He spoke not a word of English and had none of Verlaine's enthusiasm for leanirng. He sulked at meals and Mr Andrews soon found that he was incapable of keeping order. As for the Miss Granthams, who had recommenced French lessons with him on their old master's recommendation, they could not bear him. He was taciturn, unkempt, 'a great contrast to Verlaine',[107] and altogether a great disappointment.

Verlaine advised, admonished, with the affectionate gravity of a true father:[108]

> O ses lettres d'alors! les miennes elles-mêmes!
> Je ne crois pas qu'il soit des choses plus suprêmes.
> J'étais, je ne puis dire mieux, vraiment très bien,
> Ou plutôt, je puis dire tout, vraiment chrétien.

By the end of the term it had become evident that Lucien's place was not in Stickney. When Verlaine met him at King's Cross at the end of December, it had probably been decided already that the experiment had been a failure and the two of them should return to France.

Verlaine had once spent Christmas day in London. He had been sad and lonely then, when all the rest of the world seemed gay. When he decided that Lucien and he should spend the holidays there together, it was surely part of the planned antithesis between the old and the new love, between the first departure:[109]

> En compagnie illustre et fraternelle vers
> Tous les points du physique et moral univers,
> —Il paraît que des gens dirent jusqu'à Sodome.

and this new, pure love that would lead the father and son:[110]

> Par un chemin semé des fleurs de l'Amitié;
> Exemple des vertus joyeuses, la franchise,
> La chasteté, la foi naïve dans l'Eglise.

As for what really happened, one can only guess and choose between two equal possibilities.

'J'ai la fureur d'aimer. Mon coeur si faible est fou', Verlaine admitted and it seemed that the flesh too was less completely tamed than he had liked to think. He himself has told us all we shall ever know about that terrible Christmas day in the 'monstrous city':[111]

> O l'odieuse obscurité
> Du jour le plus gai de l'année
> Dans la monstrueuse cité
> Où se fit notre destinée!
>
> Au lieu du bonheur attendu,
> Quel deuil profond, quelles ténèbres!
> J'en étais comme un mort, et tu
> Flottais en des pensées funèbres.
>
> La nuit croissait avec le jour
> Sur notre vitre et sur notre âme,
> Tel un pur, un sublime amour
> Qu'eût étreint la luxure infâme;
>
> Et l'affreux brouillard refluait
> Jusqu'en la chambre où la bougie
> Semblait un reproche muet
> Pour quelque lendemain d'orgie,
>
> Un remords de péché mortel
> Serrait notre coeur solitaire . . .
> Puis notre désespoir fut tel
> Que nous oubliâmes la terre,
>
> Et que, pensant au seul Jésus
> Né rien que pour nous ce jour même,
> Notre foi prenant le dessus
> Nous éclaira du jour suprême.

Monsieur Jacques Borel and Mr Vernon Underwood believe that these verses refer to the 'noble avowals' made by the 'son' to his 'father' and concern a liaison between Lucien and some girl in Boston. But the semi-admissions, the quick withdrawals behind the 'it was as ifs', the 'sincere insincerity' that pierces through every line, are typical of Verlaine when he has something to hide—something so close to his heart that he is forced—almost physically—to translate it into poetry, but which he dare not describe exactly as it happened. It seems more likely that the couple celebrated their reunion and Christmas Eve with too much alcohol, and that this was followed by an upsurge of Verlaine's old, irresistible sensuality. Did that Christmas night in London mark a turning-point in the relationship between the two or, more probably, a single incident which marred an otherwise successfully sublimated love? One can only speculate. At any rate, they returned immediately to the Ardennes, and Verlaine continued to speak and write of his 'son', until Lucien's death from typhoid in 1883.

So far as we know, that dreary, guilt-ridden Christmas day was the last he was to pass in England before reappearing in 1893 as a lecturer and literary lion. There had been many plans for exploring the country more thoroughly. 'This year we shall probably go to Brighton, perhaps to Scotland and Ireland', he had written to Emile Blémont early in 1873, and two years later, in a letter written from Stickney to Delahaye, we find him daydreaming of 'travelling by short stages all over this country, and perhaps in Scotland and Ireland'. It was probably through lack of funds that these excursions never materialised, but there is a mysterious reference in 'Souvenirs et Promenades' to a visit to London, which seems to have taken place in 1883. This was the year of Lucien's death, and Verlaine tended in times of stress to take refuge in England, to seek the peace he had always found there when life became too much for him. He may well have crossed the Channel, seeking comfort in the gentle, orderly life he loved, yet which he could never support for long. England was the Mother-Image, incarnate in geographical entity, adored and resented as were all Verlaine's loves.

4

Lecturing in England: Mallarmé and Verlaine

'Serious Instants': Verlaine in London, Oxford and Manchester

By the time the 1890s had set in, the French colony in London had been to a great extent dispersed or assimilated. The Communards had died or had returned, forgiven, to their own country or were settled, now elderly and respectable, in steady jobs in various parts of England. Soho still had its French shops and cafés, and a certain characteristic flavour, but there was no longer a steady trickle and occasional flood of refugees to swell the population and inject new life into it. With revolutions apparently out of fashion, there was no more excuse for the ephemeral newspapers and semi-secret societies that had enlivened the quarter over the centuries. Nor were there any outstanding figures like Vermersch[1] to stir things up. The colony, in fact, had become rather insipid. Soho was no longer a fascinating and slightly dangerous place, but a quarter in which London's artists and writers could meet in the little cafés and restaurants that evoked their beloved France.

For literary London was almost aggressively Francophile now. Things had changed a great deal from the time when Mallarmé, drifting miserably in a hostile city, had been unable to discover a single young poet with whom he could talk of the Ideal. Nearer still, Verlaine had glimpsed, but been excluded from, a circle in which British intellectuals were pillars of Victorian society and foreigners—especially if they were French—were still distrusted. Now the day of the Eminent Victorian was past. Madox Brown's miching and mowing greybeards were dead or had lapsed into senile silence, and no new Tennyson or Carlyle had arisen to replace them. There were some great names like those of Meredith, Hardy, Housman, but these were nonconformists, almost fringe geniuses compared with their predecessors. Swinburne indeed wrote on, though he was a reformed character now, living in Watts-Dunton' sprim villa, his latest volumes a little tired and dim compared to the fine days of the sixties. His disciples, however, were beginning to make themselves known. There were the members of the Rhymers' Club—Arthur Symons, its chief mouthpiece, Oscar Wilde, Yeats, Lionel Johnson, Ernest Dowson, Richard Le Gallienne, Theodore Wratislav and others—young men who believed in art for art's sake, who despised the great British public with its great British materialism, and refused to compromise with it. To turn to France for one's inspiration was a gesture of defiance.

Everything about France fascinated them. The naturalism of Zola and Flaubert, the dandyism of Baudelaire, the aestheticism of Gautier and Huysmans, the rediscovery of the visual world by the Impressionists . . . all these seemed like avenues of escape to island-bound artists and writers. French Symbolism, above all, suggested possibilities of flight from sordid reality, though, like Payne and O'Shaughnessy before them, the poems it inspired them to write were rather thin and insubstantial. It is said that a guest at a meeting at the Cheshire Cheese was driven in desperation, after listening to the various poets reading, in alphabetical order from Dowson to Yeats, from their own works, to suggest a fine of sixpence for every use of the word 'lily', singular or plural. They dreamed of Paris, of Mallarmé, the Father of Symbolism, of Verlaine, who had cast off the trammels of conventional society and wrote in a new free style. The liberty and free-and-easy Bohemianism of the Left Bank was a magnet, too, for these Londoners, so was the gay indifference of a city where one could live as an individual unhampered by laws enacted by the hated and ubiquitous philistines.

So everyone went to France, and some even settled down there. Whistler had been one of the first to shake the coal-dust of London off his feet and take up residence in Paris, where he had become the friend —or more often the enemy—of almost everyone who counted in the world of art. George Moore had studied art there and considered himself practically a Parisian; Oscar Wilde, who considered French art 'the only art in present-day Europe worth talking about',[2] made long stays and was a friend of Marcel Schwob, Rémy de Gourmont and most of the rising young writers. Symons, Edmund Gosse, John Payne, Charles Whibley, John Ingram, went busily back and forth, meeting people, giving and gathering news, translating, introducing new French poets to a restricted but receptive English public.

For all of them Mallarmé or Verlaine, or both, were poles of attraction. Each held his own court, one in the rue de Rome, where his Tuesdays were famous and he had drawn around him, 'a magic circle within which he accomplished the rites of his mysterious incantation';[3] the other in the cafés of the Latin Quarter—the Procope, the Harcourt, the François Ier—where he reigned, sick, poor and drink-sodden, but with ever-increasing prestige. Returning visitors wrote about them;

their names became familiar to the widening circle of those interested in French literature. Not all the people who spoke ecstatically about Mallarmé seem to have actually read him[4] and though Henley allowed himself to be bullied by Whibley and Henry James into publishing Mallarmé's very esoteric 'Vers et Musique en France' in the *National Observer*,[5] he did so under protest, admitting freely that he found it a lot of incomprehensible nonsense. Verlaine was a more accessible and familiar kind of poet and by this time he had become a real influence in English poetry. Unmistakable echoes sound in works as antithetical as that of Henley and Symons, as well as in that of most of the poets of the Rhymers' Club.

It was towards the end of the year 1893 that the artist William Rothenstein had the idea of bringing Verlaine to lecture in England. Rothenstein was only twenty-one at the time, but he had been studying in Paris for several years and had become acquainted with the old poet (everyone thought of Verlaine as old, though he had not yet turned fifty). Hearing that he was ill in hospital, Rothenstein visited him and found him destitute and horribly discouraged. He had changed greatly in the last few years.[6]

> His baldness [recalled his young visitor] made his head look higher than it really was, and his small brown eyes with yellow lights and with their corners turned up, looked queer. He was very pale. His eyes had a half-candid, half-dissipated look, the effect of drink and white nights; but they also had an engaging candour. Beneath were broad cheek-bones, a short, socratic nose, heavy moustaches and an untidy, straggling beard, turning grey.

Verlaine was sick, discouraged and miserable, and had no idea how he was to live when he left hospital. He told his friend of the readings from his works which he had recently given in Belgium and Holland, and which had been well received. Kind-hearted Rothenstein, seeking for some helpful idea, suggested that something of the same sort might be arranged in England. He had useful contacts, both in London and Oxford and with their help and Verlaine's growing reputation there should be a sufficient audience to make the journey worth while. His friend Arthur Symons was an obvious choice for the chaperon and agent needed on the London side.

Symons was considered at this time as one of the chief figures in the literary *avant-garde* and he remains the most important theorist and exponent of a certain aspect of the nineties. He was a very aesthetic young man, with a curiously high-pitched voice, whom his mother, at least, considered 'rather pettish and childish'. He had revolted early from a strict nonconformist background and adopted paganism, art for art's sake and a curious mixture of urban romanticism and Celtic twilightery. As a critic, his judgments were often brilliant and penetrating. As a poet, he was perhaps a little too consciously decadent. When *London Nights* appeared in 1894, Verlaine, to whom it was dedicated, discovered in it[7]

> all the subtlety and brilliance of night life, seen through the eyes of a man of imagination who is in love with Beauty. He moves among the splendours of a London that is intelligently free-living, exceedingly modern and at the same time Parisian, yet with something essentially English which lends it a supreme distinction.

The volume caused a scandal and was violently attacked for its immorality, but the *Saturday Review*, whose critics were often both perspicacious and unkind, suggested: 'One feels Mr Symons is merely posing, anxious to appear a more depraved sensualist than he really is.'

Like most of the young men who wrote in the same spirit, Symons was fascinated by France and French art and did his best to identify himself with the French. (He even went to the length of buying himself a ready-made, French-cut suit from La Belle Jardinière in Paris. 'One is not exactly proud of him', wrote Arthur Condor, another French fan, when his friend appeared in this outfit.) Verlaine was one of his heroes, and he could not have been unconscious of the prestige he would acquire by producing the famous poet in London. He agreed to make all the arrangements in London, and Professor York Powell, another great admirer of the poet's would do the same in Oxford.

As for Verlaine, he was, of course, delighted. He retained the tenderest memories of England and seems to have forgotten the horrors of his early years in London. He had always felt that England was in some way lucky for him and now, with his usual resilience, he began to plan ahead. 'An era of lectures—perhaps lucrative—awaits me',[8] he wrote from hospital to Robert de Montesquiou, and to Rothenstein; 'My intention is to speak of French poetry at this moment of the century (1880–93), with plenty of quotations, several of them from myself.'

He set out on 19 November 1893, after a series of rather frantic letters: How was he to get there? What would the journey cost him? How much would he be paid? In spite of all misgivings, he arrived safely, though not till two o'clock on the morning of the 21 November, owing to rough seas in the Channel which had delayed the crossing. Symons, excessively worried, was waiting for him in his rooms in Fountain Court in the Temple, 'that vast caravanserai of the Law and of Silence'[9] where Symons's friend, Havelock Ellis, another Francophile had lent him his room. He later described this charming spot in a poem entitled 'Fountain Court', which he dedicated to Symons:[10]

> La 'Cour de la fontaine' est, dans le Temple,
> Un coin exquis de ce point délicat
> Du Londres vieux ou le jeune avocat
> Apprend l'étroite Loi, puis le Droit ample:
>
> Des arbres moins anciens (mais vieux, sans faute)
> Que les maisons d'aspect ancien si bien
> Et la noire chapelle au plus ancien
> Encore galbe—aujourd'hui . . . table d'hôte.

Verlaine was exhausted by the journey, but he was even more hungry than tired. The two men had much to talk about: 'Paris, poetry, money too—poets think of nothing else, and for good reasons— my future lectures', recounts Verlaine.[11] Thus they gossiped for two hours, consuming an entire box of Osborne biscuits (Verlaine thought they were muffins), washed down by gin and water. Verlaine said afterwards that it was one of the best and gayest meals he had had in his life. As for Symons, he was in the throes of a passionate and hopeless love affair with the 'ambiguous child' he celebrated in 'Liber Amoris', and the evening seems to have cheered him up considerably:[12]

> My dear Master and friend [he wrote to Verlaine on receiving the poem on Fountain Court] You are too charming to me. The poem is delicious and I thank you for it a thousand times. Nothing could have given me greater pleasure. Now, if my poor verses are soon forgotten, at least my name will be remembered.
>
> But, you must absolutely evoke the memory of the biscuits and gin of that truly immortal night! It is a worthy subject for you, 'a subject made to your hand', as Browning said, and you could very well write something both funny and exquisite. We simply must have that poem.

At midday, Edmund Gosse arrived to take them out to lunch, so Verlaine found himself in the stimulating company of the two men who were the chief English experts in contemporary French poetry. Then he returned to a whirl of activity in the Temple. There were the finishing touches to be put to the evening's lecture, but everyone wanted to see the legendary poet, fresh from Paris, and there seems to have been a constant coming and going. William Heinemann and William Rothenstein dropped in, so did the publisher, John Lane, in whom Verlaine had great hopes; Meredith had written to say he would like to arrange a meeting, but for some reason this does not seem to have materialised; Mrs Belloc Lowndes came to tea, and it was on this occasion, apparently, that Verlaine confided in her and poured out the nostalgic memories of his married life which so touched that kind-hearted lady.[13] It seems curious that he could have been preoccupied with thoughts of Mathilde at a time when his sentimental life was so complicated. For Verlaine had left behind him in Paris two mistresses—Philomène the unfaithful and Eugénie (Esther) the avaricious—to each of whom he had promised marriage when he should return rich from his English lectures. A good deal of time during his stay was indeed spent in writing pacifying letters to these two harpies and begging friends for information about their behaviour, for 'I am jealous in this land of Othello', he confided to Cazals. 'I am dying of jealousy.'[14]

In the middle of all this agitation, someone thought of asking the poet what he meant to wear that evening. Verlaine had not given the matter a thought and it now turned out that he had nothing but the disreputable clothes in which he had arrived. Symons—less unconventional evidently than he liked to think—rushed out and borrowed hastily, here and there, a suit, pumps and a nice clean shirt. Stuart Merrill, who was not present but had the account from Symons, says Verlaine, redressed, looked like a respectable clergyman.[15]

The lecture—entitled 'Contemporary French Poetry'—was held in Barnard's Inn, near Holborn Viaduct, in a hall of 'rustic Gothic, sincere, natural and marvellous in its simplicity'[16] which pleased Verlaine so greatly that a year afterwards he was still begging his friends to send him a photograph or drawing of the building. The lecture had been well advertised in a number of newspapers, some of which had described the lecturer enticingly as 'the convict poet', so there was a sizeable audience, mostly feminine. The two ladies who wrote under the pen-name of 'Michael Field' were there, and to them he seemed like 'Satan in a frock-coat, reading religious poetry and darting pitch-dark glances at a company incapable of understanding the tragedies of hell (even the devils believe and tremble), still less its bouts of free revel.'[17] But Verlaine's glances were evidently not as dark as 'Michael Field' imagined. Far from disdaining his audience, he was intimidated, for after his return to France he sent a small drawing to Edmund Gosse, who had been in the chair. It shows a tiny Verlaine looking lost in an immense armchair before a gigantic table and was accompanied by a poem giving his own account of the occasion:[18]

> Dans ce hall trois fois séculaire,
> Sur ce fauteuil dix fois trop grand,

A ce pupitre révérend
Qu'une lampe, vieux cuivre, éclaire,
J'étais comme en quel temps ancien!
Et l'âme, un peu, du Moyen Age
M'investissait d'un parrainage
Grave, à mes airs mûrs séant bien.

Ma parole en l'antique enceinte
Ne jurait pas trop, célébrant
La Foi du passé, sûr garant,
L'éternel Beau, vérité sainte!

J'entretenais de mon pays,
De cette France athénienne,
Une élite londonienne
Dont les voeux furent obéis,

Puisque de l'estrade sévère
Il ne tombait conformément
Au réel devoir du moment,
Que ces mots: 'Bien dire et bien faire',

Et tel bel autre et caetera
Dont s'esjouit la bonne salle.
—Coin de la ville colossale
Où, ce soir, l'Esprit se terra ...

Je conserverai la mémoire
Bien profondément et longtemps
De ces miens sérieux instants
Où j'ai revécu de l'histoire.

The lecture consisted, in fact, almost entirely of readings from his own works, accompanied by a running commentary in which the poet described the occasions that had inspired him. Verlaine was in fact presenting a biography of himself, in a carefully revised version, suitable for the tender ears of the young girls in his audience.

When it was all over he, Symons, Gosse and a few others went to the Crown Inn in Charing Cross Road to celebrate. Verlaine, having played his part in such a satisfactory way, was once more his incorrigibly friendly and convivial self and was soon in conversation with an ex-ballet girl who was overheard proposing to him that he should accompany her home. Verlaine had enough strength of mind to decline the offer, but Gosse—a prudish young man—left in a hurry.[19]

Next day, there were friendly reports in the morning papers and

John Lane reported to Rothenstein—back in Oxford, where he was busy preparing his album of *Oxford Portraits*—that 'Verlaine was a great success last night.' Verlaine himself was in an exultant mood and wrote to his mistress, Philomène Boudin: 'I gave my lecture yesterday. Success and, I have every reason to believe, money. But as there were three people selling tickets from door to door, I don't know how much, nor, alas, can I get at it.' It seems in fact that Symons and his friends, knowing their Verlaine, were inventing pretexts to prevent him spending his fee before returning to France.

More friends dropped in during the day, but Verlaine found time to take a stroll through Soho and revive old memories. Symons was amazed at the extraordinary exactitude of his memory and the way in which he recalled every detail of streets and houses he had not seen for so many years.[20] As for Verlaine, he found the city much changed 'at all events in its purely "continental" quarter, and much to its advantage from the point of view, somewhat narrow perhaps, of an old Parisian'.[21] Soho had indeed been considerably cleaned up, physically and morally during the past few years. It had become almost respectable now, with just enough aura of departed vice to make it exotic and exciting. The sordid old chop houses against which he and Rimbaud had railed in 1872 had been smartened up, 'changed with our new mood', says Holbrook Jackson[22] and replaced by larger and brighter restaurants. The pubs, though still much frequented by prostitutes, were no longer thieves' kitchens; the streets no longer ran with filth and the proximity of Notre-Dame-de-France, erected on the site of Burford's famous panorama, shed a certain aura of decency over its vicinity. 'All this', noted Verlaine, 'did but increase my long and profoundly felt sympathy for a city which I have praised so often for its force, its splendour, its infinite charm too, in fine weather and foul.'

That evening there was a dinner in Symons's rooms, with Theodore London, an artistic clergyman from Manchester, William Heinemann, the poet Herbert Horne, editor of *Hobby Horse* and son of Mallarmé's old friend, and others. This time, some ladies had been invited and Verlaine mentions an elderly Englishman, teased and flattered by a young girl:[23]

> . . . et poésie!
> La jeune anglaise à l'anglais âgé ment.

This old Englishman was probably Richard Horne, for Verlaine brought back news of 'that young gentleman', who seems to have been as anxious as ever to be accepted by the rising generation as one of themselves.

The Empire Promenade was at that time the favourite late night haunt for young writers, and the whole company repaired there after dinner. The ladies had been primed in advance; it was their role to watch over the poet and keep him out of mischief. They carried out their mission successfully and Verlaine, on his best behaviour, spent a delightful evening watching the slightly daring *tableaux vivants* on which the fame of the establishment largely rested.

Next day, 23 November, he was embarked by his friends in the train for Oxford, where he was to discover some quite unexpected aspects of English life.

From an academic point of view, the university in the early 1890s was an ebullient place, ringing with controversy and split into clans whose mutual hostility and divergent views contributed to intellectual liveliness. On a deeper level, however, the reigning atmosphere among faculty members seems to have been rather dim and stuffy. Eccentrics abounded indeed, but their eccentricities were of the donnish kind, recognised in the university as part of the attributes of learning. Professors were expected to write weighty volumes on their special subjects, so they often confined their university duties to droning lectures, while the less majestic job of tutoring was left to variously competent private teachers engaged by the students at their own expense. Learning was sacred and not to be taken lightly. Political opinion was generally conservative or non-existent; there was much preoccupation with religion, but it was mostly confined within the bounds of the many shades of Anglican belief, varied by a heady tendency towards Rome. There was, in fact, a sort of underlying pattern of mind and notorious nonconformists made themselves conspicuous by their tastes and habits—some of which seem to have been indeed peculiar—rather than by any great divergence in their attitude towards life.

There were exceptions of course. One of them was Walter Pater, at this time Fellow of Brasenose, whose growing reputation left Oxford perfectly indifferent. Oscar Wilde had acclaimed his *Renaissance* as 'my treasure, the flower of decadence', and some of his students seemed to have listened enthralled when he urged them to burn with a hard, gem-like flame. The faculty, however, had little regard for him and Sir Charles Oman recalls that 'As for Walter Pater, whom some folk in literary London seemed to take quite seriously, he was of little account in Oxford, being regarded as a *poseur* and not at all a leader of thought.'[24] Frederick York Powell, the man responsible for bringing Verlaine to Oxford and who was now waiting to receive him, was not so easy to dismiss. He was a genial, bearded, burly person of extraordinarily untidy appearance, always dressed in a crumpled blue serge suit, a tie like a piece of string and an old-fashioned, battered top hat. Endlessly toying with an evil-smelling pipe, he gave an impression of total disregard for his appearance and William Rothenstein, who knew him well, tells us his mind was 'as untidy as his dress . . . a jungle of knowledge'.[25] He was an expert on many and unrelated subjects—medieval history and literature, Roman law, boxing—on which he contributed articles to the *Sporting Times*—Icelandic poetry, racing (when Lord Rosebery, then Prime Minister, appointed Powell Regius Professor of Modern History in 1894, unkind tongues suggested the appointment had more to do with racing than with history), modern French painting and poetry. He knew Hebrew, High Dutch, Provençal and most of the European languages and could discuss practically any subject in an endlessly entertaining and erudite manner, but the idea of writing anything serious filled him with horror. The huge *Corpus Poeticum Boreale* on which he was working in collaboration with the Icelandic scholar Vigfússon, would certainly never have been finished if Vigfússon had not been a man of iron determination, prepared to sit on indefinitely in Powell's rooms when his collaborator had to be forced to finish a chapter.

It is not surprising that the university mistrusted this dilettante, who refused to take learning seriously, confessed himself a free-thinker and aggravated his case by flaunting his socialism, and introducing a number of most disreputable friends into his college. His friendships were indeed as eclectic and unpredictable as his interests and he valued his friends far above all the languages, literatures and schools of painting with which he was so disconcertingly familiar. One of them was the poet-chimney-sweep, William Hines, whose *Songs of Labour* he had prefaced. Another, though less close one, was young Bernard Shaw, considered at that time, by a few people who had heard of him at all, as a dangerous firebrand. He had also been a great supporter of the Commune and was in touch with numerous ex-Communards in Paris. Occasionally one of them would visit him in Oxford and their host no doubt enjoyed the effect on his colleagues when he introduced them to Christ Church. The Rev. Charles Dodgson—Lewis Carroll, the creator of *Alice in Wonderland*—used to refer to them sourly as 'Powell's assassins'. He too was a famous eccentric, but of a very different kind, and he was noticeably lacking in cordiality when the two men met at the High Table.

Powell, of course, knew practically everyone in the literary world. To his rooms came Meredith, R. L. Stevenson, William Morris, Henley, William Blunt, visiting Scandinavian writers and an endless stream of French painters and poets, bringing news of all that was happening in the *avant-garde* in Paris. Naturally he knew all about Mallarmé and Verlaine, and was one of the few people in Oxford who read and understood them. It was, in fact, Mallarmé whom he had hoped to bring to Oxford this year. As Curator of the Taylor Institute, it was his privilege to arrange an annual lecture on some subject connected with foreign literature and Charles Bonnier, a teacher of French in Oxford and an old colleague of Mallarmé in the Paris *lycées*, had put forward his name. Powell had written to Paris, but it had been too late to make arrangements for that year. Then Rothenstein, who had become very friendly with Powell, had suggested that Verlaine be asked to give an unofficial talk to follow up his lecture in London. Powell had been easily persuaded. He was a great admirer of the poet's, had a complete edition of his works, 'nobly bound', on his shelves and had made a very neat translation of one of Verlaine's prison poems, 'Le ciel est, pardessus le toit'.[26] Thus it came about that Powell was now waiting to welcome his guest at a luncheon party organised in his honour, while Rothenstein waited at the station for his arrival.

In spite of all his bohemian friends, young Rothenstein was in many ways a conventional person, who respected Oxford and all it stood for. Verlaine's appearance thus came as a shock, for the clergyman-like attire had been returned to its owners and the poet was curiously arrayed in a long flapping greatcoat, a scarf wound round his neck and his diseased foot bulging in a cloth shoe. He was whisked off to Christ Church, where Powell had retained a room for him, and presumably redressed in time for lunch.

Powell lived in vast, dim rooms lined with books from floor to ceiling; piles of books encumbered the floor; there were folders crammed with Japanese prints; on the walls, antique arms alternated with Impressionist paintings, and Rodin's *L'Homme au nez cassé*—a work of startling modernity at the time—presided over the library. 'The great room', says Charles Bonnier, 'looked less like a museum than a mobile gallery which opened up in front of you. . . . Few places gave such an impression of being lived in.'[27]

Charles Bonnier was present at the party and has left a lively account of it:[28]

I can see the scene now [he recalls], the great room overlooking shadowy Broad Walk, some indeterminate and rather scared students, come to admire a poet in the flesh, feeling they were taking part in a slightly daring pleasure-outing; Powell striding up and down, smoking and laughing; and Verlaine! But not the

Verlaine of the Concert Rouge, or one of the cafés in the Latin Quarter; what a transformation! He had no doubt been told to behave himself in Oxford, to be 'good', and so he was, with the most comic efforts. Waves of laughter and cunning creased this face that reminded one of a good old Silenus who was a genius at the same time. It was obviously amusing him to play a part and to wear formal dress for once. He talked the whole time, but all in half-tones, like his portrait by Carrière. He recounted his memories of the time when he had taught French and drawing in English schools, of his role as Press Censor during the Commune, and of his play about Louis XVII. The eternal background of Oxford absorbed the faces of the students; the only ones that stand out in the full light are Verlaine, talking, reminiscing, Powell applauding with his boisterous laughter.

After lunch, the company piled into several hansom cabs and set off to visit Oxford. Verlaine found the town[29]

deliciously dainty, almost rustic in its commercial quarters, tiny shops, as it were illuminated with cheap confectionery, sweets for little people with little purses; sweet little houses, little gardens full of rest, trees showing their last red leaves, above the red, comfortable red roofs, somewhat like the proper and modest little streets of Boston . . . and unique in its mediaeval majesty, its buildings, colleges, churches, of the good periods.

He was enjoying himself obviously, touchingly, but he made no mention of the evening's lecture. When his hosts began to worry and brought up the subject, it became clear that he had brought no material with him and was relying on a very faulty memory to recite the poems—mostly from *Sagesse*—that he had read in London. Perhaps Powell and Rothenstein would have done better to let him alone, for, after all, the London lecture had been a success. Instead, they hurriedly produced a few volumes, and perhaps made recommendations that intimidated poor Verlaine, who easily lost his nerve.

At any rate, the atmosphere of Oxford was very different from that of London and the lecture was not very successful. It was held in the back room of Blackwell's bookshop and Verlaine spoke to a sparse audience of undergraduates, clad in the cap and gown which gave them, he noted 'a half clerical, half magisterial air'. The only poems he knew by heart were a few of his own, the rest he read in a muffled and sometimes inaudible voice. The *Oxford Magazine*, whose reporter was present, was charitable, however, and wrote:

Last Thursday, a small number of enthusiasts met in the back room of Mr Blackwell's shop to hear M. Verlaine lecture on contemporary French poetry. M. Verlaine had the happy idea of speaking chiefly in this lecture of his own work, rather than that of poets little known in Oxford. Thus he gave us a sort of biography of himself, illustrating the various phases of his life by quoting from poems in turn tragic and dramatic. 'The poet must live, live in all possible ways'. Such was his justification, the theme of a truly interesting and original lecture. The audience was scanty, too scanty, but it saw and heard the poet with great pleasure.

The following day, Verlaine's hosts expected him to return to London, but it soon became clear that he had no intention of doing so. Oxford, with its beautiful buildings, jolly company and good wines, delighted him and he settled down in his room in Christ Church with the air of one preparing for a long stay. He was in fact, having the time of his life and even York Powell, so careless normally of other people's opinion, grew worried and wondered what the Dean and Mr Dodgson would think. Finally Rothenstein was sent to explain, with all possible kindness, that guest rooms were available for short periods only.

In his own account of his stay, Verlaine says he spent only twenty-four hours in Oxford, but it seems to have been on 25 November 1893 that he took the train back to London. During the next few days—or perhaps even in the train to London—he wrote a poem about the city that had so impressed him:[30]

> Oxford est une ville qui me consola,
> Moi rêvant toujours de ce Moyen Age-là.

The 'toujours' was not just poetic licence. Verlaine had really been haunted, if not 'always', at least since his conversion in Mons, by nostalgia for an age when God was the centre of the universe, when that universe rested on a solid structure of faith, and art was the representation of faith. In Oxford, this lost Eden seemed for a moment to materialise again and Verlaine saw in its ancient stones 'le Moyen Age énorme et délicat'[31] living on again.

But modern London had its delights, too, and he was prepared to taste as many of them as his friends would allow him to do. There is a certain mystery about the way in which he spent his time for the next few days. Symons was away and it seems that William Heinemann first received him in his rooms at No. 3 Cork Street. 'I'm living like a lord and everything for free', he wrote gaily to Eugénie Kranz, but he seems to have stayed in Cork Street only one day, since his next letters to Cazals and Philomène Boudin were addressed from No. 63 York Terrace, Regent's Park. M. Jean-Aubry suggests that this was the house of a prostitute he had picked up in Soho and with whom he spent all his Oxford earnings.[32] At any rate, he seems to have disappeared completely until 29 November, at which date Ernest Dowson and some other friends dined with him at the Constitutional Club. Whatever company he had been in, it must have been expensive, since he seems to have been practically penniless when he arrived on 30 November at St Pancras Station, 'all brick, marble, pointed arches and bell towers',[33] which he had watched the workmen building when he was living in London in 1873.

This time he was bound for Manchester where Theodore London, with the help of a French-speaking Swiss named Emile Bally, had managed to arrange a lecture in Salford. Both men were, says Verlaine, 'steeped in literature to their fingertips' and the three of them spent an enjoyable evening at the Vicarage of the Congregational church, where London lived with his sister and young brother. There was little time for visiting Manchester next day, but Verlaine caught a glimpse of the city, 'all swathed in smoke, with open promenades by the side of a low-lying river'.[34] He regretted a little that there was no time to see his own portrait and that of Rimbaud in Fantin Latour's *Coin de Table*, which was just then on show in the city's art gallery, but he and his friends dragged around Salford, Verlaine limping terribly. It seems to have been a rather trying day, for he recalls:[35]

> Je n'ai vu Manchester que d'un coin de Salford,
> Donc très mal et très peu, quel que fût mon effort
> A travers le brouillard et les courses pénibles
> Au possible, en dépit d'hansoms inaccessibles
> Presque, grâce à ma jambe male et mes pieds bots.
> N'importe, j'ai gardé des souvenirs plus beaux
> De cette ville que l'on dit industrielle,—
> Encore que de telle ô qu'intellectuelle
> Place où ma vanité devait se pavaner.

The lecture this time was a rather more formal affair, since it treated of Shakespeare and Racine. Verlaine had prepared it in hospital 'between two crises and some cries'. There was an appreciative audience, come, says Verlaine, 'to applaud in Verlaine the author of *Esther*' and to listen to some comparisons. Racine, according to Verlaine, was 'more distinguished by passion than anything else', while Shakespeare was 'a man more intellectual than passionate'. Their attitude to women varied in the same way, since Shakespeare's 'divine imagination' created impersonal, idealised types, while Racine revealed 'the innermost recesses of her nature'. Shakespeare 'borrows his jests from all sources, and invests them with a charm peculiarly his own, free, fantastic, reminiscent of the artisan, the peasant, even the courtisan', while 'Racine's gaiety, light and smart as it is, savours slightly of the student and the gentleman.'[36] Verlaine's knowledge of his subject was really profound and it was a joy for him to be able to proclaim thus, in public the 'culte énorme pour Shakespeare'[37] that had once transformed Stickney common into the setting for *A Midsummer Night's Dream*, and the New Forest into the Forest of Arden.

He returned to London with a substantial fee in his pocket and stayed again with Symons. This time, his friends were determined he should not get into trouble and they kept a careful watch on him. By now he had become the centre of a little group of clever young writers who loved and appreciated him, understood his weaknesses and were truly eager to help him. Thus they managed, not only to amuse their friend, but to ensure that his stay should bring in a substantial profit. Several more readings were arranged in friendly *salons*, notably in that of Henry Harland, shortly to become editor of the *Yellow Book*, where he recited a number of poems.

> I spent a few days there [he recounts[38]] and I brought back deep love, a boundless admiration and a spontaneous, ever-ready sympathy for these good, kind people, who are so cordial beneath their apparent coldness and—this is a national defect—so eccentric that they consent to return from long journeys by land and sea— and in books—far from the motherland they rightly love, with a taste for good continental literature . . . with a pleasant and flattering touch of preference for we 'French ladies and gentlemen'.

Thus he spent 'some delightful days dawdling through a London of theatres (a very fairyland), music-halls (a very Paradise!), of good and excellent visits received and returned'. Some of these visits were for publishers—notably John Lane, whom he hoped to spur on with the publication of his works in English—and he met Frank Harris, 'the sympathetic editor of the *Fortnightly*', whom he was later to accuse of cheating him over the payment for 'Myself as a French master' and other contributions.

When Verlaine returned to France, probably on 6 December, he had earned £80, a really considerable amount in those days. It had been arranged among Symons, Gosse and other friends that the sum should not be given to him in England, but should be forwarded to him in Paris. This was supposed to be a safeguard against ill-advised spending, but Rothenstein at least—who knew all about his friend's private life—might have guessed what would happen. Philomène and Eugénie were waiting for him when he arrived in Paris, each vociferously claiming her share, and each determined the other should get as little as possible. It did not take long for his two terrible mistresses to get their hands on his money and within a few days every sou was spent. From a financial point of view, Verlaine was back where he had started.

Yet the visit had not been a failure. In London, in Oxford, in Manchester, he had made precious contacts and left devoted friends. During the next two years, they worked to make his name known and to provide him with small sums of money. Powell's plan for an English edition of his works never materialised but the young critics wrote articles about him and translated his poems. His name became familiar to readers of the *Fortnightly Review*, the *Pall Mall Gazette*, the *Athenaeum*, the *Oxford Magazine*, *Hobby Horse*, the *Saturday Review*, the *New Review*, the *Senate*, and other smaller magazines. Philomène and Eugénie, it is true, stole the letters and took the money, so that Verlaine was always complaining that he had not been paid for his contributions. After his death Eugénie, who seems to have been the greediest of the pair, but who looked after him to the last, wrote several letters to Rothenstein, pretending that Heinemann and Harris owed sums which should be made over to her.

Verlaine never saw England again, as he died in January 1896.

'Marble Cities built for Thought': Mallarmé in Oxford and Cambridge

Meanwhile, Mallarmé had received through Charles Bonnier York Powell's invitation in the name of the Taylor Institute. His first reaction, though it was expressed in different terms, was curiously like that of Verlaine:[39]

Dear Monsieur Bonnier [he wrote]. These latter days, the *Walkyrie*, Maeterlinck's *Pelléas et Mélisande* and a general feeling in the air of things about to happen, have delayed my reply. Yet the offer of hospitality added by M. York Powell is so charming and touches me so greatly, that I would not wish to wait before begging you to thank him with all my heart, until I have decided, if not on the subject, for I hardly ever go beyond my own, but the title of the lecture. Shall it be 'Literature and

Music'? I shall reflect on this for a few days among the shadows
of Fontainebleau and will soon send you a letter for M. York
Powell. Quite between ourselves meanwhile, and without a
word to anyone, do tell me, as a friend, if there are any pecuniary
conditions attached to this delightful project, so tempting in
itself: how, etc.

As I have now retired, I shall have a hundred things to do at
that time of the year, and I want to be in a state to travel
properly.

The problem of the relationship between music and poetry had
indeed been preoccupying the minds of poets for some time past.
'Les parfums, les couleurs et les sons se répondent'[40] but where exactly,
they were asking themselves, was the limit between the different types
of perception, between sound and sense, and did, or should, that limit
exist? And what is, in truth, the difference between two arts, 'identical
in their principle, which resides in the same need to express an interior
sound, and in their aim, which is the representation of a state of fictive
joy'?[41] Mallarmé, whose own poetry sometimes seemed almost to
invade the domain of music, had of course reflected at length on the
problem.

He had frequently attended the Lamoureux concerts during the
year 1893 and had found in them even more mental anguish than
aesthetic delight. Paul Valéry, who had accompanied him on at least
one occasion, has described how:[42]

> as a great artist his mind would be full of protest and of a striving
> to decipher what the gods of pure sound could utter and pro-
> nounce in their own way. Mallarmé would leave the concerts
> filled with a sublime jealousy, seeking desperately a means of
> recapturing for our art the marvels and the significance which
> Music, grown too powerful, had stolen from it.

The prospect of this lecture, with its free choice of subject, was an
encouragement and an opportunity to formulate his ideas, to try to
discover—for his own satisfaction first of all—what was the true,
elusive relationship between music and poetry.

The invitation had come well in advance and he had a good many
months before him to prepare his discourse. Meanwhile, news of
Verlaine's success had seeped into literary society and reached the rue
de Rome. Verlaine and Mallarmé, the extrovert and the introvert,
were temperamentally poles apart and their mode of life could hardly
have been more different. Yet the two men, though they seldom met,

loved each other dearly. (Verlaine, indeed, said a little later that Mallarmé and François Coppée were the only two friends who had always remained true to him.) So Mallarmé set about trying to track down Verlaine in view of some useful information. He was not to be found in any of his usual haunts, however, since he was living at this period with the terrible Eugénie Krantz, who knew how to keep him at home and out of the *bistros*. Meanwhile time was drawing on, so a letter went off to London:

And now, dear Mr. Gosse, I am writing for some information. Tell me, I beg you, on a postcard, which is the most popular lecture hall in London; and the name of the agent, if something of the sort exists. I know that Verlaine whom I cannot get hold of, since he is out of Paris lectured somewhere last winter. I am going myself to Oxford at the end of February, in answer to an invitation from the Taylorian Association, and I should be pleased to repeat, as I pass through London, a lecture on the effect of which I may hope to count a little. The chief thing for me (apart from this additional project) is this most unexpected opportunity of shaking some hands out of the past, and yours first of all, dear Mr. Gosse.

Mallarmé was not so lucky as Verlaine—or perhaps his friends thought his style less suited to a public lecture. At any rate, nothing was arranged for him in London. However, a second lecture was organised in Cambridge by his old friend Charles Whibley whose brother Leonard was a professor at Pembroke College. He accepted without comment, a little bewildered perhaps, since he would probably have agreed with Henry James that 'when I say Oxford, I mean Cambridge, for a visiting savage is not in the least obliged to know the difference, and it suddenly strikes me as very pedantic and very good-natured in him to pretend to know it'.[43]

Mallarmé seems to have been even more flustered than Verlaine as the time for his departure drew near. Certainly he took infinitely more trouble preparing for it and towards the end of February we find him writing to Méry Laurent, 'I am late with the text for my lecture, a bit anxious and not leaving the house'. The title had finally been chosen: *La Musique et les Lettres* and it was agreed that York Powell should make a translation, to be read by the speaker, whose accent was generally admired by his French friends. On 21 February, the *Oxford Magazine* announced the lecture in rather flat, unenthusiastic terms:

Monsieur Stéphane Mallarmé, who lectures during the coming

week at the Taylorian, has kindly allowed us to reprint one of his poems. Although reputed highly as a gifted poet, Monsieur Mallarmé has published little, and authorized versions of his works are not easy to obtain. One special claim upon an English audience Monsieur Mallarmé would seem to have in that he has for years dedicated himself to the study of English literature, and some of his well-known publications in prose are translated from the English.

The poem was a translation by 'L.D.' (no doubt Louis Dyer) of 'Soupir', a very early poem, possibly written in London, when Mallarmé was still under the influence of the Parnassians.

According to Dr Mondor, he arrived in Oxford on 27 February 1894, but he was evidently in England before that date, since he wrote from Paris to Edmund Gosse: 'I shall be lecturing next week, Wednesday in Oxford and Friday in Cambridge and am going meanwhile to stay with a friend, in a place I know only under the name of "Sussex Bell".' The friend has been identified[44] as Charles Whibley, an associate of W. E. Henley, who was still at this time editor of the powerful *National Observer* and had introduced Mallarmé, Verlaine, Schwob and other contemporary French writers to the English public. As for Whibley, he was really only on the outskirts of literature, since he was primarily a journalist and his published works were limited at this time to a guide to the cathedrals of England and Wales, and an anthology entitled *Three Centuries of Cambridge Wit*. However, he was Whistler's brother-in-law, a fact which had opened many a door to him during the years when he had acted as correspondent for the *Pall Mall Gazette* in Paris. It was Whistler who had first brought him to the rue de Rome, and for some reason no one had ever quite understood, he and Mallarmé had become firm friends. No two men could have been more unlike. Whibley prided himself on being a plain, downright sort of person, who said what he meant and had no nonsense about him, and he appears to have had little understanding of any sort of poetry, let alone that of Mallarmé. However, he was not the first nor the last to fall under the spell of the poet's personal charm without being able to appreciate his work.

As an anonymous friend wrote in his obituary notice: 'Charles must somehow have penetrated the barrier of innocent pretence which Mallarmé raised to shield his sensitiveness. Art they also had in common, though Whibley's art eludes by its apparent facility, Mallarmé's by its studied difficulty.'[45]

At any rate, it was to Whibley that Mallarmé went first of all when

Plate 1 Mallarmé, aged twenty

Plate 2   Portrait of Verlaine by E. Carrière, Louvre, Paris

he arrived in England after an absence of nearly twenty years. The 'Sussex Bell', which he took for a place name, was in fact an inn near Whibley's home in Haslemere, and Mallarmé lodged there on the night of the 24th, and possibly until the 26th.[46] Nothing is known, unfortunately, of this stay, but it seems likely that Henley would have come down to discuss the worrying contributions to his paper, of which he confessed he could not understand a word and felt them to be 'a great fraud'.

A letter dated 27 February shows he had been enjoying York Powell's hospitality at least since the previous day.

> Oxford is a miracle [he informed his daughter Geneviève]. Twenty or more cloisters, exquisitely Mediaeval, among parks and water; there is even a town and people, but one forgets them. Under my window, there is a field full of cows, deer and centuries-old trees, all lacy now the leaves have gone. Yesterday, visited a good deal of all that, in the sun, dined in a refectory as fine as a cathedral, with long gas-pulls on panelling hung with portraits of famous men who were former students. Here is the menu. . . . I stole it for you from the high table. Then we spent an hour in hall, where the professors drink various wines after removing their robes, which they wear at table, with the queer hats, something between a chapska and a blotting pad.

Meanwhile, Mallarmé and York Powell had been making each other's acquaintance. In appearance, one could hardly have found a greater contrast than that of little, quiet, reserved Mallarmé, and huge, boisterous Powell, receptive and curious of all life had to offer. Yet the sympathy that sprang up at once between them went much deeper than a common love of literature, and perhaps had its roots in the fact that each of these two agnostics had a deeply religious temperament. Charles Bonnier, writing about Powell, whom he loved and admired, says that his atheism 'conferred on him a calm resembling that of the great mystics', but that his special form of mysticism was 'an infinite élan towards knowledge'.[47] Powell himself admitted that the only two books he truly loved were the *Imitation* and the *Confessions* of St Augustine, because, he said, they proclaimed 'abandon of self-will, love of suffering, abnegation'. Mallarmé's dedication to poetry was of the same nature, as profound and absolute as was Powell's to knowledge.

One would like to know more about what passed between two men of such exceptional quality, but their talk went unrecorded and their correspondence is not yet available. We only know that they liked and appreciated each other: 'We are as thick as thieves', wrote Powell.

'He made me laugh with the most delightful reminiscences of queer Parisian types. He is a charming man; beautiful manner and speech', and after Mallarmé's death he recalled that his guest had the simplicity he had found characteristic of all the great men he had known.[48]

Perhaps there was not much time for talking, for the lecture was billed for 1 March and there was much work to be done. Powell had undertaken to translate the text, but the thick manuscript of *La Musique et les Lettres*, with its beautifully polished, long, difficult and tortuous phrases, must surely have been more than he bargained for. It was presumably while he was plunged in this practically superhuman task that his guest was handed over to Louis Dyer, a Greek scholar from Balliol, to be shown round Oxford. They visited the colleges and the Bodleian Library on a grey, rainy morning, and Dyer wrote to his friend Alidor Delzant in Paris, 'What originality and what depth. I found his conversation in some respects even more interesting than his writings.'[49]

Walter Pater had been invited for lunch. It seemed a natural choice, for Pater's work was probably closer to Mallarmé's, at least in intention, than that of any other English writer. Moreover, he was a friend of John Payne, as he had been of O'Shaughnessy until the latter's death. The two should have had much to talk about, but communication with Pater was notoriously difficult. Obsessed by his own ugliness, he had retired long since into a shell from which very few people could persuade him to emerge. Though he knew French perfectly, he dared not speak it in public and his shyness seems to have affected Mallarmé, who suddenly found it impossible to speak English. So they sat in silence, gazing at each other while Powell talked, alternating between English and French that was more fluent than correct.

The terrible translation was presenting insurmountable difficulties. Mallarmé was requisitioned to help and explain; the two men worked, with Powell for once attentive to his task. In fact, he kept his guest so hard at it that next day, when Mallarmé wanted to scribble a note to Méry Laurent in Paris, he had to slip away on the pretext of curling his moustache in readiness for the lecture.

They sat up most of the night and Mallarmé grew more and more nervous. Finally he declared he felt incapable of reading the text in English. He would lecture in French and Powell would follow with a reading of the English version.[50] The solution was adopted not, perhaps, with the happiest of results, for the English translation according to Dyer, was even harder to understand than the French original.

The lecture was held in the afternoon, in the Taylor Institute. Mallarmé had been mindful of his daughter's admonitions to 'dress quietly and not just anyhow, as you often do. We daren't advise you to get someone to look you over, to see your appearance is correct enough for a lecturer, but it would be wise. A mirror might help.' He had imagined, no doubt, a brilliant gathering of the élite of Oxford. The reality was disappointing:

> Oh dear, If I had only known! [he reported next day to Marie and Geneviève] Two or three professors, a few students; all the rest women. I'm not complaining, everyone behaved perfectly, applauding at length and correctly, a bit automatically at the end. But I came there to give them a difficult piece of aesthetics, whereas I might just as well have talked without any preparation. Fasting, in daytime, and wearing a morning coat. . . . It seems strange to have come so far and taken so much trouble to amuse about sixty society people who were either studious or just taking the opportunity to hear some French.

La Musique et les Lettres is indeed 'a difficult piece of aesthetics' and the audience could hardly be blamed for finding it bewildering. Arthur Symons reports that a freshman who had been present remarked as he came away: 'I understood every word but not a single sentence.' As for Louis Dyer, he found it hard to make up his mind.

> M. Mallarmé gave us his talk in French [continues his letter to Alidor Delzant] and was so clever at coming down to our level that he was better understood than was M. York Powell. Several people have spoken to me admiringly of his graceful elocution with its beautiful rhythm. Yet it must be admitted that old Oxford was a bit puzzled by the novel style and people complained they had not understood a word. We simply must have it in print.

The Oxford audience remained, apparently, impervious when Mallarmé announced from his rostrum, with solemnity, for this was indeed a thing that touched the very core of his existence: 'J'apporte en effet des nouvelles. Les plus surprenantes . . . On a touché au vers' (I bring news for you. Most surprising news. Something has changed in poetry), and went on to develop his theme, in obscure and graceful arabesques, to arrive at the conclusion which summed up, modestly and triumphantly, before this mediocre audience, the fruit of thirty years of reflection: 'La Musique et les Lettres sont la face alternative ici élargie vers l'obscur; scintillante là, avec certitude, d'un phénomène, le seul, je l'appelai, l'Idée' (Music and Writing are alternative aspects, sometimes broadening out into obscurity; sometimes glittering with certainty, of a single phenomenon which I have called the Idea).

After a luncheon held in his honour, at which he was forced to drink sherry and champagne—both of which disagreed with him—Mallarmé took leave of his 'friend of three days and for ever',[51] of 'that excellent York Powell who has been like a mother to me'. He must have reached London late, but John Payne, the 'brother' of his youth, was waiting for him. 'What joy to drink my first glass of beer!' Mallarmé wrote home. There was not much time for talking, however, for he was due next day in Cambridge, where he was to repeat the same lecture.

He was not in the best of tempers when he set out because, he explained to the family, anxiously awaiting news in Paris, 'I was sure, in spite of all Whibley's kindness, that it wouldn't bring in much money.'

He was right, for a travelling theatre company formed a rival attraction that evening and only twenty tickets were sold, at five shillings each. The quality of the audience, however, made up for the quantity.

> If ever I missed you, my poor absent ones [he wrote next day to Marie and Geneviève], it was last evening. No lecture has ever given, or ever will give me, such an impression of rarity and beauty, it was more than one could dream of. The twenty people in the audience—with two ladies among them—were an absolute élite, as friendly as they were discreet. Listened to in a religious silence, felt their sympathy welling between each word, and their intelligence. I must add that the setting was exquisite: a superb panelled hall, fine furniture, evening, nine o'clock, the audience in shadow, one or two tables with a few candles on them; and in front of his own, Papa, enthroned, framed—he alone in the light—by two great silver candlesticks. The applause at my entry and exit was in no way banal, and perfectly tactful. The lover of rarities in me was enchanted.

The English universities, in fact, made a profound impression on Mallarmé, and though he approached them in a spirit very different from that of Verlaine, he came away with the same impression of an idyllic existence spent among the marvels of mediaeval architecture: the life of the Fellows especially, seemed to him the most ideal that could be imagined. Looking back on the 'déplacement avantageux'[52] that had been his visit to Oxford and Cambridge, he concluded that these Fellows—'men unique in Europe and the world'—represented 'the culmination and result' of the ambient, historic beauty of the universities. Their lives seemed to him infinitely gracious; they lived as he, no doubt, would have loved to live, exempt from all material cares, able to dedicate themselves entirely to the things of the spirit:[53]

Each collegial lodging has secreted from age to age, a group of these amateurs, who succeed each other, follow each other. A vacancy: 'such a one (they agree), somewhere, might join us'. A vote, and a call goes out to him. One condition only: that he be a university graduate. For the rest of his life, he has only to draw his stipend. Should he, to the daily contemplation from his window of some British landscape, to compulsing in his usual arm-chair one of the volumes that line his walls, before repairing to the refectory vast as a cathedral, built over an admirable wine-cellar, should he prefer to travel in Italy or any part of the globe, then he will find his income awaiting him in the bank of his choice. Most of these men live in, respecting the clause that excludes married couples from these monasteries of science. . . . Such exceptional lives, the charm of which still haunts me, can only flourish, in all their elegance and elevation, in a soil of undisturbed tradition . . . in marble cities built for Thought.

York Powell knew what the other side of the picture could hold, but did not disillusion him with stories of envy, gossip and malice. Mallarmé had seen only 'quelques messieurs délicieux', infinitely privileged, knowing nothing of the struggle against poverty that had weighed on him all his life. Oxford and Cambridge, the one 'imposing' the other 'cosy', blended together, all minor irritations forgotten, in a single, near-celestial city.

Then once more, and for the last time, he was in London—'this London I have loved so much and that I shall love again'.[54] This time, there was no room in Payne's lodgings and he stayed at No. 93 Jermyn Street. There were friends to be seen: Gosse, Whibley, Henley —a plum cake to be bought for the family. The sun shone through a dry mist 'the colour of dead leaves'. Perhaps like Verlaine a few months earlier, he slipped away to Soho, to visit the familiar places, or make a pilgrimage to Panton Square and gaze up at the window behind which Marie had sat sewing and weeping, and that he had opened so often to toss down pennies to the vagrant singers.

For him, too, it was the last visit to England. Four years later, in 1898 he died at the age of fifty-six, worn out with the incessant effort of creation that forced him relentlessly: 'de creuser par veillée une fosse nouvelle—Dans le terrain avare et froid de ma cervelle.'[55]

5

Aestheticism and Imperialism: Paul Valéry in London

Fin-de-siècle

Francophilia and Francophobia had been twin features of British literary life long before the 1890s. France was evil or heroic, depraved or seductive, a menace or a promise. Opinion on the subject was often bigoted and ill-informed, but it was rarely absent. France, on the other hand, was far from returning this almost obsessive interest. Except in the eyes of a few romantics, England was a dull country and people went there chiefly because they had nowhere else to go. Nor had English writers much audience across the Channel. The possession of Shakespeare was the one irrefutable superiority to which the nation could lay claim, and his existence was one of the few widely-known facts about English literature. Though the names of Dickens and Tennyson had become fairly familiar before 1890, only a limited circle of initiates had heard of Swinburne and his disciples. All the comings and goings of Payne, Gosse, Horne, Ingram or O'Shaughnessy had indeed created a current of information flowing from the English shores, but it had reached only a small group, comprised chiefly of professional poets. Men like Banville, Heredia or Catulle Mendès kept in touch with literary events in England, but they seem to have distrusted the glowing accounts of Mallarmé and Verlaine and felt small urge to go and see for themselves.

And now, as the century drew to its close, here was France becoming as avidly curious of England as England had long been of her. It was partly a reaction against the climate at home. The Third Republic was boringly secure, prosperous and cautious—the very antithesis of Carlyle's gloomy prophecies. Nothing happened. The bourgeoisie reigned supreme, reflected in a literature that was largely a pale imitation of Zola, Maupassant and the Goncourts, purveying the gossip of high life or political society to those who had no chance of experiencing it at first hand. One saw, it is true, the first symptoms of the nationalistic spirit that was to culminate in the Dreyfus affair. Maurice Barrès and a few other young writers were already veering in this direction, in the wake of noisy patriots like Déroulède and Drumont, who occasionally ruffled the complacent surface of the nation's life. The real adventures, however, were those of the spirit; the real adventurers were the Symbolists, who were doing their best to destroy certainties and open up the universe of the imagination. It was easy to ignore them and the great French public did so. Yet something was lacking. The Republic was suffering from 'the disease of habit, of boredom, of being something that the new generation now coming to maturity had not made for themselves but had inherited from their fathers'.[1]

It was partly by contrast that England began to seem at once threatening and fascinating. She was perhaps even more prosperous and secure than France, but she was far from cautious. The imperialist spirit was rampant. Adventure was very much on the earth; men whose names were on every tongue were planting the British flag in the farthest corners of the world. Africa was the main focus of interest. Britain and Germany were racing each other to secure concessions south of the Equator. France, who had her own investments in the region, watched with nervous interest. This ever-increasing dynamism on the part of 'La perfide Albion' was alarming and fascinating at the same time. Emulation, as it so often happens, vied with suspicion. It became fashionable to adopt an English accent, to dress and look as much like an Englishman as possible. There were long articles in the main reviews, dissecting the British national character. 'Today', wrote Maurice Jusserand, 'the English are themselves and no one else. Despite their close relationship with the peoples of the Continent, they have forged for themselves a character, manners and ideas so categoric that they have struck the imagination of the masses.'[2]

So it is not surprising that English literature should have become fashionable too, though it lagged behind English clothes and customs. By 1890 various reviews were introducing safely-established writers. De Quincey's *Confessions of an English Opium-Eater* had been one of the first classics to arouse curiosity, though still in a limited circle; now the widely-read *Bibliothèque populaire* began to devote whole numbers to English poets and novelists. It carried translations from Burns, Keats, the Brownings and a certain Philip Bailey, in whom it discerned 'a worthy successor to Goethe'. George Eliot's *Scenes from Clerical Life* appeared in 1890; there were new translations from Walter Scott and so on. Then in 1892, the *Revue des deux mondes* forsook the past and published a long, analytical essay on Rudyard Kipling who, at the age of twenty-seven, had recently published *The Light that Failed*. Adventure, an exotic setting, a touch of brutality . . . this was the England the French wanted to hear about. Kipling typified it, so did Rider Haggard, whose novels began to appear in France at about the same time, so to some extent did Stevenson, whose *Treasure Island* had been translated back in 1885 and whose other works were gradually becoming familiar.

So everything about England, and especially about London, became suddenly interesting. Curiosity was notably rife in literary circles, stimulated in March 1892 by the publication in *La Mercure de France* of translations from *The Book of the Rhymers' Club*, preceded by an essay on the English 'Decadents', in which they were described, presumably to their annoyance, as 'somewhat Parnassian'. All this suggested a puzzling contrast. Writers and artists were increasingly intrigued and even tempted to see for themselves just what was happening in this strange city, whose name evoked Dickensian vice and a pea-soup fog that lifted only to reveal the bloody, tormented skies portrayed on Turner's vast canvases.

So they began to venture in increasing numbers across the Channel and to find an enthusiastic welcome in various hospitable houses. There, they discovered that English life was not at all what they had been led to expect. The England they told of on return was no longer that of Taine or Dickens, but more like that of Verlaine: innocent and poetic, with voluptuously cosy homes, where burned huge open fires and foreigners found generous hospitality, strange foods and copious quantities of drink. Moreover, the hypocrisy Verlaine had deplored was on the decline; philistinism was momentarily out of fashion. London had its eyes fixed on Oscar Wilde and aestheticism was penetrating insidiously into the most unlikely circles. 'This people is becoming as sensuous as the Italians of the Renaissance,' reported the Comtesse de Puliga.[3]

The young generation of rising writers was specially intrigued. Many of them frequented the rue de Rome and had heard Mallarmé speak nostalgically of the city he loved so much. So Léon Daudet went there and discovered 'something elemental, like a Shakespearean drama, a limitless store of historical possibilities'.[4] Paul Bourget, already a confirmed Anglophile, and always with an eye to the main chance, hurried to publish an account of various visits to an island which he had found 'drowned in mist, where each object melts and fades and the landscape seems to bathe in dream'.[5] Henri de Régnier slipped over to visit Oscar Wilde; Pierre Louÿs was invited by the young aesthetes John Grey and André Raffalovitch, met their circle of friends and was enchanted by their elegant manners and the climate of poetry in which they managed to envelop their life; the painters Ricketts and Shannon, who were living what they liked to call 'the life beautiful' in Chelsea, welcomed visitors from France to their home; Marcel Schwob visited Symons and Gosse and returned with a booty of novels and poems to be introduced to readers at home.

It was chiefly through Marcel Schwob that the Symbolists and their friends were kept informed of what was happening in England. In 1904, he was still only twenty-seven—a little, fat, flabby young man, so obsessed with his own ugliness that he used to paste newspapers over all the mirrors in his home—but his immense erudition and a sort of globular timelessness in his appearance, led many friends hardly younger than himself to accept him as a mentor. He was a polyglot, a classicist, familiar with long-dead civilisations, and his biographer, Pierre Champion, recalls,[6] 'He used to read to me from the ancients or from English authors, bringing life to them, recreating them. Then he seemed to me like an alchemist of words, or a marvellous conjuror. . . . He was like an echo from the past, and at the same time a sounding table for all that was happening in Europe.'

Schwob was specially well-suited for interpreting the climate of the English 1890s since he was by temperament a bizarre mixture of aesthete and lover of adventure. Though himself a sedentary young man and haunter of libraries, his chief admiration was for adventurers and outcasts, for the daring or the macabre. He had been enthralled by Villon, then by Poe and de Quincey. In *Hamlet*, he saw 'an adventure story, a continual coming and going of emotions that correspond exactly to the development of external events'.[7] Defoe's anti-social heroes became his own[8] and the Goncourts have left a picture of him, a guest in their Japanesy drawing-room, entertaining them with an extemporary translation from *Colonel Jack*, hesitating a little, but amazing them by his gift for conjuring up the exact, irreplaceable word. Then he had discovered R. L. Stevenson, with his brigands and pirates and exotic settings that sparked off his own creative imagination. The enthusiasm for R. L. Stevenson of this haunter of libraries and lover of comfort was indeed such that he actually set out for Samoa to follow in his hero's traces through the South Seas. The voyage was not a success. Schwob hated every minute of it and decided from then on in favour of purely vicarious adventures.

At this point in his life, however, Schwob was rather disillusioned with English writing, comparing it unfavourably with the work of the new American writers and reserving his admiration solely for Stevenson, Henley and Meredith. He had been in touch with the latter for some time, though he had not actually met him, and was fascinated by his extreme intellectuality. Meredith seems to have appeared to him as a sort of necessary phenomenon—a writer for intellectuals difficult and demanding, who, introduced to France, might prove a counter-influence to the vast, Zola-like constructions and laborious, naturalistic documentation which had become so boring. So, since he was a great propagandist, there was constant talk of Meredith in the apartment in the rue de l'Université where Schwob—who was almost alone among French writers of the time in disliking café life—used to receive his friends.

Among the closest of these friends were three young disciples of Mallarmé—André Gide, Pierre Louÿs and Paul Valéry. All three were in their early twenties and had yet to make a name for themselves, but they were already known to an inner circle as being among the most promising of their generation. They were tremendous aesthetes and intellectuals and Meredith, who had 'exalted his cerebral activity far above all human limits',[9] who had called despairingly in the sonnet-sequence 'Modern Love' for 'more brain, O Lord, more brain!' was exactly the sort of writer to capture their imagination. He was known too to be a tremendous Francophile and to welcome visitors from France. Altogether, there seems to have been something of the father-figure about Meredith, and one suspects that Valéry, at least, discerned in him a possible insular pendant to Mallarmé himself.

Curiosity for Meredith was one of the motives that led Valéry to visit England that summer. So, of course, was the encouragement of Mallarmé who had often assured him, 'London is a very captivating city;' so was the general atmosphere of interest for all things English. It was not actually his first visit, since his parents had taken him to London when he was seven years old. His memories of that occasion were hazy. He had crossed the Channel in an antique boat like the one on which Rimbaud and Verlaine had embarked a few years earlier. It had pitched and tossed as it had done then, and he had been terribly ill. Then, when he arrived in London, he had been taken to Madame Tussaud's, where he had been terrified by the masks of famous criminals. The only other recollection he retained of this visit was a vague one of an operetta called *Fantanitza*, with music by Suppé. There were slender women dancing amid a shower of snowflakes, and he never forgot the languid rhythm of their movements.

That had been sixteen years ago and now, at the age of twenty-three, he had passed through a number of mental experiences of unusual intensity. He had left school 'not knowing where to go and feeling he was good for nothing', with the vague impression that 'art was the only thing one could count on in life'.[10] During his military service in Montpellier, he had read Mallarmé and Rimbaud and had fallen 'madly and deliberately in love'.[11] Next year, he had 'come up' to Paris, as the southern French say, and met Mallarmé, who became and remained the greatest influence in his life. He was invited to the rue de Rome, petted and encouraged. Heredia and Henri de Régnier appreciated the promising young poet. Few young men have shown such intellectual precocity or seemed more clearly predestined for greatness.

Yet Valéry seems to have been passing at this time through a period of depression that came near to nervous breakdown. His meeting with Mallarmé had inflamed his passion for the older man's poetry, but accentuated his tendency to doubt himself and everything else. He despaired now of his own poetry and felt it would never fulfil his immense aspirations. Art, which had seemed for a moment the only solid thing in a world of uncertainties, became problematic. 'I was led by I know not what demon to oppose the awareness of my mind to its productions', he recalled later.[12] A sort of exacerbated intellectuality was constantly at war with the creative instinct. One night, when he was staying in Genoa, he had passed through a veritable crisis, a night which he compared later to the night of prayer and vision that had determined the destiny of Descartes. When morning came, he had reached the conclusion which was to rule over the rest of his life: the chief function of the mind is the study of its own action.[13] He was no longer, in fact—and he noted this himself at the time—in the state of mind in which he could envisage literature as a career. Even less could this ex-law student imagine himself as a future lawyer. There seemed to be no way of reconciling the pursuit of pure conscience with any recognised form of activity. He was, in fact, at a loose end, ready for everything and for nothing.

So in June 1894 he came, armed with various letters of introduction, to stay with his aunt Paulette at No. 10 Highbury Crescent. Paulette Grassi was in fact a great-aunt, sister of his paternal grandfather on the Italian side of the family. She had married a Mr de Rin, an Anglo-Italian and they had a daughter, Pinetta, who was about Valéry's own age. She was interested in poetry, knew how to listen intelligently, and the cousins became close friends.

Highbury at this time was still almost a village, and Valéry recounts:[14]

I had below my windows a large lawn, brightened by the golden morning sun in June; it was called the Crescent, where sometimes football matches were being played, whilst often strollers were lying enjoying a 'far niente' which I should never have thought possible elsewhere than in our southern latitudes. In fact, I discovered on that day that there are lazzaroni in the North. I started roaming about London from morning till evening, very much alone, but in the company of thoughts within, and I found delight in wandering aimlessly and without any particular purpose, in the streets of the capital, either too full of life, or else too lonely.

Valéry, it must be remembered, was of Italian and Corsican descent and had spent his whole childhood and adolescence in southern towns like Sète and Montpellier. This northern city was for him a contrast far more vivid than it had been for Mallarmé, Verlaine or Rimbaud, and it was perhaps this contrast that produced what he called the 'intellectual intoxication' of London. 'I can say that my mind was amused at everything, and since then a general impression of nervous and indefinite merriment was left in my mind, associated with a town and country which are not generally regarded as calculated to impart such cheerful excitement'.[15]

He visited, of course, the usual sights: the Tower; Madame Tussaud's, which was no longer terrifying; the National Gallery, where he was bored by the Parthenon frescoes that looked so un-Greek and out-of-place in the surrounding greyness; the Houses of Parliament, where he was able to listen to a debate, thanks to an obliging neighbour in Highbury who had procured him a ticket. But it was the City that enthralled him. It was no longer the Dickensian 'cesspool' which Mallarmé had hastened to visit during his first day in London, but rather the reflection of a new, materialistic dynamism, of vast fortunes made almost overnight in 'Kaffirs', of new plutocrats setting out to conquer Society.

The City suggests this to me [he wrote to André Gide on 9 July]. One day, no doubt, people will look back at this place, with its characters and its setting, as we look back on bits of history, comburant, ashes there where we see flames; yes, my friend, trade, and the trade we see here, is the most ardent, the most 'natural', the most sublime thing in our times. And I note, ironically, that not a single artist has shown any interest in it. Oh for a Zola! . . . I believe we see here the most significant mechanism of our age, a festival of complexity for the mind.[16]

And again: 'It's the atmosphere of a machine-room, or the interior of a heart. All our heroes are to be found there . . . Loyola, Tristan, Perseus. . . .[17]

It was indeed an exciting city from the point of view of a young man just arrived from the Paris of the Symbolists. The second half of the nineteenth century had become something of a golden age for writers. It had seen the foundation of an amazing number of literary and political reviews of high standard, wide interests and great liberality towards their authors. (The *Nineteenth Century*, notably, had paid Tennyson three hundred guineas for his poem 'The Revenge'.) The *Cornhill*, *Macmillan's Magazine*, the *Fortnightly Review*, the *Saturday Review*, the *London Weekly*, the *National Observer*, the *New Review* and many others offering fine opportunities had been securing a steady income for many years for established writers. Now, they were opening their pages to younger men and to more advanced ideas, and at the same time, a whole host of smaller reviews were springing up, ready to print anything that showed talent and originality. Contrast provided excitement; moral attitudes were changing and writers were seeking for new forms to express them. Shocking the bourgeoisie had become a form of sport, though sometimes a dangerous one. There was, above all, an unparalleled ambiguity about intellectual life. Oscar Wilde was at his zenith, Symons's fame was spreading—but so was that of Kipling. Decadence was the fashion—but so was a romantic imperialism which we have come to identify with reaction, but which represented in those days an authentic, though different, *avant-garde*. The two co-existed and sometimes blended in a way which evidently appeared normal at the time.

Nowhere was this ambiguity more in evidence than at the receptions held by Joseph and Elizabeth Pennell. They were Americans—he an engraver, she a writer—with the tireless, pioneerish energy their race still displayed at the end of the nineteenth century. They lived sometimes in London sometimes in Philadelphia, holding court in one city or the other, but disappearing frequently to the Continent, where they 'gypsied', as they liked to call it, recording their travels in volumes of etchings: Provence, Tuscany, the Judengasse in Vienna, Norway, Greece, and so on. When in London, they lived at No. 14 Buckingham Street—a dingy old house with a view over the Thames which had caused Mallarmé, who had visited them during one of his stays in the city, to exclaim: 'Now I can understand Whistler!'

Whenever the Pennells appeared in Buckingham Street, they immediately became the centre of a heterogeneous group of writers and artists. Henry James came to their house whenever he was in London (Joseph Pennell illustrated his *English Hours*); one met wicked, Portuguese Howell, the villain of so many dramas connected with the Pre-Raphaelites, Charles Whibley and, above all, Whistler, the star of their collection, whom the Pennells were apt to regard as their private property and to whom they showed—according to William Rothenstein, who could not bear the anti-semitic Pennell—a jealous and syco-phantic devotion. Lately, the *Yellow Book* group had been very much in evidence too, for Joseph Pennell had more or less invented Aubrey Beardsley by writing an enthusiastic article in the *Studio* about the still unknown young artist. Beardsley was grateful and had con-sulted him frequently about his daring aesthetic experiment of found-ing a review edited exclusively by and for artists and writers and destined to serve no practical purpose whatever. The house in Bucking-ham Street had indeed become a sort of unofficial editorial office and Beardsley, Henry Harland, Ella d'Arcy, Kenneth Graham, Sickert and other contributors were nearly always present at the Pennell at-homes.

Valéry was introduced into the Pennell circle by Charles Whibley—that almost professional go-between—whom he had met at Mallarmé's Tuesdays in the rue de Rome. As Whibley had married Whistler's sister-in-law, any protégé of his was sure to be welcomed, and Valéry seems to have been received very kindly. Thus he found himself plunged, one evening soon after his arrival, into a gathering that could hardly have been more representative of London's literary and artistic life. Aubrey Beardsley was there, of course: 'a butterfly who played at being serious and yet a busy worker who played at being a butterfly'[18] and the two young men were soon involved in a long discussion on Toulouse-Lautrec, of whom Valéry thought Beardsley spoke with great appreciation and intelligence. Then he was cornered by Edmund Gosse, another ardent purveyor of French poetry. Hearing that the young Frenchman knew Mallarmé, he launched into a monologue on the subject of Mallarmé's poetic art. It lasted for one and a half hours. Nothing could stop him and Valéry, in any case, was too young and polite to try.

The gathering must have seemed much like those Paris *salons*, in which Valéry had taken so little pleasure. It was here, however, that he met W. E. Henley, who was to play an important role in his life as he did, indeed, in the lives of most of the English writers of the day and many French ones.

Henley had come a long way from the days when Verlaine claimed to have met him as an impoverished cripple among the Communards in London. He was a much-feared critic now and a power in Fleet Street, making and unmaking reputations, as well as a poet whose imperialistic 'Song of the Sword' was thrilling the nation. Henley's poetry tended to deify strength, whether moral or physical; his criticism was bombastic and prejudiced (his attacks on Ruskin, Wagner and Ibsen are more like those of a rude schoolboy than a serious writer), and his taste geared to what was becoming known as the 'Rumbustious

School', appears today uncertain to say the least. Altogether, he was as typical of the extrovert, majority aspect of the late Victorian age, as Symons and Beardsley were of the introvert minority.

It is hard to see how Henley, or even Whibley, fitted into the Pennell *salon*, or what he can have found to say to Beardsley. Yet the Pennells managed to combine them, in the mysterious way known only to creators of these sorts of *salons*, and, in actual fact, the aesthetic young men who mocked at his political views, could not entirely reject him. Henley knew at least as much about French art and poetry as they did, and was certainly more effective at introducing it into England (the fact that he loathed obscurity and intellectuality and believed that no decent poetry had been written in France since the Romantic era, only made his merit the greater). There was also the appeal of his themes, his choice of the hospital, the street, the poor, the sick and the wretched; there was the undeniable originality of his broken rhythms and French verse forms, which recalled those of Verlaine and forced even Arthur Symons, who detested him as a man, to admiration; and there was the attraction of his advanced views on morals. He had been one of the first to dare use the word 'sex' in a poem and even Valery Larbaud, who detested his 'materialistic fatalism', later admitted that his 'action and influence as a critic, as well as a discoverer of young talent and a liaison agent with the Continent, specially France, was considerable. His influence against the Puritanism and anti-cultural attitude of the general public in England is unquestionable'.[19]

Valéry was impressed and rather intimidated as were most young men by this famous master. Henley's physical presence was immense: 'He commands a larger atmosphere, gives the impression of a grosser mass of character than most men',[20] his bosom friend R. L. Stevenson said of him, though less well disposed observers, such as Wilfrid Scawen Blunt, noted 'a dwarf's malignity of tongue and defiant attitude to the world in general'.[21] To Valéry, he seemed to have 'a face like the masque of a lion, a formidable face, though his imposing aspect was sometimes joyously transformed by bursts of immense laughter'.[22] The two talked together. They had a common friend in Marcel Schwob, who ranked Henley with Meredith and Stevenson as 'one of the noblest of living writers', perhaps because he shared Schwob's own passion for Villon. Valéry was invited to an evening at the poet's house in Muswell Hill—a rendezvous for the great names in literature, as well as for coming young writers like Kipling, Barrie, H. G. Wells, Alice Meynell, Kenneth Graham, Katherine Tynan, W. B. Yeats. Even Bernard Shaw came for a time but Henley's rabid anti-Socialism—he had changed a

great deal from the Communard days and preferred to forget them—
soon put a stop to that budding friendship. Valéry felt shy and ill at
ease on this occasion, but Henley evidently took to him. He was in
fact to be the first link in the curious chain of people and events that
brought the young man to an unlikely desk in the offices of the
Chartered Company.

There could have been no better introduction to a certain side of
English literary life than the Pennells' hospitable house. It was there, too,
that he had an experience of a different kind which made a deep impression
on him. He was living now in a state of moral and material uncertainty,
the old beliefs discarded, new ones still only tentatively formulated.
'For a long time now, I have accepted the fact that I have reached the
limits of my own power of supporting uncertainty,' he had written
to André Gide in February that year.[23] Thus he found himself in a state
of special permeability, when one of those rare moments when life
and art combine in a single aesthetic experience was certain to provoke
a fleeting but incomparable ecstasy. Such a moment occurred one
evening at about eleven o'clock, when Mrs Pennell's guests were gazing
idly out of the window over the Thames.[24]

> Nothing could have been more beautiful [he recalled over thirty
> years later] than the fantastic sight that met our gaze. A great
> conflagration had broken out in the direction of Finsbury; no
> flames were visible, but the reverberation of the fire from the sky
> imparted a rosy hue to the atmosphere. A London as seen in dreams
> was being produced before us: we saw masses of azure and gigantic
> turquoise and sapphire forms. The dome of St Paul's was
> silhouetted in the luminous sky and one felt the sensation of
> seeing a unique masterpiece which would have satisfied all Turner's
> and Whistler's ambitions combined.

That evening, London had been transformed into a sort of ideal work
of art, on which he preferred to reflect in silence.

Meanwhile, there was Meredith who was one of the motives for
his visit to England. He was not quite a stranger to Valéry, for a few
years earlier the young Frenchman had written an admiring letter from
Montpellier to which Meredith had replied in the most charming
manner. Now he sent off Schwob's letter of introduction, and shortly
after received a reply, written in impeccable French:

> Cher Monsier, The friend of Marcel Schwob has every right to
> ask for the hospitality of my home. You will be welcome and I
> hope you will do me the honour of dining with me at 7 pm.

English cooking, alas, but the wine is French. I shall be at home
every day this week, and I could see you after 4 pm. on Friday,
Saturday, Sunday. There is a train to take you back at 8.25.

On the following Sunday, Valéry took the train to Box Hill, where
he found himself, alone and lost at the station, with no idea of the
direction to take. After a time, a servant appeared, announcing himself
as 'the faithful Coles' come to lead him to his master. They set out
together, 'plunging into the verdure of the English fields where there
are neither walls, boundaries nor hedges; green everywhere.'[25] Conversation was difficult as Valéry's English was not up to understanding
a country accent, but he did gather that Coles was recounting a visit
to Paris, when his master had paid his fare so that he might see the 1889
Exhibition. On his arrival at the Gare du Nord, he had made the
acquaintance of some person whom he took to be a policeman on leave;
the two had started on a drinking bout that had lasted three days and
three nights, after which he had returned to England. He spoke fervently of Paris, seen from this limited, but apparently delightful angle.

> I was beginning to wonder where Meredith's abode might be
> [recounts Valéry]. All at once Coles said to me, 'Here we are:
> all you need do is walk straight ahead,' and he went off, after again
> raising his cap with a happy smile. Still I could see nothing before
> me but green pastures without walls, hedges or houses. I walked
> on in the direction indicated. Gradually the ground rose and I
> soon observed against the sky, at the top of the hill, a mass of
> something sweetly reflecting the golden rays of the setting sun
> and consisting of a few trees clustered together round a hut, and
> the hut in front. I began to distinguish a few persons sitting who,
> little by little, proved to be ladies and gentlemen taking tea.[26]

All these people looked very large, and were dressed in informal
country clothes. Valéry was very small, slight and dark, looking a
thorough southerner, in spite of his bright blue eyes. He was wearing
his neat black suit, a tall, stiff collar, and probably the monocle which
had become a sort of insignia of the French Symbolists. Suddenly, he
became acutely conscious of his incongruous appearance. 'I imagined
the impression necessarily produced upon them by this little foreign
personnage, a black marionette on a green background, advancing
awkwardly towards them.' His confusion increased when a strange-
looking old man arose with difficulty and came towards him. Meredith,
in his old age, was tall and thin like the dead branch of a tree and he was
dressed in an exceedingly un-French way, in a blue suit with a red

handkerchief round his neck. He was already suffering from creeping paralysis and walked with difficulty, leaning on a stick. To Valéry's horror, when he was within three paces of his guest and just in the act of raising his cap to bid him welcome, he fell forward, flat on his face.[27]

> I have the recollection [he recalls] of having picked up with wonderful ease the very thin body of this rather tall man. I felt confused by the incident, which increased my awkwardness; but Meredith at once manifested so much kindness and such marked sympathy, that this painful impression almost at once gave way to the pleasure his gracious reception gave me. He spoke with difficulty and roughly, with a strong guttural and rather indistinct voice.

Meredith's other visitors on this occasion were Sir Frederick and Lady Pollock. Sir Frederick was at that time a barrister of some renown, who later became a member of the French Institute. He combined a passion for mountaineering and for the philosophy of Spinoza, so that Valéry found himself, probably for the first time, in the company of an intellectual who was also a man of action and an extrovert. The phenomenon was at that date peculiarly British, or at least peculiarly non-French, and the late Victorian period was notable for a philosophy of action which underlay much of its expansionist achievement. This encounter and his later relationship with the Pollocks were not without importance.

After tea, Meredith took his young visitor into what Valéry calls his 'cottage', but which was in fact a sort of study, built separately from his dwelling-house and communicating with it by means of a telephone and an electric bell. There were two small rooms, their walls covered with books. Valéry noted that many of these were in French and consisted largely of memoirs of the Consulate and the Empire. Conversation was difficult because Meredith had a disease of the vocal chords and spoke through a hoarse, cackling speaking-trumpet. However, Valéry soon discovered he was 'in love with Napoleon', of whom he now said, to his visitor's increasing surprise, 'Napoleon was a man so great, so great, that the gods could only get rid of him by turning him against himself.'[28] He also revealed 'a kind of worship for Joan of Arc'. It was indeed a contrast with the conversation he had known in Symbolist circles.

Meredith had placed his writing desk in front of a little window almost entirely obscured by shrubs and trees so that hardly any light fell on it. Valéry asked him the reason, whereupon the old man replied, 'The brain requires darkness.' Then, recounts Valéry, 'We started talking about this awful brain, the eternal and invisible collaborator of the man of thought, both a very capricious friend and foe. Meredith said to me: "The brain never gets tired. It is the stomach".' These aphorisms of Meredith's on the subject of the brain impressed Valéry sufficiently to be noted on his return and remembered long afterwards. Marcel Schwob, who visited Box Hill a few months later, was equally impressed and also took careful notes of the conversation.[29] A comparison shows that his host made the same remarks, word for word, on the two occasions. One can only suppose that the Great Old Thinker had a stock of these humorously profound remarks which he produced for the benefit of disciples. Valéry himself, once he had had time to reflect on the interview, seems to have been a little puzzled by the old man, for he wrote the following year to Marcel Schwob:[30]

I felt I knew Meredith too little. I'm not sure that his opinions on women, or on Nature, which in Boxhill is like the softest of billiard tables, would bear examining in bright sunlight. . . . In any case, Meredith is something of an unknown quantity for me. His tall, slow-moving figure, the hoarse trumpet that compensates his aphonia, his wavering charm, *Harry Richmond*, which I have read, and your admiration, which I follow undoubtingly, are enough. I never saw such a man before! Oh, how I wish I could talk to him without any of these ridiculous obstacles, have two really transparent hours with him now!

The most positive result of the visit seems to have been the immense curiosity concerning Napoleon it aroused in him. As a half-Corsican, he must have heard a good deal about the Emperor, but battles and strategy had not been among his interests up to that date. Meredith had put the question in a new perspective. 'B. interests me,' Valéry wrote in the first of a long series of notebooks he filled throughout his life with his meditations, 'like a word in an imaginary language. For me, he definitely signifies the exterior face of a conscious intellectual power over the material world in its most complex aspect.'[31]

Valéry returned to London in company with the Pollocks and was later invited to their house. There he made the acquaintance of Sir Frederick's mother and mother-in-law, who 'both spoke the purest and most elegant French' and one of whom had been a friend of Victor Hugo. Although Sir Frederick was an exceptionally shy man, his fine mind and the charm of the three ladies drew a good many visitors to the house. In all likelihood, it was there that Valéry met Lord Kelvin, the brilliant mathematician and inventor. A letter written the following year, congratulating Kelvin on the Jubilee of his professorship at

Glasgow University,[32] was answered in roneo, but with a note added by hand, so the two must have met fairly frequently.

Now Lord Kelvin was greatly interested in Far Eastern affairs and had dealings with Japan sufficiently important for the Emperor to bestow on him, some two years later, the 'Order of the First Class of the Sacred Treasure of Japan'. Presumably, then, it was through him that Valéry heard of Torio Koyata. This distinguished soldier, scholar, philosopher and politician had been sent by Ito Hirobami's government to Europe in 1885 in connection with its policy for the westernisation of Japan. Exactly what Viscount Torio did or where he went during the year he spent in Europe remains a mystery, but Lord Kelvin must have met him, been impressed by him and discussed him with Valéry, for a quotation from Torio: 'Civilisation, according to the interpretation of the Occident, serves only to satisfy men of large desires', introduces the oriental tale entitled 'Le Yalou'.[33] Various jottings from Valéry's notebooks for the following year show that he was preoccupied with and planning this strange, difficult story—or rather meditation— of a Western traveller in China.[34] Under its political overtones, 'Le Yalou' is really an examination, in the context of the Sino-Japanese war, which broke out in August 1894 and which Lord Kelvin had probably foreseen, of the same relationship between the intellect and the material world so fascinatingly illustrated by Napoleon. This relationship always seemed to Valéry the key to the true meaning of civilisation, and Napoleon and Torio had each provided, through Meredith and Kelvin, one of the early clues to the problem that pursued him through his whole life.

The sort of people Valéry met at the Pollocks' were very different from those he had known at the Pennells', and it was here he had his first glimpse of an England he never ceased to admire—the England he described many years later as[35]

> the empire of fact, the country where, more than anywhere else in the world, a choice, whether made among men or things, is always made in relation to experience. It is this that has made her powerful, slow, strange and sometimes, for us inconceivable. Her strength, her mystery, her charm seem like elements of nature.

Soon he had further opportunities of observing this empirical spirit that attracted him all the more because it was so utterly foreign, so un-latin. Charles Whibley was a faithful and efficient friend to visitors from France, especially when they came with the aura of the rue de Rome still upon them. He had taken his young friend to see the

Pennells; now he introduced him to a new literary milieu. The *Pall Mall Gazette* had recently been bought up by an American, William Astor, who had transformed it in an amazingly short time from a rather limp and characterless magazine into one of the most dynamic periodicals in London and certainly the one which expressed most forcibly a new current of ideas that was sweeping through England.

The ruling spirit of the 1890s had, of course, nothing to do with the *Yellow Book*, the Rhymers' Club, Art-for-Art's-sake, or *fin de siècle* decadence. It was not Aubrey Beardsley who could command the attention of the public, but the young Rudyard Kipling, whose manner, as York Powell—veering unexpectedly in the direction of the new nationalism—remarked, was 'that which his age admires and recognises, because he has something new to say which he must say plainly and does say well.' For these were the years of Rhodes, of the Chartered Company, of the penetration into Central and Southern Africa. The comfortable certainty that England was right had flared up, almost suddenly, into a new style of patriotism, challenging, aggressive and romantic. It was a feeling that Henley, who was one of its most enthusiastic exponents, summed up when he wrote:[36]

> We English have been recaptured by certain influences whose hold we had, or seemed to have escaped. We had waxed fat and we had learned to feel a sort of pride in getting kicked. We were bloated with peace and believed that war, being a costly business and one most ruinous to trade, suburban amenities and the smiling self-complacency which comes of consciousness of virtue and a pleasing pass-book, had no more terrors for us, that it had passed for ever from our tale of ways and means. All that has changed. We have renewed our pride in the Flag, our old delight in the thought of a good thing done by a good man of his hands, our old faith in the ambitions and traditions of our race.

Many of the staff of the *Pall Mall* had worked with Henley on the *National Observer*. Max Beerbohm used to refer to them as 'Henley's regatta', and they habitually lunched at a restaurant called the Solférino, in Rupert Street. Soho, as Verlaine had remarked a few months earlier, had changed greatly and now offered, among other delights, a wide range of cheap little French restaurants where Francophile Englishmen could revive memories of happy holidays in Paris. Kettner's, for instance, had become positively fashionable since, back in the 1860s an adventurous diner had written a letter to *The Times*, expressing his amazement at discovering in darkest Soho an establishment where one could dine not only safely but well. The Solférino had become popular with a more bohemian crowd. It was a favourite haunt of Whistler and Sickert; Rothenstein loved it, and most of the Pennells' friends came there from time to time.

Whibley brought Valéry there, and introduced him to George Steevens of the *Pall Mall*. Henley later described Steevens as 'a rather gloomy and socialistic junior don', but he was on the way to becoming one of the finest 'imperialistic' journalists.[37] There was Ernest Williams, who edited the *Gazette* under Astor, sometimes Henley himself and often occasional contributors who strayed in during brief visits to London. The talk was naturally about Africa, about Rhodes, 'Matabele' Thompson, Lugard and the explorers and concession hunters everyone was discussing at the time, about the difficult negotiations with King Lo Bengula. All these young men were what the latest slang was beginning to call 'jingoists'. They put England above all else, defended her against any attack, thrilled to her exploits. They were romantic and idealistic, ready to worship those who were shouldering 'the white man's burden' in the mysterious lands of which strange tales were beginning to make headlines in the English press. Imperialism, in the *Pall Mall* offices and the Solférino, meant youth, enthusiasm, exaltation. It was even, Henley assured them, a divine mission:[38]

> We are the choice of the Will. God, when He gave the word
> That called us into line, set in our hand a sword;
> Set us a sword to wield none else could lift or draw,
> And bade us forth to the sound of the trumpet of the Law,
> East and West and North, wherever the battle grew,
> As men to a feast we fared, the work of the Will to do.

That was the African adventure as Valéry and his new friends saw it. Over in Park Lane, the new millionaires were raising mansions built on sudden fortunes into whose origins it was better not to enquire; in the City one saw greed at its most hideous paroxysm; fine words and fine sentiments were a cloak for vulgarity and sordid self-interest, but 'Henley's Regatta' lived in a dream of chivalry and believed sincerely in the inevitability and rightness of British supremacy.

It must have seemed like a new world to Valéry. The Symbolists in Paris hardly knew that politics existed. His closest friends were pacifists like Marcel Schwob, or like André Gide, were in revolt against all authority, whether personal or political. He listened, not speaking enough English to take much part in the talk, but understanding all that was said. Soon he discovered Cecil Rhodes or rather, the Idea of Cecil Rhodes, which went far beyond the figure of the explorer himself, romantic and exciting as he appeared in the conversation of the *Pall Mall* journalists. He had been surprised and impressed during his visit to Meredith, by the old man's devotion to Napoleon. Returning from Box Hill, he had reflected on it and had come to the conclusion that 'It is the zenith of glory to be able to attach to one's person, or the idol of one's person, at the same time, the soul and hazy devotion, so to speak, of the people, and the minds of most deep-thinking men'.[39] Rhodes evidently shared this quality for he seems to have caught the national imagination on several levels, appearing to simple minds as a sort of schoolboy's hero, and to the more thoughtful as a symbol of action, of an inward energy directed to the conquest of the outer world.

It was thus that Valéry, who had been alone among his friends in Montpellier and Paris in questioning the absolute supremacy of Art, fell under the spell of Rhodes and British imperialism, and found himself, to his own amazement, becoming a nationalist, a 'patriot'. It was a mental attitude that was to remain with him all his life and Marcel Schwob, for one, considered his friend to have picked up some kind of obnoxious germ in London. It was due to this difference of opinion that a coolness grew up between them. 'When one becomes a patriot late in life—and in London! one is lost to intellectuality', commented Valéry ironically.[40]

Then the visit was over.

I returned from England absolutely enchanted with my stay [he recounts]. I had seen London under the most favourable conditions. The month of June, the facilities I had had to come into contact with so many minds differing so much, and, for me, both so different and so attractive. Briefly, everything left upon me one of those impressions which necessarily create an increasing desire to experience them again and lead us to that strange conclusion that different causes must produce the same effects, and that it is possible to return to the same place as if it were a rendezvous with one's own self.[41]

The Chartered Company

This rendezvous with himself came about two years later, after a period that appears extraordinarily fruitful to the objective observer, but which to him seemed merely frustrating. Perhaps the 'intellectual intoxication' of London was responsible for the intense mental activity of this period? At any rate, by the end of 1895, he had completed both the *Introduction à la méthode de Léonard de Vinci* and *La Soirée avec Monsieur Teste*, two curiously contradictory yet complementary works, one turned towards the conquest of the exterior world by the creative mind; the other, the apotheosis of interiority. An amazing achievement for a man of twenty-four, but Valéry seems to have dreamed of a sort of Human Comedy of the intellect, a vast panorama parallel to Balzac's *Comédie humaine* or Dante's *Divina Commedia*. What he had actually accomplished seemed terribly inadequate when weighed against such vast ambitions, and it left him feeling useless and hopeless.

On another plane, he was desperately worried by his material situation. A rich bourgeois like André Gide could allow himself to dedicate his life to literature without calculating immediate financial returns, but the Valérys were both bourgeois and poor. They had to maintain middle-class respectability on an insufficient income and could hardly be expected to keep one of their two sons in apparent idleness. Valéry's parents and everyone else expected him to follow one of the professions normally adopted by young men of his class at that time: the civil service or the law, for instance. This was precisely what he felt himself incapable of doing. He was in fact caught in a very difficult dilemma. He might have defied public opinion by proclaiming himself a poet and accepting everything entailed by such a decision. It was a romantic attitude not uncommon at the period. Unfortunately he was not certain that he really was a poet. 'I distrusted literature and even poetry, which demands a certain precision,' he explained later, adding, 'The act of writing always implies a certain sacrifice of the intelligence.'[42] Nor, though, could he imagine any other kind of existence that could be defined in the context of his social milieu.[43]

> I was still following within myself a certain clue which I felt to be continuous [he says], but the end of which I could not see. . . .
> I lived waiting for I know not what incident to turn up and change my life. My trunk was always at the foot of my bed as a symbol of the departure I was ready to take at the slightest token from Fate.

Everything seemed to suggest that this departure, when it came, would be once more in the direction of England. Valéry had maintained his connections across the Channel. He had written several articles for Henley's *Art Journal*; he was in correspondence with Meredith, who had tempted him with a charming letter, dated 11 July 1895 and written in his usual confident French:

> Dear Monsieur Valéry. We are in the middle of the travelling season and perhaps you intend to visit England for your studies. Perhaps you even have friends whom you would like to see and

who would help you to discover some of the pleasures of this country which foreigners find rather depressing. In that case, I hope you will count me among them and come to visit me. It would be a real pleasure. Sir Frederick and Lady Pollock, whom you met in my cottage, have kept a most pleasant memory of this occasion. As for me, I look through the literary reviews, seeking your name and your contributions: I know you are working and that you have the skill and enthusiasm that bring great results.

M. Georges Hugo has spoken of a study of da Vinci—but, I beg you, don't call me Master. I am merely your elder brother. . . .

But Valéry was unemployed, poor and for the moment terribly uncertain of himself. He could not travel to England, or anywhere else, and could only wait in Paris, with as much patience as possible, for the expected 'sign'.

It was to arrive the following spring, in the last days of March. Valéry had not been forgotten in London, where a number of people had been impressed by his intelligent interest in politics and especially in the situation in Africa. No doubt, his natural discretion had been noticed too, and perhaps something unexpectedly British in the appearance of this pure Latin told in his favour.[44] At any rate, his name had been put forward in connection with a highly confidential mission that seemed opportune in view of recent developments in the South African adventure.

The British Association Chartered Company had been founded in 1889 by Cecil Rhodes at a time when the scramble among the European powers for the territory and trade of the African interior had begun in earnest. Most of the original capital had been supplied through French sources, largely through the influence of Baron d'Erlanger, of the great Anglo-French banking family, so that the Company had close connections with France. Rhodes himself had established his offices in the City and gone off to negotiate with native kings, hew roads and establish his personal empire in Africa, leaving the running of the Company to a curious band of often inefficient and not always completely honest associates. The thrilling tales of the British flag planted in almost unexplored territory, the setting up of a British magistrature, of a British police system in these new and far-flung outposts of the Empire, the legend of Rhodes and certain of his famous associates, no doubt deflected attention from balance sheets and administrative details. All the same, shareholders must have wondered why, with the company's capital holdings rising vertiginously, they were never paid any dividends.[45] Then, in December 1895, came the

Jameson raid. Public opinion was shocked; Rhodes repudiated it, but was forced to resign his governorship of Cape Colony. For the first time, people began to ask themselves questions, even to doubt the flawless, Crusader-like image of certain of their heroes.

If the British were worried, the French were openly, righteously indignant. Over in Paris, *Le Temps* was describing the raid as 'this expedition of brigands',[46] accusing the British Government of using the Chartered Company to foment troubles that endangered the vast sums invested by France in the South African mines. A few days later, it had adopted a definitive policy with which the greater part of the French public heartily agreed. 'For history, for the Boers, for ourselves, the saviours of the Transvaal will be the Germans.' In fact, the Boer war already appeared inevitable and it looked as though French sympathy would be all on the side of the Boers struggling to free themselves from 'the British yoke'.[47] It was more than time for the British to present their own point of view in the few papers prepared to give it space.

Valéry was in bed on a Sunday morning at the end of March when the postman brought a letter from England. It was signed by a name he had never heard before—a certain Lionel Decle, who had heard of him through Charles Whibley, and who suggested he might translate some articles on South Africa for publication in the French press. The work must be done on the spot and, if he accepted, he was to wire a single word, 'agreed', fetch the money that was waiting for him in a Paris bank and take the boat next evening for Newhaven. From thence he was to travel to Victoria, where he would find a secretary ('Mr. Juniper, a blond young man', specified the writer) waiting with a cab. The job would last two weeks and possibly longer and he was to be paid one hundred and twenty-five francs a week, plus all travelling expenses.

This letter, coming as it did at a moment when Valéry found himself in such a curious state of availability, really seemed like the 'sign' he had been waiting for.[48]

Coup de théâtre! [he scribbled hurriedly to his mother] I leave for London Monday evening at 9 o'clock, by first class. I am to do some important translations for M. Lionel Decle, 12 Burleigh Mansions, Charing Cross Road. I have not hesitated a moment, for it's perhaps the chance I have been dreaming of. I shall work from 11 to 3. This letter that came this morning made me leap out of bed. I had to take an instant decision.—It's done. I am off to wire the word agreed on, and to fetch the price of my journey. I am writing at once to Aunt too. But I shan't be staying with her, at least at first.

Everything went according to plan. Valéry arrived at Victoria on the Tuesday morning; the blond Mr Juniper was waiting with a cab to convey him to Burleigh Mansions and the man who, in his own account of the affair, he refers to only as 'the writer of the letter' or, even more mysteriously, 'X'. Here is his own story of the meeting:[49]

I found myself in a house where everything was negro and all bristling with more or less poisonous assagais and arrows and adorned with obviously equatorial photos. I was then introduced into this home by an individual of magnificent black who, as I afterwards learnt, was the son of a king of Bechuanaland or something of the kind. I waited a considerable time among these African weapons and spoils, very anxious to know what I had come here for.

A tall gentleman appeared in white silk pyjamas. He first of all gave me a full account of his life which did not concern me, but at the same time interested me very deeply, as it was most graphic and varied, and his story was especially the story of a professional explorer in the central parts of Africa.

He related stories which made me shiver, stories of negroes given up alive to giant ants, stories of negro kings like the famous Lobengula. He seemed to have known this king fond of wit who, it appears, formed words by having the tongues, hands, feet, etc. cut off people who had not shown him enough respect or whom he disliked.

At the most pathetic moment, it occurred to X—that I must be dying of hunger. I availed myself of this little oasis in the form of eggs and bacon, to ask him what I was expected to do and why he had asked me to come.

Now X, as we have seen, was Lionel Decle, a Frenchman whose role in African politics remains as mysterious as it must have seemed to Valéry on this first morning in London. He was a tall, lean man, with a long, cadaverous face, who had been brought up in England and had spent much of his boyhood travelling with his parents in Europe and the Middle East. He retained his French nationality, however, and had returned to France to go through his period of military service. He seems to have spent most of his time in the army in prison, and was regarded, according to his own account, as 'an incorrigible rogue'. He later recounted the story of his inglorious military adventures in a book called *Trooper 3809* and his picture of the French army is such that one can hardly be surprised to find him, once restored to civilian life, choosing England as his home. Thereafter he spent most of his time travelling in Africa, where he was soon fired with an immense enthusiasm for 'the genius, the indomitable energy and the greatness of the conceptions of Mr Cecil Rhodes, Mr H. M. Stanley and other Englishmen who have left wherever they have been the imprint of their great minds'.[50] Back in London, he became friendly with Henley, Steevens and Whibley. The *Pall Mall Gazette* was glad to publish articles by a great hunter and collector, who also turned out to be a shrewd political observer. Decle, in fact, was in the invidious position of a French national (complete with a slight accent, which he never entirely lost, in spite of his English upbringing) who explained British Imperialism to the British.

His situation was in fact even more complicated than it appeared, for Decle was also a French agent, acting directly for the French Secret Service. He did not, perhaps, advertise the fact at this time, but later he made no secret of it and wrote quite openly, in his preface to *Three Years in Savage Africa*, of the mission he had carried out for this Service in Madagascar. On that occasion, he had gained great credit by solving a complicated mystery concerning the death of a certain Stokes, which turned out to be a particularly sinister murder. His employers were much less pleased when he returned from his first long journey in Africa.[51]

> I was treated with marked coldness by my countrymen [he complained]. The official world had no abuses strong enough for me. I had committed the great crime of openly expressing my admiration for the British administration in South Africa, Rhodesia, Nyasaland and Uganda, and when I tried to prove that I had merely been fair and impartial, I was told by a high official that I had no right to be fair and impartial with regard to Anglo-African questions.

When Valéry had finished his eggs and bacon, and his talkative host had come to an end of his stories, they took a cab to the City, and Valéry was put at once to work.

The Company had its offices in St Swithin's Lane, and there the young man was given a room of his own and a desk that was kept piled high with documents relating to the Transvaal and South African problems. Each day he saw his chief, a Mr Bourke, for half an hour, after which he was left to his own devices. Thus he was able to observe the comings and goings of 'an unparalleled collection of the most diverse types of humanity, that is to say, a humanity of adventurers'.[52] These men, whom the Company had recruited from all possible sources, seem to have been typical of the bands of mercenaries who still descend from time to time upon Africa—that is to say, they were unemployable elsewhere. The company's official biographer says they were 'a force of pioneers and police, as daring a band of adventurers as ever Pizarro or Cortes led',[53] but on visits to London they cut a less glorious figure and Valéry adds that, 'occasionally could be seen strange wrecks, men to whom no other perspective was left than suicide or life in its most dreary form.' Among the officers and 'magistrates' of Rhodesia, he even recognised members of the French aristocracy who had adopted a mode of life more like that of their ancestors in the early Middle Ages than anything to be found in modern France.

The weather was evidently horrible; the town was veiled in fog and mist—it was probably for this reason that Valéry's memory so soon betrayed him and caused him later to situate this visit in February instead of April. He was lonely and often depressed. A pencil sketch, showing a row of forbidding-looking and typically English chimneypots (a view from the window of his office or from his lodgings in Greville Street?) has the word 'solitude' scribbled above it. To Marcel Schwob he wrote:[54]

I brought your fine Descartes here, but I never open it. I couldn't make anything of it now. But when I see it lying there, my mind is brought back from the Transvaal and I reflect on both at once. Have you ever thought of the pleasure of the helmsman when he feels the boat sway to left or to port, following the wheel—and the wheel sliding beneath his hand—and beyond his hand, the flow of ideas starting from that point, and its intoxicating passage along the current between the idea and the sea, the various resistances. . . .? Hush. Just think that I talk to my chief for half an hour each day about business—and the rest of the time I'm alone, like the king in his lavatory. And then, when I leave my South Africa, I feel a fool, I have the impression I'm taking a cure here. Perhaps silence, toast and gold mines have been prescribed for me.

A letter to André Gide[55] reveals even more clearly how strange and lost he felt himself in these new surroundings:

By eleven o'clock [he wrote on 2 April, describing—in an expurgated version—his arrival in London], I was at work. I had entered into a new world that I don't yet understand. I have rented a room nearby. I live absolutely alone and speechless, except at the times when we attend conferences where we are given explanations and orders. And afterwards I go straight home, cut off suddenly from my whole former life and from any ideas except technical ones. A maid brings me disgusting food—oh! disgusting—at the usual English times and I eat, watching the fire, without ceasing to reflect on serious business. Sometimes I make faces at myself in the glass, so as to give myself at least the impression that I am laughing and not too constantly serious.

You must know that I am caught up among immensely clever people. Thanks to my job (a confidential one) I have discovered some very important things. I have access to some pretty significant documents. I beg you never to say anything about what I am telling you now. I awoke on Tuesday to find myself face to face with one of the thousand parts of a colossal machine called the Chartered Company, which is taking possession of South Africa. Its policy is extraordinary. The general public has only heard about it since the Jameson affair and the events in the Transvaal. You can have no idea of the power, the depth, the wisdom, the brutal simplicity of these people. They are always right. I understand their ethics. In France, these will never be understood.

The letter was signed: 'Prometheus (raped by fire)'.

Valéry had been engaged primarily as a translator, but some scribbled notes suggest that he also prepared rough drafts of articles, presumably for his colleagues, since his own English was too elementary to allow him to write them himself. The absent figure of Rhodes, which had so impressed him during the discussions at the Solférino, became tremendous, overwhelming, now that he was at the heart of the Chartered Company.

'One will attempt to explain—without any fulsome praise—the work and energy represented by the organisation of a territory', he suggested in some pages apparently prepared in view of a magazine article. 'One will explain how such a task ordinarily demands centuries, and the evolution of a given territory, of a race'. . . . Then, carried away, one feels, by his subject, he sketches a portrait of Rhodes himself—a strangely intellectualised Rhodes, whom the British public would hardly have recognised:[56]

We see him now, acting for the sake of action, drunk with pure action, just as one can be drunk with pure science; one imagines him burning with this passion, with this amazing debauch which can only be satisfied by the feeling that huge territories are changing form in one's hands, that men are travelling, fighting, growing rich, within the circle drawn around them by a powerful mind, and accomplishing by means of their instincts and temperaments, that which the grandiose gamester has foreseen for them.

Yet at the same time, Valéry, as we have seen, was discovering 'some very important things'. These things seem chiefly to have concerned Rhodes, and they did not always match the heroic image he had conceived. Some notes, scribbled in English on a piece of paper evidently torn from an exercise book, record certain discoveries:[57]

Rhodes' contempt of married people.
Rhodes' dream of creating a Rhodesian empire for himself.
Difficulties with the imperial government.
Rhodes' recent words: 'I have only commenced politics.'
Rhd's journey from Cape to London for one hour's interview with Mr Chamberlain.
Rhds' cynical method of buying people when opposite.
Report of Ch. Company's forces management. Ammunitions and weapons.
Curious war directions.
Dr Jameson's acquaintance with R.
Royal Charter granted on 29/10/89.
U.S. of South Africa.

Were these notes destined for communication to Decle and from thence to the French Secret Service? Or were they elements of the portrait the new employee was trying to form for the satisfaction of his own curiosity? They suggest, at any rate, that he was puzzled, perhaps even dismayed, by some of the revelations in the 'pretty significant documents'.

Physically and mentally, Valéry found himself marooned, now, on the desert island which the Company offices turned out to be, once his first curiosity was spent. There was none of the busy, exciting literary life he had enjoyed during his first visit. The trial and condemnation of Oscar Wilde had brought about what William Gaunt has called 'a wholesale literary and cultural fumigation'. First the *Yellow Book*, then the *Savoy* had disappeared; the Decadent movement was dead, and a great many people connected with it had gone temporarily underground. His own mood had changed too and he felt himself less and less in tune with what Holbrook Jackson has described as 'a perverse and finicking glorification of the fine arts and mere artistic virtuosity.' Literature and almost the whole of philosophy now seemed

to him 'vague' and 'impure', a 'sacrificing of intellect'.[58] 'In England I
have only very sensible ideas and I think according to the words I
know', he wrote to Schwob.[59]

Meredith had not forgotten him and he seems to have dined at least
once at Box Hill. Conversation must have been difficult, for the old
man by no means equated Rhodes with Napoleon and was strongly
opposed to colonialist policy. He had been furious at the Jameson raid
and took a point of view exactly opposite to that of Henley.

> This exposure of Cecil Rhodes and the masterly attitude of the
> Boers in defence should be a lesson to England [he wrote to Alice
> Meynell on 2 May 1896]. Foiled at every turn by a small body of
> wild Dutchmen! We see the first result of our turning under
> Haggard's wand to a beast with bloody jaws for auriferous Africa.

One may suppose that, since both were notably courteous men, they
agreed to avoid this controversial topic.

So when work at the Company's offices was over, Valéry returned
to Greville Street to sit before an inadequate fire waiting for the maid
to bring him the 'disgusting food' that constituted his dinner. His
spirits sank lower and lower:

> There is a certain way of thinking, for just three seconds, in the
> evening, as one is taking off one's trousers [he wrote to J. K.
> Huysmans[60]], about oneself, one's body and the end it will
> come to, that suddenly intoxicates one with horror and freezes
> one. Then, all the dark part of the brain pursues its vast,
> mysterious work.

He was part of the City now, but seen at close quarters, these
bustling streets seem to have lost their power over his imagination.
The Thames, however, still exercised its rather awful charm. When he
could escape from the claustrophobic office in St Swithin's Lane, he
wandered down to the river, to watch the loading of ships and perhaps
dare brief conversations with sea-faring men. Certain English terms—
'log-book', 'docks', 'engine-room'—begin to appear in the jotted
reflections—the *Analecta*—transcribed in his notebooks in the very
early morning, 'between the lamp and the light', before the working
day began. From then on, he used these and other technical terms frequently, since a certain category of ideas would always seem to him to
belong to England and be best expressed in English.

It was while he was wandering one day by the Thames that he was
inspired to write the prose poem, or 'meditation' he entitled 'London
Bridge'. It portrays the strangely dual mental world in which he felt

Plate 3   Paul Valéry, aged twenty-four

Plate 4 Valery Larbaud in London, 1910

himself to be living at the time—a duality personified in *Léonard de Vinci* and *Monsieur Teste*, those two antithetical masks which he had fitted the previous year to his own face.[61]

> A little while ago [he wrote] I was walking across London Bridge and I paused to contemplate what is for me an endless pleasure—the sight of a rich, thick, complex waterway whose nacreous sheets and oily patches are loaded with a confusion of ships, their white smoke-puffs, their swinging davits, their strange balancing-acts with crates and bales, bringing themselves and the whole panorama to life.
>
> My eyes halted me; I leaned upon my elbows, as if in the grip of a vice. Delight of vision held me with a ravenous thirst, involved in the play of a light of inexhaustible richness. But endlessly pacing and flowing at my back I was aware of another river, a river of the blind eternally in pursuit of immediate material object.
>
> This seemed to me no crowd of individual beings . . . rather I made of it, unconsciously, in the depth of my body, in the shaded places of my eyes, *a flux of identical particles*, equally sucked in by the same nameless void, their deaf headlong current pattering monotonously over the bridge. Never have I so felt solitude, in a mingling of pride and anguish—a strange and obscure sense of the danger of dreaming between the water and the crowd.
>
> I found myself guilty of the crime of poetry upon London Bridge.

Solitude, the uncertainty as to his future, the sensation of 'a nameless void', poetry 'a crime against the intellect' . . . Valéry was indeed experiencing a mood of almost pathological depression during these sad, wintry spring days in London. Much later, he confided to a friend that he had been tempted by suicide as he gazed down into the water from London Bridge. He resisted, but the temptation returned—as it was to return recurrently throughout his life—on that or some other evening, when he was alone as usual in the gloomy Greville Street lodgings. Perhaps it was as he was undressing for the night, at one of the terrible moments he had described to Huysmans, that he was overcome by the sentiment of the terrible inanity of his existence. The story as he told it to Dorothy Bussy[62] and the version given to Henri Massis[63] vary slightly, but the essential fact—that he had decided to hang himself—is the same. According to these two accounts, he was searching for a rope in his cupboard (or had already found it) when he noticed a yellow, paper-back book on the shelf above his head. The literary instinct was evidently irresistible even at this supreme moment. He reached for the book, opened it at hazard. In one version, it was by Alphonse Allais, in the other, by Aurélien Scholl. At any rate, it was funny and, he told Henri Massis, 'these funeral preparations seemed to me so intolerably ridiculous that I rushed out of my room . . . and found myself outside on the pavement, under a gas lamp, still laughing with the same irresistible laughter that had saved my life.'

The story is a little too well-arranged to ring true and the determination to put an end to it all cannot have been very serious. Valéry was certainly miserable, but he still found life interesting. One evening, for instance, he dined with Charles Whibley in 'a massive club, full of heavy, reddish things, newspapers, lamps and a few silent, pretty-faced footmen'.[64] After dinner, they took a cab to Muswell Hill and called on Henley. Valéry was more at ease on this occasion than he had been during his previous visit and he surprised Whibley—and incidentally himself—by his fluent English. It was probably on that evening that he talked with Henley's assistant, Williams, who was engaged at that time in writing a series of articles in the *New Review*, destined to awaken the public to the dangers of German competition in South Africa. These articles were being widely read and discussed and had done a good deal to arouse English mistrust of German motives. A good many reports on this subject had no doubt arrived from various sources at the Chartered Company's offices. Valéry must have read them. He was in a nationalistic mood and, as a Frenchman born only a few months after the Prussian invasion of France, he had no love for the Germans. Both Henley and Williams were evidently impressed with his grasp of the subject, which he viewed from a quite different, a more philosophical angle than they did themselves. They discovered in him, in fact, a political philosopher—a species rare in England at that time and practically non-existent in France.

So it came about that Valéry was invited to contribute a sort of philosophic conclusion to Williams's series—a strange commission for a young man who, only three years earlier, had been considered by himself and his friends as a dedicated aesthete of the *fin de siècle* type. He hesitated. 'Several good reasons pressed me to accept what reason itself would have ordered me to refuse', he recalled later.[65]

Reasons won; 'reason' lost, perhaps because Valéry felt about German activities in Africa rather as he had done about the Sino-Japanese War that had sparked off 'Le Yalou'.[66]

I myself had no special reason [he explained later], for taking an interest in the far-away things which corresponded to nothing in my ordinary occupations and cares. . . . I felt that these events were not mere accidents or limited phenomena, but something in the nature of symptoms or premises, like significant facts, the meaning of which went far beyond their intrinsic or apparent importance.

So he wrote his article, calling it first, 'Une conquête méthodique' then, 'La conquête allemande'. It was a masterly piece of analysis and synthesis and Henley published it, in French, in January the following year. Valéry was evidently pleased with it, for long afterwards, in the middle of the First World War, he considered republishing it and wrote to Arnold Bennett on 8 April 1915:

'I published in January 1897, in no. 92 of W. E. Henley's *New Review*, an article in French on the Boches; a solid, prophetic, improvised article that was épatingly thorough and thoroughly épating.' The Second World War was to confirm his prophetic insight even more surely, for Valéry had foreseen in this article a development which had once seemed purely fantastic: the coalition of Germany, Italy and Japan.

He was not there to see its effect on the English public, which was apparently considerable. On 16 April, when he had been just over two weeks in London, a letter had arrived from his chief:[67]

Dear Mr Valéry, I have sent off your article by tonight's post; and I want to take this opportunity to say how pleased we have all been to have you here, but the Matabele situation is likely to absorb the whole attention of the English press for some time to come; therefore, I do not really see that we are likely to get material for translation out of our papers in the immediate future, and that naturally leads me to consider that it is not worth your while to remain here with no great possibility of work; therefore I should suggest that so far as we are concerned our arrangement may come to an end this week, through want of material. Yours very truly, Hubert E. M. Bourke.

Valéry had arrived in England ready for anything, and he seems to have had the vague idea that his destiny lay across the Channel. He had even written to Gide of a possible departure for South Africa or Rhodesia—a prospect which he seems to have viewed with the greatest nonchalance.[68] More seriously, he considered making his home in London. England at that time seemed to offer more than France could do. There, he found himself in a world of significations, which appealed to him, at that juncture, more than the world of signs he had left behind him in Paris. 'If some politician had got hold of me at that time, I should no doubt have made a career in politics,' he confided later to his friend Valery Larbaud.[69] His daughter has confirmed that he really considered following that career in England.[70]

Instead, he returned to France and, to the amazement of his friends, entered the French War Office. There, André Fontainas tells us, 'his subtle mind, eager to seize on and classify this new knowledge according to highly personal methods, led him to reflect on the most arduous problems concerning the development of military material, technical improvements, a better use of the rules of commandment.'[71] The visit to Meredith had sparked off an interest in Napoleon; Valéry was soon an expert in the Emperor's campaigns and writings, and Fontainas recalls that he would constantly quote the hero whom he so admired for his firm decisions, prompt initiatives and a will that was never weakened by doubt or hesitation. Napoleon had replaced Rhodes, but this new hero, like the old one, was a man who allied thought and action and, by doing so, created an Empire.

The English experience had been short, but its intensity could not be measured in days or weeks. It had confirmed the intuition that had overwhelmed him four years earlier, during that stormy night in Genoa. For the next seventeen years, Valéry succumbed, like his own Monsieur Teste, to the seductions of silence, deserting poetry for mathematics, architecture, psychology, philosophy, political science and above all, an incessant curiosity concerning the processes of his own intellect, observed with implacable attention and consigned in the monument to human thought which he called simply his *Notebooks*. 'We have seen a man struggle alone with an almost unknown territory', he had written of Rhodes. For him, that almost unknown territory which he had sworn to discover, was the human mind.

6

Valery Larbaud and the 'Heart of England'

Birth of A. O. Barnabooth

August 1902: a new century. Queen Victoria had died the previous year and peace with the Boers had been signed during that spring. The violent eruption of jingoism that had shaken England at the end of the century had partially subsided now, and there was even a certain embarrassment over the whole South African affair. Edward was a man of peace, a cosmopolitan who loved France and was much distressed by the violent anti-British feeling roused there by the Jameson raid and the Boer War. He had always had a great many rich and beautiful friends among the French aristocracy, though his absolute refusal to have anything to do with the outstanding figures of the Third Republic suggests he understood the country less well than he believed.

There was a new jollity now in the London air, as well as signs of slackening moral standards. As Wilfrid Blunt noted in his diary that year, the new King had 'certain good qualities of amiability and a philistine tolerance for other people's sins which endear him to rich and poor, from archbishops down to turf bookmakers and the man in the street'.[1] The mental climate of the country, or at least of London, still depended greatly on the mood of the Palace. People were ready to enjoy themselves; money could get one anywhere; there was a great deal of it about and the people who had it flaunted it unashamedly.

This new London was no longer the Mecca she had been for impecunious French writers and artists in the early 1890s, but a new class of tourists was crossing the Channel for new reasons. It was a strange paradox that, as political hostility to England had mounted, fanned by the Boer War, Panama, Fashoda and other incidents, so interest and admiration for Britain and her institutions had become more and more fashionable, first among intellectuals and then among the bourgeoisie. More and more books appeared in translation; articles and analyses multiplied in the press. A study by E. Desmolins: *Pourquoi les Anglo-Saxons sont-ils supérieurs aux Français?* had been widely read, though hotly disputed, in 1898. It contained a long list of British superiorities, one of the chief of which was the English educational system, which the French were beginning to view with almost mystic reverence. 'Never', complained a dissident, 'has France nourished in her bosom so many convinced and aggressive anglo-maniacs. . . . For the anglo-maniac, the Englishman is his model, his ideal, his god.'[2]

Now, with most of the reasons for hating the English removed, this cult was fast losing its last taint of nonconformism. The rich bourgeoisie, traditionally hostile to foreigners, sensitive to historical oppositions and generally disinclined for travel, began to cross the Channel. England offered immense opportunities for having a good time. It was fashionable, as well as educational. The rich middle classes installed their young in Oxford or Cambridge, rather as the English sent their daughters to acquire polish in French finishing schools. They were welcome everywhere, popular with everyone. The *entente cordiale* was already in the air and would soon become a reality.

The rich middle-class tourists from France liked their comforts. Poorer visitors and intellectuals stuck to tradition and chose the neighbourhood of Soho; aristocrats and minor royalty made for the Ritz or Claridges; but they had discovered the delights of the Savoy, new, plushy and opulent, with such ultra-modern conveniences as six lifts and a bathroom to every bedroom.

Madame Nicolas Larbaud arrived there late in this month of August. She was that rare thing, a French business woman, widow of the proprietor of the famous St Yorre curative mineral waters in Vichy. She was already elderly, stout and imposing, with an unquestioning belief in her own infallibility that struck people as impressive and sometimes terrifying. She was accompanied by two young men: her son Valery, a fragile boy with large, globulous dark eyes, and his schoolfriend Paul Colombier, who was presumably in Madame Larbaud's good graces because he had just come into a considerable fortune.

Madame Larbaud's personality was to be an important influence in her son's whole life, and the key to that personality was her attitude towards money. On the death of her husband, she had come into a very large income, the capital of which was held in trust for her son until he attained his majority. She loved to display her money, but disliked spending it. The French critic, Robert Mallet, who knew her in her old age, describes her as 'a megalomaniac with the tastes of a housekeeper; a squiress who played at being a cook', and adds that her son was brought up in an atmosphere that was 'a curious mixture of simplicity and inordinate vanity'.[3] When he was ten years old, he had been sent, on account of delicate health, to a boarding school near Paris. Sainte-Barbe-aux-Champs was a curious choice, for it was a

Catholic school, whereas Madame Larbaud was a Protestant and her husband had been an old-fashioned die-hard atheist. It was frequented chiefly by immensely rich Spanish-speaking South Americans and no doubt the mother considered it a suitable establishment for the future proprietor of the St Yorre waters. She paid the fees gladly, but saw no reason to give the child pocket money. Later, he was to recall his impressions of this school in his novel, *Fermina Marquez*, describing how 'At first he [Joanny Léniot] had been so lonely among all these school-fellows who spoke among themselves in an unknown language—so like a prisoner, so abandoned, that he had begun to work feverishly so as to forget his misery. He had taken to study as others take to drink.' He recalled later that he had felt it to be a terrible humiliation if he was not first in his class.

In Joanny Léniot, Valery Larbaud traced his own portrait as a child, but the intervening years had changed him considerably. He still had what Robert Mallet has called 'the Croesus complex', but the preco-cious ambition and taste for hard work had greatly diminished. For the moment, in fact, he was causing his mother a good deal of worry. Back in Paris, he had been expelled from one school, had failed his first examination for the *baccalauréat* and has passed now at a second attempt—brilliantly, it is true, but much too late. For the last five or six years, indeed, he had been wasting his time writing poetry and collecting a library of English and American books. The latter interest was inexplicable since his already considerable travels had taken him all over the Continent, but never across the Channel, and his library revealed a curiosity for the less frequented byways of Anglo-Saxon literature, rather than for the great names figuring in the text-books. 'I am an anglicist', he had written the previous year to Karl Boes, editor of the *avant-garde* review La Plume, adding, 'I am specially interested in the popular songs of Scotland and Ireland.' Soon afterwards La Plume had published translations of an Irish ballad called 'The Lass of Loch-royan', of a 'tobacco song' dating from 1719, 'Mollee', a song in Northumbrian dialect popular in the days of Cromwell, and an old Scottish complaint entitled 'Saphia'. During the same period, when he should have been studying German for his *baccalauréat*, he had trans-lated long passages from a *History of Canada*, all Nathaniel Hawthorne's *House of the Seven Gables*, Poe's *Marginalia*, pages from de Quincey, poems by Rossetti and Swinburne and Coleridge's 'Ancient Mariner'. The latter had even appeared in a limited edition. Madame Larbaud was tyrannical and possessive, but indulgent to the whims of her only child and it was with her help that a publisher was found for the translation and Valery had the pleasure of seeing his work in print.[4]

Now the *baccalauréat* was passed, the question of a degree at the Sorbonne arose. Valery had decided to choose modern languages, and had pointed out that it would be difficult to specialise in English without having even visited England. His mother agreed. A certain doctor in Oxford had been recommended as tutor and she planned to do a little sightseeing in London with the two boys before settling him in the university city.

They left for Oxford a few days later, but the visit did not turn out as planned. The highly recommended doctor had far too pretty a wife. Madame Larbaud snatched her son away almost before he could get a glimpse of potential temptation, and took him back to the Savoy.

It was there, on 29 August, that he celebrated his twenty-first birthday and succeeded, in principle, to the family fortune. In principle only—it soon turned out that his mother had no intention of letting the boy she still considered as a mere spoilt child, get his hands on her money. She would buy him anything he wanted. He wore the most expensive clothes, travelled with the most costly luggage, ate the most delicate food—and the mother paid for everything. She saw no reason to change her attitude now, and became more evasive as her son grew more insistent. Perhaps it was to evade inevitable disputes that she returned to France soon after the birthday, leaving the two young men to continue their studies alone.

They left the Savoy immediately and made for Leicester Square: 'one of the liveliest spots and right in the centre of town', wrote Valery, to his aunt.[5] The Hotel Europe, on the corner of Leicester Street, was quite a grand place for that neighbourhood and here they took two large, finely furnished rooms. Valery wrote nonchalantly that they were 'too expensive for me'. He was expecting the business of the succession to be settled any day now, and was in no mood to worry.

For the time being, however, he had only a meagre allowance to live on. Paul Colombier, on the other hand, seems to have been positively intoxicated by his new wealth. There were wild shopping expeditions in Burlington Arcade and a Bond Street 'smelling of Turkish tobacco, Russian leather and horse-droppings. One can't walk quickly. It takes you by the waist and the shops pull you towards them. And the little horse-drawn omnibus that advances as slowly as possible from one end to the other; and the tall, gentle blonde girls dressed in blue serge!'[6] Years later, Larbaud still wrote with such sensuous longing of 'a suitcase in crocodile skin, garnished with a toilet set in crystal and tortoiseshell, with silver stoppers, lids and boxes', glimpsed by one of his heroines in Bond Street,[7] that it must surely have belonged to this period when he watched, fascinated and no doubt envious, as his friend threw his money to the winds. In fact, Archibald Olsen Barnabooth, 'one of the richest men on this planet', was already taking shape in his mind. Already he was beginning to jot down entries in Barnabooth's diary and the scene that recalls the glorious extravagance of these outings was probably noted in the Hotel Europe:[8]

> Spent the afternoon and evening undoing all these parcels, hurling myself, scissors in hand, on the strings, scattering papers over the floor, drinking in the new smell of all these beautifully-made objects, kissing them sometimes, dancing for joy around the crammed room. I think I shall never tire of buying luxurious things.

There was the usual round of sight-seeing too. Tearing themselves away from Bond Street, they admired 'les hauts monuments noirs dans l'air épais et jaune',[9] the sites that Verlaine and Rimbaud and Paul Valéry had visited before them (only Mallarmé had been too much wrapped up in his personal problems to follow the guide books). None of them, for some reason, seem to have discovered the Crystal Palace, but on these two it made a deep impression.

> Today, we went to the Crystal Palace, which is a little out of London [Valery wrote to his aunt on 6 September]. It's a great building of iron and glass, as big as a whole town, with lots of shops of every kind (motor-cars, bazaars, dressmakers, steam-boats, pictures, perfumes, etc.) and besides that, there are theatres, cafés, café-concerts, restaurants, all in the same building. All round, there are great gardens, with waterfalls, panoramas, open-air fairs, all sorts of games. There are extraordinary scenic railways.

He goes on to describe the fascinating sensation of the vertiginous ups and downs on the great slides. Into the letter was slipped a souvenir of the visit—the product of a marvellous new machine on which, he wrote, 'by pressing a lever you can write anything you want on a little aluminium plate.'[10]

A visit to Hampton Court inspired three sonnets, which were later lost or destroyed. At Madame Tussaud's, the Chamber of Horrors, which had terrified little Paul Valéry a quarter of a century earlier, filled him with sadness and the uneasy resentment he would always feel against society. He would have liked, he wrote after his return to France, to have been shut up for a whole night among those wax figures:[11]

> Surtout dans la salle des criminels,
> Des bons criminels en cire,
> Faces luisantes, yeux ternes, et corps—en quoi?
> Mais, est-ce que ça leur ressemble vraiment?
> Alors pourquoi les a-t-on enfermés, électrocutés, ou pendus,
> Pendant que leur image muette reste ici?
> Avec des yeux qui ne peuvent pas dire les horreurs souffertes.

He wandered by 'la Tamise inexprimablement cuivrée',[12] among 'jardins verts et bleus, brouillards blancs, voiles mauves'.[13] At night, in Trafalgar Square, he saw the lions:[14]

> ... couchés dans le brouillard bleu,
> Au bord des terrasses d'eaux noires où stagnent
> Les livides reflets des globes électriques ...

and Piccadilly Circus where,[15]

> Sous le ciel de cendre rose incandescente
> Ou entre dans un brouillard d'or,
> Dans un voile fait d'étincelles derrière lesquelles flamboient
> Trop de globes électriques devenus fous de resplendir;
> Les façades de Scott's, du Criterion, du London Pavilion
> Sont éclairées comme par un soleil de l'Océan Indien.
> Et, au centre, du sommet d'une colonne noire,
> Un jeune archer me darde une invincible flèche.

One day the pair visited Abingdon and saw more mist:[16]

> Les collines dans le brouillard, sous le ciel de cendre bleue
> Comme elles sont hautes et belles!
> O jour simple, mêlé de brume et de soleil!
> Marcher dans l'air froid, à travers ces jardins,
> Le long de cette Tamise qui me fait songer aux vers de Samain.

Then Paul Colombier returned to France. The days that had been so filled with pleasure became lonely and the young man had time to meditate on his future. Lucas Letheil, one of Larbaud's thinnest disguises, writes in the story entitled *Mon plus secret conseil*, in a passage dated 1902:

> In a few weeks, as soon as the business of my trusteeship is concluded and I am freed from all material and social constraints: begin to live like a prince. That is: gain more self-control each day. That is: while experimenting with everything (so as to become capable of making a definitive choice) remain

constantly objective: keep myself free of any habits, friendships, liaisons; of any kind of team spirit or set of people, of any fashion.

Valery Larbaud's lifelong quest for freedom had begun already, and as the years passed, the word was to gain new meanings that became constantly more profound.

For the moment, however, it meant chiefly freedom from petty financial worries. Back in Vichy, the mother was using delaying tactics. Instead of the papers relating to the inheritance, she sent spies to report on her son's behaviour (Barnabooth, already jotting down passages of his diary, knew himself to be surrounded by invisible spies, delegated by a well-intentioned guardian to report on his movements and keep him from harm). Her suspicions were not perhaps entirely unfounded. The spoilt boy, accustomed to be given everything he wanted, was surrounded by the endless temptations of the city (and the pretty women to whom he was so susceptible), living on a small allowance, parsimoniously doled out from the fortune that legally belonged to him. Paul Colombier had set an example he was all too inclined to follow:[17]

> Oh, acheter tout ce qu'on voit, et dont on n'a,
> Ne serait-ce qu'une seconde, le désir!

exulted Barnabooth, who could dispose of his money as he wished.

Credit was easily come by in those days. Presumably Valery got into debt. At any rate, his life in London was sufficiently irregular to provide an excuse for a 'conseil judiciaire'—a weapon frequently used by French families against profligate or mentally unstable sons. It carried a good deal of stigma with it and the indignant young man promptly issued a summons against his mother. Relations between the two became more and more strained. Twice during the autumn, Valery was forced to hurry to Paris to defend his cause. At last an agreement was reached. He would receive a yearly allowance, equivalent to the substantial income derived from his father's fortune, but the capital was to remain in trust. The hated poverty was at an end, but his fragile nervous system had been terribly shaken. It was in a German sanatorium, where he slowly recovered his health, that Valery Larbaud wrote the first Barnabooth poems, that were to appear in 1908 under the title, *Poèmes par un riche amateur ou Oeuvres françaises de M. Barnabooth*.

Archibald Olsen Barnabooth, whose *Journal* is considered by many connoisseurs as one of the masterpieces of modern French literature, is a composite figure, and it was during this first, rather chaotic visit to London that he came into being. His name, Larbaud once confided, came from a combination of the suburb of Barnes, and the word 'booth', which probably refers to the little shops set up in the Crystal Palace. He can be traced to several origins. There is something of a schoolfriend at Sainte-Barbe, portrayed in *Fermina Marquez*, under the name of Santos Iturria, the free, brilliant, insolent rival of Joanny Léniot; something of the profligate Paul Colombier; something of a certain Max Lebaudy, heir to a vast fortune amassed in the sugar industry, who had died a few years earlier during his military service because his exemption for reasons of health would have caused a scandal in the press. But Barnabooth is above all Valery Larbaud himself, painted against a purely imaginary background of fabulous wealth and romantic parentage. His confessions are always fragmentary; he himself sometimes adopts several disguises in the course of a single story, while people who have impinged on his own life take on heroic, almost magical dimensions. Thus the father he had hardly known is transformed here into an intrepid cowboy from the Far West, who discovers—instead of a mere source of mineral water in Central France—gold mines in South America. He creates railways, speculates in Caucasian petrol, in Australian platinum, becomes the master of all Peru and founds 'probably the largest and certainly the most secure fortune in the modern world'.[18] His son, like Larbaud himself, is an incessant, an obsessive traveller, 'a great cosmopolitan patriot', the poet of trans-European express trains, great liners, sumptuous luggage and distant cities juxtaposed in the ellipsis of speed.[19]

> J'ai senti pour la première fois toute la douceur de vivre,
> Dans une cabine du Nord-Express, entre Wirballen et Pskow.

confides Barnabooth, echoing the adolescent Valery Larbaud who had once set out, suitably chaperoned, on a Grand Tour of Europe arranged by his mother. Barnabooth, like Larbaud, feels himself the slave of his social position, hopes to find freedom on his travels, and discovers that it is not so easily come by. He is constantly spied on, his movements reported. Invisible guards, paid by his intendant to keep him from harm—and to save him from himself—watch over him day and night. Even when he falls in love with a chorus girl, she turns out to have been in the pay of the same faithful steward. Here in fact, in the guise of a legendary multi-millionaire, struggling against his fate in Florence, is a recognisable portrait of Valery Larbaud in London, battling to break free of the conventions 'in which Destiny sought to keep him a prisoner'.

The first version of Barnabooth appeared in 1908, six years after the personage had been conceived, and the earliest poems were written in

London. These *Poèmes par un riche amateur* were preceded by a short story and a biography of the imaginary author. He is, according to this biographer,

> a charming young man, barely twenty-four years old, small, always plainly dressed, slight, with reddish hair, blue eyes and a very pale complexion, wearing neither beard nor moustache. At first sight, he is not at all remarkable; common people and servants are even apt to take him for a person of little consequence. Add to all this that he is very shy and somewhat untidy, and you will not be surprised to learn that certain shopkeepers have been tactless enough to inquire offhandedly what he wanted. . . . He seems to enjoy these misunderstandings, which reveal, as he says, the baseness of mankind and permits him to amaze these people when he suddenly reveals his power.

Up to this point, the other models for Barnabooth are more to the fore than Larbaud himself. He becomes more recognisable when his 'biographer' depicts him as 'somewhat naïve and sentimental' and when he relates—with admirably feigned reluctance—certain love affairs, which reveal his subject as an easy victim for any scheming woman, but quick to resent all attempts to hold or constrain him. And it is Barnabooth-Larbaud, in the section sub-titled: 'Barnabooth the poet: his ideas on art', who proclaims his contempt for the public and insists that he is, and will always remain, 'an amateur'.

The Barnabooth of the *Biography* is, on the whole, a chilly and ironical young man. Another, parallel, Barnabooth reveals himself, however, in the *Journal* that was only published in 1913, though the first entries date from 1902. Here we find the young millionaire seeking not only for freedom from constraint and convention, but also for freedom of the soul, through the channels of renunciation and charity. It was a gradual evolution, foreshadowed by 'Lucien Letheil's' programme for a 'princely' life, and each of the stages of that evolution took place in London.

The Meynell circle

Several years passed before Larbaud came to England again. Only one article bears out his claim to be an 'anglicist'; a study of Meredith's *The Egoist*[20] which had sparked off some reflections that give a clue to the strangely rootless life he was leading at the time. Meredith—for whom Schwob had by now generated a vast reverence among a little group in France—had written rather obscurely of 'literary angels', and

Larbaud translated this as meaning 'the aptitude of things (or people) to be transformed by the writer into the matter of literature', adding that 'it is the mission and duty of the writer to discover these Angels'. In this case, he himself was a sort of literary Angel, for he was already beginning to transform himself, not only into Barnabooth, but simultaneously into a number of other characters: Joanny Léniot, Lucien Letheil, Felice Francio, and later Marc Fournier. 'His poems are full of his personality, but his person is absent from them,' he was to say later of Coventry Patmore,[21] but he might have been speaking of himself.

Genoa, Naples, Greece, Algeria, Sweden, Belgium, Spain . . . for five years Larbaud travelled tirelessly, obsessively, accompanied sometimes by his adhesive mother, sometimes by one of the women who appear under various disguises in *Mon plus secret conseil, Amants, heureux amants*, various short stories and *Barnabooth*. The diaries in which he recorded these travels were almost constantly those of A. O. Barnabooth, as were all the poems of this period. Episodes were transferred from one land to another, so that, for instance, Paul Colombier's spending spree is described as taking place in Florence instead of London. One has the impression of a sort of kaleidoscope, of[22]

> a vagabond free to sleep anywhere, drinking at every fountain, citizen of all the world's finest cities. . . . For him, at the end of the Avenue de la Grande Armée one comes on Oxford Street and Holborn, and these give onto the Roman Corso, with the Chiaja forking off it, cut across by the rue Saint-Lazare, which ends at the Piazza di Duomo in Milan.

So it was not till May 1907, that Larbaud returned to England, still accompanied by his mother. The date of the final examinations for his degree in modern languages was drawing near and both were probably getting anxious. Valery had been in bad health during all these years, and far more preoccupied with travel and love, than with work. Now his mother planned for him to do some intensive cramming with Sir John Rhys, professor of Celtic languages and principal of Jesus College. For some reason, this plan was abandoned, perhaps because Larbaud never felt at ease in Oxford and greatly preferred Cambridge which he visited that summer. At any rate, mother and son were soon back in London and a few days later Valery was installed at the de Vere Hotel, near Kensington Gardens, where he was left to brush up his English in his own way.

After the chaotic life of the last few years, he was happy to be back in[23]

> this country so well suited to study, where overstrained con-

tinental nerves relax, where the tastes and habits and even the eccentricities of a man of leisure who works for his own sensual pleasure, can be revealed without embarrassment, where they will be respected and humoured, and where he can enjoy rural peace and solitude among the pleasures of the greatest capital in the world.

South Kensington in May was flower-filled and peaceful ('Voici que les tulipes, aux jardins de Kensington / Vont s'ouvrir au bord des allées, dans les flots du brouillard tiède'[24]). The hotel was quiet and old-fashioned, frequented by provincials and studious foreigners. He was working simultaneously at *Barnabooth* and *Fermina Marquez*, inter-weaving the complicated pattern of his own and other existences, of childhood, adolescence and young manhood. The university pro-gramme was neglected, as the school curriculum had been a few years earlier, and it is not surprising that he should have failed to get his degree when he took his examination in July.

It was while he was staying at the de Vere Hotel that Larbaud met Daniel O'Connor, an Irishman, born in Mauritius, who had once trained for the priesthood. O'Connor—who sometimes used the name Stephen Langton—was to play a certain role in his life and he is one of the models for Maxime Claremoris, Barnabooth's impulsive and vigorously independent Irish friend. 'His conversation amuses me—I'll go even further: he takes me out of myself to a point where I almost become him. My personality expands to include his own. . . . When I talk with him, I begin to imitate the intonations of his voice and his charming Irish brogue.'[25] Maxime Claremoris, like Daniel O'Connor, is older than Barnabooth and continually irritates him by making him feel in the wrong. He is a Puritan who disguises his Puritanism as 'love of Beauty'. His conversation is all of the past. 'How far he is from me!' exclaims Barnabooth. 'He knows nothing of love, pity or this kind of fury that urges me to do good or harm—I hardly know which—to certain persons.'

The real-life O'Connor was a minor man of letters, who wrote in various magazines and had put Barrie's *Peter Pan* into book form. He was also a specialist in French literature and was working at the time as part-editor on Dent's series of French classics. His taste seems to have been uncertain, for his new friend soon discovered that he believed an anthology of speeches made by members of the Academy at their reception ceremony, would contain the finest treasures of French literature. 'A charming chap, apart from his literary tastes', reported Larbaud to his friend Marcel Ray in Paris.[26]

As a Catholic and a literary man, O'Connor had access to what at this time was the strangely restricted, cut-off, yet fecund circle of English Catholic intellectuals. He was thus doubly connected with Wilfrid Meynell who, besides being a tireless journalist, was then director of the Catholic publishing firm of Burns & Oates. It was O'Connor who took Larbaud to see Meynell, at first, apparently on a purely business visit, since a letter dated 1907 refers to a possibility of Larbaud doing some kind of work for him. The collaboration never materialised and the friendship with the Meynells ripened only gradually, but this visit brought Larbaud for the first time into contact with what certain French reviews had been describing, with a curiosity stimulated by almost total ignorance, as the 'English Catholic Revival', and—even more important—with English Catholic poetry.

The Meynells' *salon* had been built up long ago around Coventry Patmore, much in the same way as the Pennells' had been built around Whistler. It was above all a centre for Catholic intellectuals, though a great many non-Catholics—including Oscar Wilde in his heyday—drifted there in the endless round of calls and conversations that made literary life so pleasantly convivial at the end of the century. Things had changed a little in the last few years. Coventry Patmore had been dead for some time and the Meynells, with their family growing up and marrying, had moved from their big house in Palace Gate to a flat in Granville Place, near Portman Square. The Sunday evenings continued though, and Alice Meynell at sixty-three retained her queenly beauty and an intellectual prestige so immense, that her name had even been put forward for the post of Poet Laureate, left vacant by Tennyson's death.

Both the Meynells were of Quaker stock and showed a Quakerlike tolerance in the matter of religious opinion. The Catholics who came to Granville Place represented every possible tendency, some of them highly unorthodox. Patmore had described himself as an esoteric mystic and had been violently anti-clerical; Wilfrid Blunt, poet, diplomat, traveller, politician and fighter for lost causes, had gone through a spiritual upheaval caused by Darwin's evolutionary theories and had become first a Modernist then what he describes in his diaries as a 'logical materialist' though he still felt nostalgia for the certainties of his youth; Father Tyrrell was an ex-Jesuit and another Modernist, who rejected papal infallibility and felt uncertain about a future life. ('His views seem quite incompatible with any Church teaching I have ever heard of,' commented Blunt.) In contrast, there was Hilaire Belloc, brilliant and facile, with his uncomplicated faith and love of exactly those outer trappings of the Church that Blunt and Tyrrell hated. His sister, Marie Belloc Lowndes, was simply, sweetly yet intelligently pious, as was the Irish novelist Katherine Tynan; the poetess Mrs Hamilton King had a social conscience and had been converted to Catholicism when Cardinal Manning had taken his famous stand for the workers during the dock strike. Larbaud, very much out of things and a little dazed, observed the comings and goings with his usual insatiable curiosity and remarked that any foreign visitor might well have supposed 'that the whole of England was becoming Catholic and lived in the shadow of Newman and the Oxford Movement.'[27]

Calm and serene, Alice Meynell reigned over this disparate assembly. Nothing could ruffle her. She had been known to return home to find a roomful of guests, sit down among them apparently oblivious of their presence, without even taking time to remove her hat, and compose on the spot some beautifully written, closely-reasoned essay. Everyone adored her, but no one, apart from her family, seems to have been really intimate with her. Her faith never wavered and her pen never tired. She reared her children, cherished her husband and had managed with consummate skill, at various periods of her career, to keep the devotion of Patmore, Meredith and Francis Thompson within unimpeachably platonic bounds. Every kind of doctrinal divergence was admitted in Granville Place, but there might be no trifling with moral standards. Alice Meynell's religion was strictly ethical. All London might succumb to Edwardian laxity, but she and Wilfrid resolutely maintained the Victorian ideals of honesty, purity and the sanctity of family life.

One could not be long in that house without hearing about Francis Thompson, though one rarely caught sight of him now. Everyone knew how Wilfrid Meynell had received an almost illegible manuscript, been struck with its unique quality and had finally tracked down the starving vagrant who was its author. He and his wife had supported Francis Thompson, adopted him as a member of the family, encouraged him to work and published his poems and essays, but they had never been able to domesticate him. Now he lived chiefly with Franciscan monks in Wales, but occasionally he would slip into the house, nearer to death at every visit, a poor, wasted little skeleton, dreamy with opium and incapable of any kind of work.

The Meynells grieved over their friend and did what they could to protect him from himself. He was not a poet easy to introduce to the general public, but in Granville Place he was loved and revered as a genius. His work could be heard there every Sunday, for the main feature of the Meynell *salon* was the readings from Catholic poets that took place before supper. There was generally a backward glance at one of the seventeenth-century religious poets: Donne, Herbert, Crashaw—who had been a Catholic convert—Traherne; there was often something by Lionel Johnson, who had been a friend of the family till his death in 1902, and some of the pathetic verses of Digby Mackworth Dolben, which touched Larbaud so deeply. But above all, he shared from the first days the Meynells' reverence for Patmore, whom he rated far above Tennyson and even Thompson, whom he considered 'the best poet England had had since Coventry Patmore and Swinburne'.[28] No Sunday evening passed without a reading of at least one poem from each of them.

The readings were followed by supper, a rather dreaded meal. Alice Meynell had the reputation of being the worst housewife in London and even Francis Thompson, who was practically immaterial, had once been heard to murmur: 'The food at Palace Gate is *frightful!*' As for the drink, the best one could hope for was a ninepenny bottle of wine from the grocer's and even this was often forgotten. The conversation, however, was generally brilliant enough to compensate for the fare. We do not know whether the young Frenchman was invited to one of these suppers this year but he certainly shared them on many later occasions.

Larbaud's discovery of the English Catholic poets and his relationship with the Meynells marked the real beginning of his career as a critic since they provided material for articles on poets who were still entirely unknown in France. Thus by 1909, he was contributing a regular article on English literature to *La Phalange*, one of the liveliest and best informed of the Paris literary reviews, which counted Guillaume Apollinaire and most of the brilliant young men of the time among its contributors. Simultaneously, other discoveries led him to a turning point in his personal evolution by forcing him to reflect on the problem of human misery. During his long travels, he had roamed in the poor quarters of many great cities. He had seen poverty in Spain, Italy, Algiers, but always in Southern climates where the sun and the colourful décor lent a romantic veneer to the most infamous streets. But during this visit to London, he had explored the slums and he had caught a glimpse, during a rapid visit, of the poorest quarters of Manchester. He had been appalled by what he had seen. English poverty still had the special quality of degradation that had shocked Rimbaud and Verlaine, horrified Taine and Louis Blanc. Larbaud's reaction was as violent as theirs had been. 'The lowest classes in England are suffering under the weight of a tyranny such as has never yet been equalled',[29] he asserted indignantly, and a little later, after having seen the worst sights of industrial Birmingham, he wrote,[30]

In the English slums, one certainly sees vice, but there is above all a wretchedness of which we have no idea in France. An Englishman in dire poverty is tragic. Like the Arab, he does nothing to pull himself out of the pit into which he has fallen; he feels abased, and then his servility becomes truly terrifying.

Naturally, these reactions were reflected in Barnabooth's *Journal* and it is significant that it was during this year, 1907, that he introduced into it the figure of the Marquis de Putouarey. Like Barnabooth, and so many other apparently fictive figures in Larbaud's work, Putouarey represents one of the facets he had discovered in himself. The *Journal* records the long conversations between the sceptical Protestant, Barnabooth, and the cynical Catholic who only maintains the formal rites of his religion out of respect for his caste. Then comes a day when to Barnabooth's amazement, Putouarey lets fall the mask and admits shamefacedly to 'a need to practise charity; the hope of satisfying the hunger for love I feel in myself.' Like his creator, the marquis has come into contact with poverty in its most degrading forms and has found himself caught up in disturbing and sometimes conflicting sentiments: pity, horror, a sort of morbid fascination, the frustration of his own helplessness to relieve or even comfort distress.

It was O'Connor who introduced Larbaud to the works of G. K. Chesterton (who was still at this time a 'high Anglican' and only joined the Roman Catholic Church in 1922. Larbaud, unaware of the subtleties of English religious life, supposed him to be a Catholic) and his ideas came like a revelation. Here at last was a religious writer who appeared as the champion of the common man, whose arguments seemed to him 'the most human our epoch has known'.[31] Chesterton's religion had nothing austere about it; it seemed to Larbaud to be a religion for free men, a humanistic religion. It suggested 'that we seek our ideas, our philosophy, our dogmas, not outside ourselves, but within us. For we have all this in ourselves, and it is the most important part of us.' And most important of all, perhaps, in Larbaud's present mood, was the evident fact that Chesterton—in opposition to the main current of Catholic opinion of the day, both in France and England— was a democrat.[32]

> The power of the common man [commented Larbaud in the same article in which he introduced Chestertonian ideas to France] appears here as inseparable from Christianity. Aristocracy is by its very nature the enemy of Christianity. And the most dangerous aristocracy of all, intellectual aristocracy, is also the greatest enemy of Christianity. All scientific and rationalistic

> doctrines are profoundly anti-democratic; Darwinism, for ex-
> ample . . . We are all children of God, part of Nature and all
> creation; therein lies the divine Democracy of things.

This thought comforted him during these lonely months when he
seems to have failed to make any satisfying contacts with the English.
Daniel O'Connor was his only friend; he had still barely penetrated the
fringe of the Meynell circle. Evolutionism was still the fashion and he
found that for most of the people he met, modern thought meant 'the
old anti-Christian ideas of our own philosophers, slightly rejuvenated
and supposedly verified by some of the latest scientific hypotheses'.[33]
At the same time, he had discovered the existence of the militant
British Philistine, 'a particularly dangerous beast'.[34] What was worse,
he found the same beast's ideas, in a slightly more sophisticated form,
rampant among the British critics whenever there was question of
some outsider, such as Aubrey Beardsley, whom they alternately
reviled and patronised.

As for Henley—still revered as one of the mouthpieces of an extreme
patriotic attitude that had been shaken but not destroyed by the disillusionments of the Boer War—he represented everything Larbaud
found distasteful at this time in England. The famous 'Song of the
Sword', that had thrilled thousands of hearts, appeared to him merely[35]

> the song of the triumph of brute force, with some vague evolu-
> tionary ideas. . . . The whole poem [he felt] shows an ineffectual
> and childish desire to be 'modern' which reminds me of some of
> the features of Henley's bust: a certain arrogance in the lower part
> of the forehead, and something proud and secretive in the eyes
> which reveals the limits of this intelligence.

In fact, at this point he loved English poetry but disliked the English,
or at least failed to make more than superficial contact with them:[36]

> Jamais, ô printemps londonien, langueur de jardin d'hiver,
> Je n'ai plus aiguëment senti mon isolement au sommet de ces
>   collines d'ordures.
> Qu'il me soit donc donné d'entrer dans le troupeau commun,
> D'avoir des visages près de mes yeux, de sentir l'odeur humaine,
> De n'être plus le spectateur désoeuvré
> Des constructions énormes, du bruit et des pavés des rues.

he wrote sadly. It was still far from the time when Barnabooth would
exclaim: 'London! I can't think how anyone can live anywhere else.'

The Provinces and a Home in Chelsea

Yet less than two years later he was back again. He had sat again for his degree and had not only passed, but done so well, that he felt obliged—or was perhaps forced by his mother—to prepare a thesis for his doctorate. As he had specialised in English literature, the university expected him to write on an English subject and Walter Savage Landor seemed as good a choice as any. Landor was very little known at the time, even among his compatriots, but Larbaud had discovered him during his random literary wanderings as a schoolboy, had admired him and had even translated some of the *Imaginary Conversations*. Perhaps, too, the choice was partly influenced by the fact that Landor had spent much of his life in Italy, which was Larbaud's favourite country at this period. Thus, what he probably looked on as a rather arid time of research in England, could be followed by a more enticing stay in Florence.

Landor-land was Warwickshire and the south-west, and it was in these regions that Larbaud meant to do most of his work. Meanwhile, as he needed a base in London, he took lodgings at No. 44 Dover Street. The house was reserved for men only and appeared in the day-time, to be extremely respectable. It became less so at night, however, as each floor was provided with a girl ready to render an essential service to these temporary or permanent bachelors.

It was not so easy to settle in Warwick in the way he liked. The town was not used to foreigners and there were several uncomfortable days in unsatisfactory hotels before he discovered the sort of lodgings he wanted. Mrs Warren was a respectable widow who had come down in the world. She lived with her daughter at No. 29 St Nicholas Church Street, and took in paying guests, who were made to understand that they were *not* boarders. Larbaud became part of the family almost at once. He spoke excellent English by now, and his cosmopolitan up-bringing made it easy for him to adopt the manners and customs of any country where he happened to settle. His room was small, his bed uncomfortable, cold pork appeared far too frequently on the menu. The daughter, one supposes, was plain, since he took no interest in her, though he listened kindly when she poured out the story of an unhappy love affair. There was a fellow guest, a Mr Smith, so four-handed whist could be played in the evenings. On Sundays, he strolled 'through empty streets, between houses whose inhabitants are so virtuous that they display their virtues on shiny cardboard notices stuck in the windows'.[37] On that day, the houses 'rumbled with hymns' ('One can hardly imagine the place these hymns take in English life' he commented) and glancing through the windows he could see the families gathered around the table in the parlour cluttered with heavy Victorian furniture. 'The eldest daughter is at the piano, and the others sing, plunged in this heavy Sunday, and in eternity.' On weekdays, he could browse in the multitude of shops that sold false antiques to the charabanc loads of tourists on their way to Stratford on Avon. There was the county library, 'full of obscure books written by country parsons, who explain the whole history of the human race and show how it has been traced by God's finger'.[38] Naturally, he made his own pilgrimage to Shakespeare's birthplace, where he was less impressed with the museum than by the skill with which the house had been restored. Then there was Leamington, which he could compare with his own native Vichy, noting the same profusion of bath chairs, but a total lack of amusement. It was here that he observed the peevish, dying little heroine of the story entitled *Dolly*,[39] which he wrote during his short stay in 'the joyous English spa'. Larbaud loved children and made friends with them wherever he went, so the stories collected in *Enfantines* are peopled with little English girls: Elsie, Dolly's friend of a single day, who was modelled on a certain Meta, encountered in Kensington Gardens; little Welsh Gwenny-all-alone; Lily of Fulham, and Ruby of Chelsea, who are no longer really children, but adolescents on the brink of experience.

Occasionally, Mrs Warren's whole household set out on an excursion to some neighbouring village and Larbaud was able to assist at a Sunday School outing in the village of Yarningdale composed, he recounts, of 'two farms and two cottages on a hillock covered with gorse and furze'.[40] The boys all belonged to the newly-formed Boy Scout movement, and Larbaud, greatly interested, noted that 'there are nearly five hundred thousand of these scouts and public opinion is becoming alarmed. It is feared that the common people will become too military-minded, to the detriment of agriculture and industry.'[41] He took long walks alone, too, visiting places where no foreigner had ever been seen: 'tiny villages and hamlets that can be reached only after opening and shutting twenty or thirty gates. . . . I have described them with the care and accuracy of the first explorer to reach the land of the Niams-Niams or the white Pygmies at the source of the Congo.'[42]

He found Warwick narrowly religious and puritanical. 'Here one really sees English provinces, which are more provincial than our own',[43] he noted. He left them towards the middle of that month and a series of postcards, dutifully dispatched to his family in Vichy, records his wanderings. He travelled by train, delighting in 'the little stations built of brick and wood, so clean, with flower-borders along the platforms. The station's pretty name is sometimes written in flowers on a well-mown lawn. The soft richness of fields and trees in the blue mist, and the towns disguised as villages.'[44] On 13 July he reached Birmingham, where he was amazed to see the cathedral cemetery separated only by railings from the main street ('Can one imagine a cemetery in the middle of the rue de la République in Lyons, or in the Canébière!'[45] he marvelled). Shrewsbury was 'all pale pink and dull white. These soft, uncertain tones seem to shield her from being too clearly seen in the delicate landscape of the Severn Valley, with its tender colouring'. Chester was 'black, yellow and red'[46] and reminded him of Seville. The smallest details—faces, snatches of talk, landscapes —were recorded in the manuscript of *Le Coeur de l'Angleterre*, on which he worked intermittently for years, but which he refused to publish during his life, delving into it however, year after year, for material. The slums of Birmingham, the pious monotony of Warwick reappear in *Barnabooth*; in the story 'Tan Callando' André, the French tourist, evokes memories of a personal humiliation among the collective humiliations of Birmingham's hungry prostitutes; the little, lovingly-decorated railway stations reappear in *Beauté, mon beau souci*; all the wayside flowers on the road to Banbury bloom again in the story 'Le Moulin d'Inigo'; and the hero of 'Une Nonnain', listening absent-mindedly in his home in the Bourbonnais, to the chatter of a young nursing-nun, dreams of England and hears the echo of a refrain: 'My heart is in England, my heart is not here.'

Towards the end of July, he returned to London for a period of research in the British Museum. (The latest intellectual snobbery, he noted, was to refer to it as 'The Mou'.) The capital had suddenly become more hospitable, perhaps because he himself was no longer quite the same unknown, unimportant person he had been on previous visits. He was no longer a boy now, but a man whose personality attracted immediate attention:[47]

> thickset and delicate [writes his friend Marcel Arland], like the little hills of his own Bourbonnais district, with an added touch of exoticism. A curious face, bold and subtle at the same time, divided between a sensuality tinged with humour (the nose and specially the lips) and the bright intelligence of the eyes and fore-head; constrained gestures, but a sudden abruptness would not have been surprising; a slowness that was constantly on the alert; hesitations which seemed to conceal a fundamental tenacity; an uneven voice, almost muffled, that hesitated too and thus suggested even more clearly how boldly that voice must sound when he was alone; beneath the well-bred reserve, a secret violence, I felt, and a taste for risks and even for provocation.

Rumours of the interest aroused by the Barnabooth poems had perhaps crossed the Channel. It must have been known that he was writing regular articles on English writers in *La Phalange*. In fact, he was becoming someone worth cultivating and a letter sent to Marcel Ray continues:[48]

> I see a lot of Daniel O'Connor, Wilfrid and Alice Meynell of the Dublin Review, theatre folk, minor poets, etc. Alice Meynell was very pleased with my translations from the poems of Francis Thompson in the June number of *La Phalange*. Apart from her talent as a poet, she is a very intelligent woman, George Meredith was very fond of her and called her his 'Portia'.

There had been changes in the Meynell *salon* since his first, brief acquaintance with it two years earlier. Francis Thompson had died late in 1907; Meredith had followed him in May of this year, within a few days of Swinburne; Father Tyrrell had died just before Larbaud's arrival, and there had been some unseemly bickering among the ecclesiastical authorities as to whether he might or might not be accorded a Christian burial. There were new faces now. Everard Meynell brought in his friends, young artists he had met at the Slade: Orpen, Augustus John—or favourite clients from his Serendipity Bookshop in Westbourne Grove. Ezra Pound was living chiefly in London and gradually became a frequent caller ('I met an odious American poet at the Meynells' the other day', complained Larbaud when he met him there later. 'He hung on to me the whole evening and I could not get a word with my hostess.'[49]) Stephen Wheeler, England's leading expert on Landor, came to the flat—possibly invited to please Larbaud. Chesterton seems to have been one of the few religious literary figures who was never seen there. His sloppy appearance and dirty eating habits would have been out of tune with the rather rarefied Meynell atmosphere. In any case, Larbaud was becoming a little disenchanted with Chesterton, whose weighty pronouncements were beginning to annoy him.

Patmore and Thompson, on the other hand, he loved more and more. Their poems were read each Sunday, just as they had been during their lives. It was through Patmore's 'sublime familiarity'[50] and the lyric ecstasy of Francis Thompson, 'the inward-looking man', the 'obstinate seeker after his own supreme good and the fulfilment of his saintliness',[51] that Larbaud felt himself drawn inexorably towards the Catholic Church, source of their common inspiration.

There was a break in the relationship with the Meynells during the August holiday month. Larbaud took rooms in Weston-super-Mare, at Florence Villa in Clarendon Road. It rained every day, an icy wind blew down from the Welsh mountains and, although it was early August, there was a feeling of winter in the air:[52]

> La pluie tombera tout le jour
> Sur les terrasses qui se dressent
> Entre le ciel en mouvement
> Et les régions solennelles
> De l'Empire au Soleil Blanc.
>
> La Montagne-Inconnue se voile,
> Et les gardiens de l'estuaire,
> Les deux éléphants échoués,
> Plongent dans l'immense brouillard
> Et partent pour l'île d'argent.

Weston held a special attraction, in spite of the terrible weather. Coleridge had been his first love among the English poets, and the moment he caught sight of the Bristol Channel, he 'recognised' the haunt of the Ancient Mariner. 'When I saw for the first time the Bristol Channel, with its bays, its cliffs and the two strangely-formed "holmes", with the Welsh mountains filling its indistinct horizon, I instantly recognised the land of the "Rhyme of the Ancient Mariner",' he recalled in his Preface to a new edition of the translation, the publication of which had given him such pleasure in boyhood.

That mysterious horizon drew him irresistibly, and a few days later he was in Wales: Cardiff, Llandaff, Abergavenny, Monmouth. He stayed at Llantony Abbey, which had once belonged to Landor, and wondered how the poet had ever stood its incredible discomfort;[53] he visited Tintern Abbey, 'that vast monument to mankind, in its solitary nest of greenery on the wooded river bank, with its arches, and the birds flying in and out of the windows'.[54] Back in England, he conscientiously visited Somerset, where Landor had lived for a time. There were rapid excursions to Glastonbury, Cheddar, Bath, Wells, with its great cathedral 'solitary in the deep valley, among its lawns, gardens and rose-covered ruins'. Everything delighted him. 'I love the English country because it is *homely*' he wrote,[55] using the English word for which he could find no satisfactory translation, and to Francis Jammes he wrote a little later, 'London does not give one a true idea of England; one must get to know the countryside.'[56]

Valery Larbaud had always hated to be a mere tourist. What he enjoyed was either the thrill of the train thundering across European frontiers, or else to settle down in a temporary home, if possible with a temporary wife, and become part of the life around him. As the autumn wore on and he found himself taking more and more pleasure in London life, he began to think of a more permanent home where he could store his books and live in the way he liked. However it was the following year before he could carry out his plan, and even then, ill-health kept him almost constantly in France. It was not till the end of 1910 or early in 1911 that he finally moved into the house where he was to have his London headquarters for the next five years.[57]

No. 1 Lawrence Mansions still stands in Cheyne Walk, much as it was when Larbaud rented the ground floor, but stripped now of the luxuriant ivy that covered the building. Chelsea in those days, was a haven of calm:[58]

> Ivy and glass, and everywhere the delicate pink of brick beneath the black veil slowly accumulated by the air laden with vapour, smoke and crimson sunsets. . . . Quiet streets, which remain quiet in spite of all the passers-by: as do the banks of river; as does Church Street, which a century ago was the main street of a suburban village, with trees and greens descending to the river.

Then there was Carlyle's house ('A curse has fallen on it; they have made it into a museum', wrote Larbaud[59]) and his statue, which reminded one 'of a good old sheep-dog'. The Chelsea-ites of the day loved silence and were determined to respect it:[60]

> The gardens, the city trees under their covering of damp soot, the chapels, hospitals, taxi ranks, all these things exist noiselessly, so that the passer-by sees nothing of their activity. Everything is solitary and discreet; even the colours are silent and must be examined more closely than elsewhere, so it is only when one is close to it, and on sunny days, that one realises that the bridge, stretched like a double garland on its high pillars from one bank to another, is painted green. And the river can only be distinguished from the mist by a muffled gleam of silver, or copper, according to the time of day. . . . The horizon is all factories, and a group of high towers, a whole family of black Babels, marks the Western limits of the city—if it has any limits.

Nearly every page of the short novel entitled *Beauté, mon beau souci* is impregnated with happy memories of Chelsea, the carefully tended little gardens, the little church with a fragment of its ancient cemetery, the respectfully cherished memories of the great men and women who had lived there: Carlyle, 'the thundering, growling prophet of the cult of heroes', Leigh Hunt, the Rossettis, Meredith, George Eliot, Mrs Gaskell, Turner, Whistler, Oscar Wilde—all of them had lived for a time, at least, in Cheyne Walk or the neighbouring streets and Chelsea was proud of them. In fact the quarter remained even now very much a village, with a distinct personality of its own. There, Larbaud gradually discovered an England unsuspected by mere tourists, the London described in Barnabooth's *Journal* 'with its tea, its fog, the days carefully regulated according to the four meals, the familiar sights'. Here, overstrained nerves grew calm. Once again, the rhythm of England brought relaxation; the city acted on him by osmosis. 'All this helps to soothe my wounds and heal me,' writes Barnabooth. 'The Sundays have nourished me with silence and I borrowed from the deserted square . . . something of its correct boredom, respectability and reserve.'

He had obviously changed a great deal during the last few years. One finds no trace now of the Croesus complex of the first stay in London. It was no longer desperately important to buy one's hats at Lock's, one's walking-sticks at Brigg's, to have one's suits made by Poole. His pleasures were more modest now, and more subtle, though he would always remain an epicurean in the higher sense of the word.[61] Barnabooth, in fact, was receding before Marc Fournier. Several years were to pass before he made the discovery of Samuel Butler, but when he traced the portrait of this new literary passion, 'a bachelor by principle, who having reduced to the minimum the expenses and apparatus of material life, led a life as free of all social conventions, as peaceful and as private as was compatible with a certain comfort and a taste for intellectual pleasures',[62] he might have been speaking of himself.

Larbaud was inclined to be shy and did not make new friends easily. His letters during these first years in London always mention the same names: O'Connor, the Meynells, Stephen Wheeler. Barnabooth dreams of 'heroic friendships', but he himself, like many people who have suffered from loneliness in their youth, seems to have resigned himself to being a spectator, participating in an amused and rather distant way in the life around him, observing provincial habits, taking long rides on top of London buses, playing for a moment with some unknown child in one of the parks. Like many unattached people he was interested in the Royal Family. King Edward had died the previous year and now it was the new king whose doings he chronicled for his mother, watching amusedly as 'King George and his wife continue their calvary of fêtes and celebrations among the pitiless enthusiasm of the mob. I am still seeing my friends O'Connor the Meynells M. Stephen Wheeler etc.'[63]

At home in Cheyne Walk he seems to have held just as aloof. In the detailed account of Marc Fournier's life in Chelsea there is nothing to suggest that the hero of *Beauté, mon beau souci* made any friends in the neighbourhood. He has the spectacle of the streets and at home, tranquil happiness with a woman he knows he will one day leave behind him. Larbaud, one can deduce from his correspondence, lived in much the same way, spending enjoyable evenings at the theatre (they were playing *King Lear* 'magnificently' at the Haymarket, he wrote home) or at the Authors' Club in Whitehall Court. It was at the latter establishment that he met Arnold Bennett, whose *Clayhanger* had just appeared. 'Dined with Valery Larbaud at the Cecil Court', notes Bennett in his diary for 29 May 1911, but there does not seem to have been much contact between them at this time. Was there really, one wonders, a gentle, loving Edith Crosland to run his house for him and welcome him joyfully when he returned home? She figures large in *Beauté, mon beau souci*, but she remains one of the Larbaud heroines no one has succeeded in identifying.

It was in Paris on Christmas Eve of 1910 that Valery Larbaud was received into the Catholic Church. With his usual discretion about his own affairs he told no one at the time. André Gide seems to have been the first friend in whom he confided but more than a year had passed before he wrote him the brief explanation that, 'My going to Rome has been quite independent from externals. It took place *outside time*.' [64] He had asked Gide to keep the matter a secret, especially from his mother, and was distinctly annoyed when Gide admitted having let it out to Claudel. Converts generally steered clear of Claudel, who was inclined to consider each of them as his personal property and hammer him into what he considered the proper shape.

That shape did not and never would suit Larbaud, and indeed it seems unlikely that he would ever have become a Catholic if he had remained in France. The French Catholic revival was terribly intellectual, terribly intransigent and the accent was not on charity. 'Catholicism is a wonderfully narrow, jealous and intolerant doctrine',[65] Claudel had written, but Larbaud never became a 'Catholic writer' like Claudel, Bloy or Jammes. His conversion had been an entirely personal process, the discovery of a religion of love and charity, that was also a kind of emancipation. The Catholic Church, seen from the angle of Chesterton, and then of 'Meynell's poets', was an escape from the puritanism that had poisoned his early life, from 'a class whose methods of education, ideas, ideals, oppressed my childhood and held my mind for a long time in a painful state of slavery'.[66] It seems strange that it should have been in England, the most puritan of all the lands he knew, that he found his road to freedom.

Nobody at the Meynells' seems to have guessed what was happening, and perhaps they never knew of the conversion in which they had played so large, though indirect a part. In fact, it is difficult to tell whether the friendship between Alice Meynell and the young Frenchman was at all a close one. Alice Meynell was a very reserved woman, a little aloof except from her family. (Typically, when Francis Thompson broke down, for the first and only time during their long relationship, and sent her a pathetic love poem, she merely returned it to him with a meticulous analysis of its rhythm and metre.) Larbaud's letters to his friends mention her constantly, always with respect and admiration, but her rigidly ethical brand of religion was completely foreign to him. He had discovered, too, that she had 'a certain prejudice against contemporary French literature'. According to him, the Meynells, and most of the Granville Place set in general, were curiously ignorant of what was going on in any country except their own, and tended to condemn everything written in France for the last twenty or thirty years as 'agnostic, immoral and inartistic'.[67] If his observations were correct, the quality of the *salon* must have declined considerably since 1907.

Larbaud was determined that Mrs Meynell should at least become acquainted with the work of Claudel. It was not easy to get this endlessly busy woman to listen, but somehow he managed to corner her while he read aloud. His guess had been right. There was an evident affinity between the two writers, and Larbaud, pleased with his success, wrote at once to Claudel asking him to send a copy of *L'Otage*. This time, Alice Meynell was truly enthusiastic:[68]

> Dear Monsieur Larbaud [she wrote], Now that I have finished *L'Otage* I must thank you again for the great experience of reading that wonderful tragedy. I think it is the most *tragic* tragedy I have ever known, because of its great spirituality. Under the impression of *L'Otage*, all other griefs seem trivial . . . I have ordered the other works of this new master.

Claudel, who had been grumbling that England was the one country where he was still totally unknown, was delighted when she published several translations from his work in the *Dublin Review*. Meanwhile he had received from her a volume of Patmore's verse, sent on Larbaud's advice, and now he was busy in his Prague embassy translating some of the poems. Would Larbaud, he enquired, preface these translations with a study of the poet? Larbaud agreed at once, and announced to Francis Jammes:[69]

> I am preparing a study of Coventry Patmore. . . . I have made some valuable contacts in the Catholic world here and thanks to

friends of Patmore's I shall be able to quote some unpublished letters and fragments of work. In the same way, I have made Claudel's name known in a circle capable of appreciating him.

The truth was that he was becoming more and more steeped in Patmore and less and less interested in Landor, whose anti-Catholic attitude had begun to irritate him. He worked on the subject in a desultory way throughout most of his life and published a translation of *High and Low Life in Italy*, but the thesis was never completed. Arnold Bennett, it is true, said of him later that he probably knew more about Landor than anyone else in the world, but the attachment never seems to have been more than cerebral. It was for Thompson and Patmore that he reserved his real love.

The long study that finally appeared in *La Nouvelle Revue Française* in September and October 1911 turned out to be somewhat explosive. Larbaud had written innocently that 'Patmore was led to Christianity by his meditations on the sexual instinct', and this idea, which he had discovered delightedly while studying the old poet's work, evidently moved him deeply, no doubt because it revealed to him something essential about himself.[70] Claudel, however, wrote that he regretted the use of the expression 'sexual instinct' (adding, kindly but incomprehensibly: 'though I know you use the word in the English sense'). Alice Meynell and O'Connor too had been pained by 'certain over-strong expressions',[71] and one phrase from the original manuscript was firmly censored by both of them. Larbaud had concluded: 'Priests know by experience that the worst debauchees are often nearer to God than the most austere puritans.' That had been too much for the moralists on both sides of the Channel and the phrase had to come out. Alice Meynell forgave him, however, and wrote:[72]

My dear Monsieur Larbaud, Let me thank you most cordially for your great kindness in sending me the copy of the Coventry Patmore translations specially produced for me. No gift could give me greater pleasure. I prize your introduction for its wise critical judgements and perfect biographical truth. Thank you for writing it.

Larbaud had been for some time in correspondence with André Gide. They had hoped several times to meet in Paris, and had always just missed each other. Now, in the early summer of that year, Gide was planning a visit to England and wrote in his usual exuberant way: 'I have never felt so drawn to London as I do now that I know you are there.'[73] Larbaud recommended his own favourite lodgings—the 'bachelor's den' in Dover Street—but something always happened to delay the visit. King George's coronation was drawing near with its attendant inconveniences. 'I am afraid that eating, sleeping, watching, breathing, will all cost a fortune,' wrote Gide as the day approached. 'So, after having longed so immoderately to go to London and meet you there, I am trying to believe I should like even more to stay quietly at home.'[74]

Larbaud had been looking forward to the Coronation, but he too took fright at the last moment and set off for the Isle of Man. After making a detour to visit the scene of Arnold Bennett's novels of the Pottery towns, he arrived in Peel and it was from that town that he wrote to Claudel describing his visit to G. K. Chesterton. Although he no longer felt entirely in sympathy with Chesterton, his interest in this 'anarchist who dynamites anarchy'[75] continued and he had published a number of articles about him in various French reviews. The interview had been difficult to arrange, for Chesterton was in bad health, saw very few people and never, under any circumstances, wrote a letter. Finally, after a series of meetings had been arranged and cancelled, Larbaud had been down to Beaconsfield, where Chesterton and his wife lived in an ugly new villa.

I did not think Chesterton had portrayed himself in his allegorical novel, *The Man who was Thursday*, but that is the truth [he reported to Claudel]. At first sight, he is disgusting; his obesity is a real infirmity and makes him look like a glutton and an idiot. His face is like the largest and most deformed strawberry in the basket. The English journalists only notice his belly and the mass of him and compare him to Dr Samuel Johnson; in reality, he has a forehead like Thackeray's, but with three superimposed layers of fat. Then, under all these rolls and lumps, one discovers two intelligent blue eyes, and from then on, all goes well. . . . He talks the whole time and talks like he writes: it's G. K. C. the whole time. While he talks, he struggles against a sort of breathlessness. But he laughs at everything he says—even when it is not especially funny—seems constantly pleased with himself and sometimes, like many geniuses, seems completely silly and childish. Yet a word here and there shows that he has penetrated far into a region of which, ten seconds earlier, one supposed he knew nothing. I am sure he has to be dressed, and that he has to be fed like a baby, for he spilt his tea all over his waistcoat while he was drinking. . . . I never met anyone more *naive*, in the full sense of the word.

Claudel, who had learned by now that when Chesterton described himself as a Catholic he meant a High Anglican, had instructed Larbaud to bring up the subject of religion and discover how the land lay. Larbaud could not give him much hope: 'For my part, I am sure it is impossible to modify Chesterton's opinions: one must wait and see how his ideas develop. He does much for the cause of truth by casting doubt on the importance of the great conceptions of our day.'[76]

Then Gide arrived at last, and the whole tempo of Larbaud's well-ordered life seems to have changed. Gide's temperament was quite different from his own. He was always passionately involved in every relationship—so much so that each of his innumerable friends seems to have believed himself to be *the* friend. Everyone confided in him, and he confided, or appeared to confide, in everyone. 'The heart of man had no secrets for Gide', William Rothenstein says of him.[77] He refused small talk, cut across inhibitions, broke down reticences. In fact, he was exactly what Larbaud needed and, no doubt, secretly wanted. He succumbed without protest, and all the more easily since Miss Agnes Tobin had come into his life just twenty-four hours earlier.

Agnes Tobin was an American—'a pious girl of a certain age' according to Francis Jammes[78]—who lived chiefly in France, and had become, like Larbaud himself, one of the rare links between the French and English Catholic revivals. At that time, she was preparing a lecture on Patmore and, having heard from Jammes of the young French writer who was an authority on the subject, she had asked for an introduction. 'Miss Tobin thought she was going to meet a prodigy', wrote Larbaud to Jammes on 6 July. 'She must have been very disappointed to find such a shy, dull man as I am.'

Miss Tobin could not have found him shy or dull, for she stayed for nearly two hours, talking all the time, and they were already firm friends when she left him. Larbaud suspected her of being something of a dilettante in literature, but she had translated *Phèdre* and Petrarch's sonnets, she had travelled almost as widely as himself and her piety appeared to him 'very sincere in spite of being transatlantic'.[79] She struck him as being truly original too, though perhaps she was merely frank and outspoken, in the manner of Henry James's American heroines who seem so surprising to his English and continental characters. At any rate, he found her worth introducing to Gide and the three soon became an inseparable trio.

Although Larbaud was the Londoner, Gide and Miss Tobin became his guides. First they took him to visit Gosse who had written a book on Patmore a few years earlier. Gosse was notorious for disliking anything he had not discovered himself, but as he had got in first on this subject he was able to receive his visitors very kindly. In fact, he turned out to be far more sympathetic to Larbaud's point of view than Alice Meynell had been, and when the study was published that autumn he wrote:[80]

> I do not think any English critic has written so well of C. P. as you have. In particular, your treatment of the causes of his conversion is luminous. 'Patmore a été conduit au christianisme par l'instinct sexuel'—that sentence contains the germ of all his poetry and all his holiness.

Miss Tobin seemed to know everyone: 'She is a friend of everyone who has a name in England—nobility and the arts', wrote Larbaud to his mother.[81] She was an old and close friend of Alice Meynell, and had frequented the famous *salon* at various times and through various vicissitudes. Another old friend was Arthur Symons, whom she had known when he was still an important figure in French and English literary life and to whom she had remained faithful during his long period of insanity. He was living with his wife at Wittersham in Kent, very much out of things now that Mallarmé, Verlaine and so many old friends were dead, and the Symbolist movement itself had somehow faded into irrelevance. In fact, though he was only forty-six years old, he gave the impression of belonging to another age and people visited him for his reminiscences of the past rather than for anything he could contribute to the present. For the French, however, he remained something of a legendary figure and Gide felt they should all get to know each other. Miss Tobin, who was rather a collector of celebrities, was enthusiastic for the plan. She was rich and unconventional, so she found it natural to hire a taxi and invite the two young men to be her guests on the trip into the country.

They set off, on 22 July, veiled and goggled, in one of the new automobile taxis that were beginning to replace the old hansom cabs. Island Cottage was reached at midday and they lunched with Symons. None of them recorded what they talked about, but Symons recorded that he found Gide 'as weird as he is fascinating, queer as he is odd, charming also'. Larbaud was presumably in one of his shy moods, since he was referred to simply as 'another Frenchman'.

Then their host suggested they call on Joseph Conrad[82] who had recently come to live in the village of Orlestone, near Ashford. He was a great recluse these days, suffering from gout and liking above all to be left alone to get on with his work. However, he had lived in Marseilles in his youth, spoke perfect French and had a romantic, nostalgic attachment for France. The callers were welcomed and invited to stay to dinner. Gide of course got on at once with Conrad who emerged from the shell into which he habitually withdrew when strangers arrived. In spite of the long years in England, he had remained very much the Polish aristocrat and Gide, in his turn, was greatly impressed by 'a sort of instinctive nobility—bitter, disdainful and rather despairing, like that which he describes in *Lord Jim*'.[83]

If Larbaud had been alone, he might not have got very far with his habitually taciturn host, who wrote to Gide after receiving a copy of *Barnabooth*: 'I am glad [he] liked my letter. I did not dare to tell him quite how much I admired his book, for he gave me the impression of a reserved man who would be suspicious of any too-great enthusiasm'.[84] As for Miss Tobin, she nearly provoked a scene by what appeared to be a passionate discourse on the genius of Georges Ohnet, a French novelist much in fashion at the time with romantic lady readers. Her claims for the 'tempered brilliance', the 'subdued richness' of his scenes grew more and more extravagant; Conrad grew crosser and crosser. Then a quotation from Pater revealed that she was talking about Giorgione, whose name she pronounced in the Italian manner. There was general hilarity and the talk became so friendly and went on so long that it was too late to return to London.

The three travellers slept at the village inn and continued their journey next day, lunching at Rye before passing through Winchelsea on the way home. Somewhere on the way, they stopped to write to Francis Jammes, dear friend to all three of them, but immovably entrenched in the Basque country. 'Gide, Valery Larbaud and Miss Tobin, whom I introduced to them, have written to me from England', he told Arthur Fontaine, adding, 'did I tell you that Larbaud wants to drag me through that poetic country in his motor-car? He wants to return to Orthez to persuade me. I shall have nothing to do with it.'[85]

Gide invariably had a catalytic effect on the people he met, so that they found themselves becoming friends with each other as well as with him. Arnold Bennett, for instance, seems to have been a mere club acquaintance of Larbaud's up to this time, but when Larbaud introduced him to Gide, the relationship evidently became intimate almost at once. 'Larbaud calls to see me nearly every day,' Bennett noted in his journal for the following February, when he was in Cannes; and in March: 'Larbaud brought Gide in at 5.30. And we kept them to dinner and had a great evening that finished at 10 p.m.' It was Bennett who later read through the articles Larbaud wrote in English for the *New Weekly* ('Arnold Bennett, whose knowledge of spoken, written and literary French allows him to reconstruct the mental process of each of my English sentences, found, in ten articles, only one flagrant gallicism,' he noted proudly[86]) and the revised edition of *Domaine anglais* was to have been dedicated to him.[87]

As for Agnes Tobin, she and Larbaud remained friends for many years. They continued to see a great deal of each other after Gide had been seen off at Southampton. Together, they even created a short-lived Donne Society, composed of twelve members—six English and six French. Austin Dobson was to edit the 'Donne Pamphlets' to be produced by the society and there was to be an annual dinner. The French members were Larbaud, Gide, Alexis Saint-Léger Léger (Saint-John Perse), Francis Jammes, Gaston Gallimard and Léon-Paul Fargue. The English membership seems to have been fluctuating. Miss Tobin proposed Herbert Trench, and Bennett, too, was approached. The Society soon petered out, apparently because of the difficulty of getting all the French members simultaneously across the Channel, but Larbaud and Miss Tobin enjoyed themselves immensely. Larbaud indeed returned most unwillingly to Vichy that August: 'Oh! I am being torn away from London', he wrote to a friend in Paris from the Times Literary Club. 'What agony! But I shall be back to spend the autumn here and work like a demon.'

It is unlikely that Larbaud was in love with Agnes Tobin. He did not care for intellectual women, preferring them—if we can judge by his various heroines—sweet and clinging, though not without spirit. However, the friendship was close enough to worry Madame Larbaud who could not bear the idea of her son marrying anyone she had not chosen for him herself. When Miss Tobin visited her in Vichy, she found her frivolous and demanded explanations. Her son reassured her: the frivolity was only apparent and in any case Miss Tobin was seventeen years older than himself.

The autumn was convivial: his circle had widened to include, besides the Meynells, Stephen Wheeler, Gosse, Arnold Bennett, H. G. Wells (who amused and disconcerted him by his passion for toy soldiers), Miss Tobin. He was working on Landor, whom he was to follow to Florence next year, seeking out the houses he had lived in, plans and descriptions of the town as he knew it, documents concerning him. Bennett had introduced him to *The Way of all Flesh* and *Erewhon*, and he had plunged, fascinated into the study of Samuel Butler. He was making more translations from Chesterton, commenting on Patmore, Bennett, Wells, Dolben, Beckford—whose work and personality began to intrigue him after a rather belated discovery of Mallarmé's *Vathek*. Crossing and recrossing the Channel, he would settle down in his Chelsea home, then, eternally restless, feel 'the need of a change after a period of work and boredom in this 'Ville de la

Bible'.[88] Then he would set off—perhaps in his own motor-car, since Francis Jammes refers to this acquisition, and Reginald Harding in *Beauté, mon beau souci*, actually takes his chauffeur's place and drives all the way down to Wells—on his tireless exploration of 'this poetic country: Cambridge, Hastings, Brighton, York, Edinburgh'.

Larbaud, in fact, fell in love with cities exactly as he fell in love with women, abandoning himself to them as if they alone were to count in his life, but always with the secret knowledge that he would one day pack his bags and seek elsewhere. He describes London exactly as he describes the women he loved, with the same powerful and delicate voluptuousness, and the same lurking fear that they may one day catch him for good:[89]

J'ai des souvenirs de villes comme on a des souvenirs d'amours

he writes, and he approaches the town he loves with the hesitations and coquetteries of a lover:[90]

One of the greatest joys in life [in English in the text]: to return on 1 May (May Day) and spend an hour or two in the first town (Dover, Folkestone, etc.). The gorse is all in flower; it has been raining; the steep, narrow streets are wet and shiny; ragged children, wearing coronets of torn, dirty flowers that have fallen in the mud, beg for pennies, etc. Then one takes the train again, for London. The well-sprung, solid little compartments, the perfection and simplicity of all that surrounds one. The Kentish fields. The first whiff of damp air, with its odour of tobacco. The first little girl in a white pinafore. The new-born lambs, huddled close to the huge, mud-caked ewes; the abundance of life, the richness of the earth. The train speeding among the roofs and hundred thousand chimney-pots; the first LCC tram, enclosed between two rows of pink houses.

London was for him 'the place where I have been most happy'[91] and, just as Marc Fournier sometimes felt a wistful temptation to marry Edith or Queenie Crosland (who are like personifications of London), so he sometimes contemplated settling down for good, or at least keeping a permanent base in Chelsea. London was gentle, discreet, eminently comfortable as Edith was, and Queenie was to become: wifely qualities, to which he might eventually have succumbed.

But the Great War was drawing near. England would soon become an inaccessible island. Larbaud was cut off from London and when he saw her again things were not the same, would never be the same again. The death of the old life had already begun.

7

Four Englands

It would be hard to find four men more dissimilar, both in their work and their psychological structure, than the four poets studied in the preceding chapters. Each is, in fact, not just an unique human being, but something of an archetype, to which may be related only pallid imitations (the end of the last century and the beginning of this one swarmed with sub-Mallarmés and sub-Verlaines, though the omnifarious nature of Valéry's intellect discouraged disciples, and Valery Larbaud was too discreet, too secret, and perhaps too physically mobile to acquire them). In each, certain facets of human nature seem to have been extended to their ultimate possibility, each revealing himself, but in an entirely different way, as what the French would call *une bête de littérature*—a literary animal.

It will have been noticed that there is a linking factor in the story of each of these four. Each came to England at an early age, when he was still porous, still retained some of the permeability of extreme youth, before the pressure of experience has diminished the response to external stimulus. Mallarmé and Larbaud were twenty when they first came to London; Valéry was twenty-three; only Verlaine had reached an age when the last vestige of childhood has normally been shed off, but Verlaine was to remain a child all his life, and to retain a child's eager awareness.

The England these four absorbed and transmuted into poetry was never, of course, the same, single country. 'If a certain assembly of trees, mountains, water and houses that we call a landscape is beautiful,' says Baudelaire, 'It is not so in itself, but through me, through the idea or sentiment I attach to it.'[1] It is obvious, through their own accounts, that the 'idea or sentiment' was extraordinarily operative in these four as well as extraordinarily different. It coloured most powerfully their perception of a new land though one suspects a certain preconception in their earliest encounters. Was, for instance, mist and fog quite as all-pervasive as the young travellers have assured us? And certain landscapes seem to have been observed through the eyes of Shakespeare rather than their own.

Here and there, then, we find a little scattered and easily discernible literary bric-à-brac. But each of these four first came to England at a point of crisis in his life, and, in each case the English landscape takes on the flavour of crisis. Mallarmé, in his first encounter with London, finds himself swathed in a *necessary* mist—the mist that was to thicken and intensify to separate him from the objective world, leaving him free to distil, in the isolated laboratory of mind, the elusive essence of things: 'l'absence de tout bouquet'. There is no recognisable trace of London in his work, none of the direct interpretations the shock of novelty provoked in Verlaine or Larbaud. But, 'a man who renounces the world attains that condition which enables him to understand it,' Paul Valéry wrote of him.[2] Mallarmé renounced the world while he was in London, and in doing so, attained the condition in which he was able to discover his own, alternative world.

No allusions, no descriptions—that first year in London, that was to mark Mallarmé's whole life, has dissolved and become absorbed into a landscape of the mind. Yet England is constantly present in his work. In spite of the great difference in temperament,[3] no one has understood this better than Valéry, and it is he who has pointed out the mystic importance Mallarmé attached to the arrangement of words.[4]

> I can imagine his state of expectancy [he writes], the intensity of his spirit as it strains to discover harmonic correspondences, totally absorbed in the effort to apprehend the genesis of a word within the universe of words, to seize the organisation of associations and reverberations invoked by an idea that clamours to be born.

Now this universe of harmonic correspondences of which Mallarmé first became aware during his stay in London in 1862–3, was inevitably coloured by his delighted discovery of the English syntax. During the long hours of study in his Knightsbridge rooms, he read Chaucer and saw in the *Canterbury Tales* how the double use of language—the Norman and the Saxon—had been put to its finest use. He had seen, too, how Chaucer had handled 'one of the most exquisite elements of English poetry . . . which consists of placing a noun between two adjectives'. This remark suggests that *Les Mots anglais*, though sometimes unconsciously funny, is also perceptive. Mallarmé illustrated it with a quotation, 'We see the woeful day fatal come', and this form, so foreign to French grammar, soon began to creep into his own poetry, as did our typically English alliteration, which he was soon to use with such surprising effect.[5]

When he absorbed these grammatical forms into his own harmonic universe, Mallarmé was doing far more than assimilating a few linguistic peculiarities. Alliteration, the double adjective, were instruments bent to the attainment of a single, devouring purpose. They became part of the alchemist's tools of transmutation, magical elements, part of the 'secret parity . . . between the ancient methods and the spell that is poetry.'[6] Like the London fog which revealed the first image representing the zone of separation between subject and object, of the no-man's-land that was to be his chosen terrain, these grammatical forms were absorbed into and became an essential part of the 'Idea'.

Verlaine was in almost every respect the antithesis of Mallarmé. His raw material was the world around him, and his own immediate experience of it. Infinitely sensitive to his surroundings, he absorbed scenes, places, people and translated them directly into poetry. The world he tells of is one of instant perceptions, and the very fluidity, the lack of consistence in his nature, resulted in an extraordinarily varied vision. Everything that England brought him is there, in the volumes of verse that mark his life like milestones and tell us where and what he was at the time he compiled them. Immediate experience or memory, but always coloured by passing mood, they can degenerate into sentimentality at one extreme and vulgarity at the other—for Verlaine was exempt from neither of these failings. Sometimes they are direct descriptions, the verbal equivalent of a delicate, century-old painting:[7]

> La chaussée est très large, en sorte
> Que l'eau jaune comme une morte
> Dévale ample et sans nuls espoirs
> De rien refléter que la brume,
> Même alors que l'aurore allume
> Les cottages jaunes et noirs.

Then there come certain luminous moments when the landscape of the outer world blends and merges with the landscape of the mind to form a pure, spontaneous, unmistakably Verlainean poem. 'L'échelonnement des haies', parts of 'Bournemouth', certain agonising memories of his *saison en enfer* in London—these *are* Verlaine's England, and *are* Verlaine in England. They are true epiphanies, as James Joyce used to call such moments of vision and no poet, perhaps, has known better than Verlaine how to capture and transmit their urgent revelation of reality.

Mr Vernon Underwood has made so thorough and comprehensive a study of the influence of the English hymnal in Verlaine's verse that there remains little to add to it. Cazals, it seems, was told by the poet himself that *Sagesse* was largely inspired by 'these English hymns to which he never tired of listening and which he could never hear without being indescribably moved'.[8] It was the sort of emotion which exactly suited Verlaine's largely feminine temperament. His idea of love was an abdication of self in the loved one, and above all an escape from the danger of self. Love, whether sacred or profane, would always be for him a refuge. Now in this refuge, which he believed himself at various times to have discovered in Mathilde, in Rimbaud, in Lucien Létinois and in religion, he sought certain particularities, above all nobility and simplicity. After his first encounter with Mathilde, we find him writing:[9]

> Toute grace et toutes nuances
> Dans l'éclat doux de ses seize ans,
> Elle a la candeur des enfances
> Et les manèges innocents. . . .
>
> L'intelligence vient chez elle
> En aide à l'esprit noble. . . .

The descriptions of Rimbaud in the early stages of their friendship, and of Lucien Létinois, are in the same vein, and in the English hymns he saw how 'nobility of sentiment can be allied to a simplicity understandable by all.' They inspired poems which are by no means his finest work, yet suggest an emotion far more authentic than the very orthodox 'Liturgies intimes' of later years. Verlaine discovered the English hymnal at the same time as he discovered the meaning of spiritual peace, and it seemed to him like an expression of that peace. The hymns were part of Stickney, of release from tension, of the simple goodness of the Andrews and Canon Coltman—of all those elements which reappear at certain moments in poems written in Bournemouth or Leamington. They represented, in fact, an England whose spirit Verlaine penetrated as perhaps no other foreign poet has done: the mid-Victorian England, stiff, proud, hypocritical, barbarous yet gentle, soothing in her timeless certainties: a refuge and a bulwark against chaos.

The London Verlaine rediscovered when he returned, old, unregenerate and famous, to England in 1893, was the city Paul Valéry first encountered a few months later. It was a changed place now, precariously poised between triumph and catastrophe, between brashness and decadence. Verlaine saw it through the eyes of an old man clinging to the past—and to that part of the past which he chose to remember; to Valéry every detail had the sharp clearness of youthful experience. Where Verlaine saw an England that was almost faded away, Valéry encountered the new England that was being born. His letter to André Gide, after his first visit to the City, his feeling that he had been at the beating heart of the world, show that he recognised a turning-point in history. England, in fact, was never for him a poetic country, as it was for Mallarmé, Verlaine or Larbaud, but rather an heroic one, a place made for action and which called for, and did not possess, a philosophy of action. Thus it was still, at this point in his development, an alien world that could be exciting but also menacing. 'London Bridge' seems to be the only poem—or rather, piece of poetic prose—he wrote during his two early visits. It has none of the plastic quality of the London poems of Verlaine or Valery Larbaud, but is rather a terrifying inner vision of multiplicity and incoherence, 'a flux of identical particles' menacing and destroying the pure uniqueness of Self. Nor did the aesthetic delight he took in the great fire glimpsed from the Pennells' windows spark off any creative work. Unlike Verlaine or Larbaud—or indeed Mallarmé—Valéry distrusted sensual impressions. A poem, in his definition was 'a long-drawn hesitation between sound and sense'.[10] The visual elements in his poetry are rare and they can nearly always be traced to his native Mediterranean shores with their classic luminosity. The London fog, so mysteriously poetic to Mallarmé and Verlaine, merely gave him a sore throat.

In any case, Valéry did not come to England seeking for its peculiar poetry, and though he had read Shakespeare and Dickens like everyone else, his own vision was uncoloured by them. What he did find in London was a new attitude to the external world, an attitude—as we have seen from Marcel Schwob's reaction—very much in contradiction with the Symbolist world, rooted in the imagination he had left behind him. Now he encountered men of action and meditated on them. Some of them, like Decle and Pollock, could be studied at first hand; others, like Rhodes and other heroes of South Africa, were at once legend and reality; Napoleon, recreated by Meredith, became a sort of magical sign representing the power of the intellect over the material world. All of these helped to spark off a life-time's reflection on the nature of action and its relationship to words and to the intellect:[11]

The rhetorician and sophist [he wrote either during or soon after the second stay in London]. Salt of the earth. All the rest who take words for things, phrases for deeds, are worshippers of idols. But the former observe these phenomena as a whole, the kingdom of the possible is within them. From which it follows that the man of bold, clear-cut, far-reaching action is of much the same type as these emancipated masterminds. They are brothers under the skin. (Napoleon, Caesar, Frederick—*men of letters*, eminently gifted for manipulating men and things—with words.)

Thus was born 'La Conquête allemande', then 'Le Yalou' and the series of essays and reflections on world events, chiefly collected in the volume entitled *Regards sur le monde actuel*, which influenced statesmen and leaders of every type in France and proved that 'a prince of the intellect may have a clearer vision of world events than a professional diplomat'.[12]

And Valery Larbaud? Larbaud was the only real traveller among the four, the other three being mainly static men, who only moved about for definable reasons. He alone was a compulsive tourist, a man at ease among half-packed suitcases and rented furniture. In fact, he was perhaps the first truly international French poet, for Barnabooth's poems precede Blaise Cendrars' 'Prose du Transibérien', which has something of the same resonance.

Yet 'tourist' is not really a word one should use in connection with Larbaud. He entered deeply, voluptuously, into the life of any place he elected as a temporary home. In London, Warwick, Weston-super-Mare, he penetrates the life around him, peers through windows, rummages in dusty libraries, plays with children, identifies himself with the life of its inhabitants. The pictures he leaves of these places tell us a little more of them than we could ever know if he had not passed by there. Though he wrote two short novels he was not really a novelist, but a poet and writer of short stories that are less in the French tradition than in the English one that produced Katherine Mansfield or Dylan Thomas. He is a seizer of insignificant scenes that are transposed into the matter of literature. His people and events are never important or imposing (Barnabooth frequents princes and statesmen but, in his presence at least, they reveal themselves humble rather than magnificent). A beggar, a child, the crowd bustling in some drab or elegant street—whether he is in London, or Alicante, or Scheveningen or Mers-el-Khebir, the place and the passer-by melt and become part of a scheme of things in which he is at once present and absent, identifying himself with people and places, yet with some part of himself remaining obstinately detached:[13]

> Et si je suis un peu différent, hélas, de vous tous,
> C'est parce que je vois,
> Ici, au milieu de vous, comme une apparition divine,
> Au-devant de laquelle je m'élance pour en être frolé,
> Honnie, méconnue, exilée,
> Dix fois mystérieuse,
> La Beauté Invisible.

It was this invisible, not evident beauty that Larbaud sought everywhere and that he served with a selfless, knight errant-like devotion. He believed that beauty was the material expression of religion and that the search for beauty, even in such unlikely places as a Birmingham slum or a luxury hotel in some dreary spa, was a sort of Quest for the Holy Grail. He believed in its power of binding people and nations together and felt, indeed, that it was the only power which might succeed in doing so. 'He was the first', says G. Angiolletti, 'to understand that a literature opening on to every horizon was the silken thread which might yet bind Europe together.'[14]

If Larbaud's personal production is relatively small, it is because he sacrificed so much of his time to this role of literary go-between, binding together writers, and peoples of different lands. Just as England provided the background for a great proportion of his creative work, English novels and poetry were the first object of his critical attention. His knowledge of English literature was immense and he penetrated the books he loved in much the same way as he penetrated into the daily life of his favourite places. 'He did not pass through them like a traveller', says Marcel Arland, the friend of his later days. 'Rather, he lived in them, as he did in cities.'[15] And he sought in them, just as he did in cities, neglected or forgotten beauties.

Translation was still, at the beginning of the century, a very minor art. Larbaud, like Schwob, was one of the few who served his chosen writers with all his talent. He loved the French language, knew how to use its most extreme subtleties, and to disguise them in an apparent simplicity. His critical career began at a time when French curiosity for England and all things English, which had been growing steadily since the early 1890s, had reached its zenith. An interest which had seemed eccentric when Mallarmé had introduced John Payne to France, and was still slightly exotic when the *Mercure de France* published Symons and his friends, had become fashionable. The result had been a spate of translations of novelists like Marie Corelli and Ouida, and of mediocre poets, who were presented as geniuses to a confused public. Larbaud did more, perhaps than anyone else, to establish more genuine values. Through him, Landor, Coleridge, Francis Thompson, H. G. Wells, Chesterton, then Samuel Butler and James Joyce[16] obtained an audience in France—certain of them at a time when they were still hardly recognised in England. His passion for Patmore may seem a little surprising today, but it arose from a personal affinity and had nothing to do with the mode of the moment.

Perhaps he did not quite realise how untypical of England was Patmore's combination of mysticism and sensuality, but he absorbed it, as he did Chesterton's combination of Catholicism and democracy.

Larbaud gave a great deal to England, and a certain religious attitude was perhaps the most important thing she offered him in return.

Journeys, contacts, friends, growing fame . . . the interwoven thread of England is clearly visible in the biographical details of these four lives, solid or tenuous according to changing circumstances, but always present. Less easily discernible, yet far more important, is the lasting effect on malleable youth of the first shock of discovery. The 'flattest opposition to foreign felicities and foreign standards' had become less evident by the 1890s, but it remained essentially unchanged except in a limited circle of aristocrats and aesthetes. England was still, in any terms but those of space, an immensely distant country, one in which previous experience lost its validity, leaving a void to be filled according to the temperament of the visitor. The stimulus to the vibrant and responsive imagination of early youth was, in the case of these poets, absorbed into later experience, but it never entirely disappeared. Over and over again, one detects an echo of that first encounter, when everything was fresh and new, when tragedy and excitement mingled and provoked a 'sentiment or idea' that became the England of Mallarmé, or of Verlaine, or Valéry, or Larbaud. A place part dream and part reality that belonged to each alone.

Notes

1 'Honeyed Poison'

1 Charles Dickens, *Pictures from Italy*, London, 1846, p. 270.
2 Hippolyte Taine, *Notes sur l'Angleterre*, Hachette, Paris, 1872, p. 37.
3 Louis Blanc, *Lettres sur l'Angleterre*, Paris, 1866, p. 36.
4 Swinburne, staying as a very young man with the Trevelyans at Wallington, was caught in the drawing-room by his host reading a book with the give-away yellow cover. Without further enquiry Sir Walter Trevelyan picked up the book with a pair of tongs and cast it on the fire. Gosse says the volume in question was Balzac's *La Comédie Humaine*, another version identifies it as the *Pensées* of Pascal. See E. Gosse, *Algernon Charles Swinburne*, London, 1917, p. 71.
5 Tennyson did, however, take an unexpected interest in one kind of French literature. Henry James has recounted how, in his youth, he was invited to a luncheon party at the great man's home, when one of the guests innocently mentioned the name of a French relative, a Mademoiselle Laure de Sade. Tennyson positively sprang to life.

> 'De Sade?' he at once exclaimed with interest . . . and proceeded admirably . . . to the very greatest length imaginable, as was signally promoted by the fact that no-one present . . . recognised the name or the nature of the scandalous, the long-ignored, the at last all but unnameable author; least of all the gentle relative of Mademoiselle Laure, who listened with the blankest grace to her friend's enumeration of his titles of infamy, among which that of his most notorious work was pronounced.

James adds that Tennyson gave, in fact, a curiously friendly analysis of the author's reputation. Henry James, *Autobiography*, London, 1956, p. 591.
6 Gosse, op. cit., p. 89.

2 The Young Mallarmé

Unless otherwise stated, letters from Mallarmé are quoted from *Stéphane Mallarmé: Correspondance*, vol. I, 1862–71; vol. II, 1871–85; vol. III, 1886–9, Gallimard, Paris, 1959–69. Mallarmé's works, unless otherwise stated, are quoted from *Stéphane Mallarmé: Oeuvres complètes*, ed. H. Mondor, Bibliothèque de la Pléiade, Paris, 1945.

1 Notre-Dame-de-France was built in Leicester Place, on the site of Burford's famous panorama, and consecrated in 1868.
2 Elizabeth Siddal, wife of Dante Gabriel Rossetti, died from an overdose of laudanum on 10 February 1862.

3   This square no longer exists.

4   See R. P. Rahb's pamphlet 'Notre-Dame-de France' on sale in the church.

5   'Autobiographie': an autobiographical letter written in 1885 at the request of Verlaine for publication in a series entitled 'Les Poètes maudits'.

6   'Arthur Rimbaud' in 'Quelques médaillons et portraits en pieds'.

7   Published in *La Revue Française*, 24 April 1859 in a translation by Baudelaire.

8   Henri Cazalis (1840–1909) is better known by his pen-name of Jean Lahor. He later abandoned law for medicine. His friendship with Mallarmé and his own reputation as a charming minor poet, brought him many literary patients, including Verlaine. See Joanna Richardson, *Verlaine*, Weidenfeld & Nicolson, London, 1971, pp. 233–4.

9   'Les hérésies artistiques: l'art pour tous', *L'Artiste*, September 1862.

10   'Sa fosse est creusée' and 'Sa fosse est fermée'.

11   The notes by Dr Henri Mondor to the first volume of Mallarmé's *Correspondance* give Ettie Yapp's full name as Juliette, but her birth certificate, consulted at Somerset House, confirms 'Harriet'.

12   Maurice Dreyfous, *Ce que je tiens à dire*, Paris, 1912, p. 59.

13   French commentators have been zealous in tracing the sister-motive throughout Mallarmé's work and have tended to ignore the Romantic convention which still prevailed among poets of this period. See Charles Mauron, *Introduction à la psychanalyse de Mallarmé*, Neuchatel-Paris, 1950.

14   'Apparition' was begun in Sens in 1862 and finished in London in 1863.

15   'Prose (pour Des Esseintes)'.

16   'Le bronze artistique' from the family chimney-piece continued long after this to play its symbolic role in the bourgeois life of France. During the civilian exodus of June 1940, refugees could often be seen hundreds of miles from their home, wearily pushing handcarts, prams, bicycles, loaded with their dearest treasure and crowned with these very objects described by Mallarmé, and whose absence so puzzled the little servant: 'Jeanne d'Arc, ou M. de Buffon, en manchettes et la plume aux doigts, ou la Géographie avec son globe et son casque.'

17   When, years later, he was asked by Méry Laurent who was his favourite hero, he replied 'Hamlet', and from adolescence onwards he compared himself, almost lovingly, with 'l'adolescent évanoui de nous aux commencements de la vie'. ('Crayonné au théâtre: Hamlet.')

18   Letter to Helen Whitman, 13 December 1876.

19   'La sottise d'un poète moderne a été jusqu'à se désoler que l'action ne fut pas la soeur du rêve', he wrote to Cazalis on 3 June 1863. The reference is to Baudelaire's 'Le reniement de Saint Pierre' in *Les Fleurs du Mal*.

20   Henri Mondor, *Vie de Mallarmé*, Paris, 1941, p. 74.

21   'Les petites Vieilles' in *Les Fleurs du Mal*.

22   Letter quoted by Lawrence Joseph, 'Mallarmé et son amie anglaise', *Revue d'Histoire littéraire de la France*, lxv, July–September 1965, pp. 457–78.

23   'Crise de vers'. This article appeared in the *National Observer*, 26 March 1892.

24   Mallarmé's projected 'Recueil de Nursery Rhymes', which he abandoned in 1881, was edited by Prof. C. P. Barbier and published in 1964 by Gallimard. Some of the rhymes are taken from Walter Crane's *Baby's Bouquet* (1878) but Mallarmé included them in *Les Mots anglais*, published a year earlier, so it seems probable that he learnt them at first hand from the only English child he knew before this date. For the instruction of his pupils, Mallarmé would

quote a rhyme, following it with a *thème* and a *devoir*. 'Cock Robin' is an example which illustrates his own reactions. Here is the *'thème'*, in Mallarmé's own brand of English: 'What a strange picture! Look at this cat with his violin; but that's not all; here is the moon and a cow jumping over it! I am like the little dog who laughs to see such a funny thing; and it seems to me that when I see such a spectacle, my ideas chase after each other, just as, in the same rhyme, the dish ran after the spoon.'

25 Jean-Baptiste François Ernest le Chatelain (1801–81), generally known as the Chevalier de Chatelain.

26 *Les Beautés de la Poésie anglaise*, 5 vols, London, 1860–72.

27 *Notre Monument*, privately printed in London, 1868.

28 Castelnau Lodge, Warwick Crescent. The house had at that time a fine view overlooking Regent's Park.

29 These remain unpublished at the time of writing. They are generally un-dated and deal more and more exclusively as the years go by with Chatelain's gout and the mental illness which preceded his wife's death (Bibliothèque Doucet, Paris).

30 Letter from Chatelain (Bibliothèque Doucet). The poem became 'Renouveau'.

31 Ibid.

32 'The Raven' and 'The Bells'.

33 'Frisson d'hiver'. This prose-poem was written in Tournon in 1864.

34 Cazalis was at this time in the throes of his first rupture with Ettie. His relationship with her was not unlike that between Mallarmé and Marie. He too seems to have loved an ideal of his own creation, rather than the real Ettie, and he wrote to his friend, 'When I cease to love a woman, it's finished at once. It's enough for her to appear to me for one day, or for a single hour, as less than sublime, and it's over.'

35 'Plainte d'automne', probably finished in Tournon towards the end of 1864.

36 This poem was later entitled 'Le château de l'Espérance'.

37 'Autobiographie'.

38 'Crise de vers'.

39 The Exhibition was organised by Henry Cole, first director of the South Kensington Museum (now the Victoria & Albert Museum). Mallarmé believed the galleries he visited to be part of the museum, but they were installed in reality in the Horticultural Society's gardens over the road where the Imperial Institute was subsequently built.

40 *Les Mots anglais*, Paris, 1877.

41 T. S. Eliot, *From Poe to Verlaine*, New York, 1948, p. 21.

42 P. Valéry, 'My early days in England', *Bookman's Journal*, December, 1925.

43 A detail reported by 'a poet of the period', in the *Dictionary of National Biography*.

44 C. Jourdanne, *Histoire du Félibrige, 1854–1896*, Avignon, 1897, p. 35 (note).

45 'Magie'.

46 'Prose (pour Des Esseintes)'.

47 Dr Mondor and other biographers have suggested that Wyse's invitation was to London and that the house at No. 1 Alexander Square belonged to him. A passage in George Sala's autobiography reveals that it was he who occupied this house, though he was usually absent, travelling here and there to produce the sensational articles that were making a fortune for the *Telegraph*. Mallarmé's correspondence with Wyse shows clearly that Wyse was not in London when he arrived there.

48 Joseph, op. cit.
49 Joseph, op. cit.
50 Ibid.
51 Unpublished letter from the archives of Madame Roman Maspero.
52 Mondor, op. cit., p. 320.
53 George Meredith, who had incautiously set out with Wyse in 1861 on a walking tour, reported on his return: 'The fact is, the dear old boy is irritable exceedingly: tiffs twenty times a day and now and then a sulk. Then ensues reconciliation. ... You may imagine this schoolboy sort of thing is not to my taste. When one does meet a woman, one prefers to have her in petticoats.' And John Payne, who had also been on excellent terms with Wyse, was soon writing to Mallarmé: 'Above all, believe nothing Wyse tells you about me.' (16 December 1872.)
54 See T. Wright, *Life of John Payne*, London, 1919, p. 31.
55 Payne dedicated the first poem in his *Songs of Life and Death* to Wagner and did much to contribute to his sudden vogue in England by causing the 'Cosmopolitan Sextet' to play certain works which were then practically unknown.
56 'Sainte'.
57 'Hérodiade'.
58 *The Masque of Shadows*, London, 1870.
59 'Les hérésies artistiques'.
60 Letter to Michel Baronnet, 3 July 1872.
61 Letter to Mrs H. Whitman, October 1876.
62 *The Poetical Works of John Payne*, privately printed, London, 1892, vol. II, p. 181.
63 See the dedication in ibid.
64 Mallarmé made a second, rapid visit to London in July 1872, to report on the second International Exhibition. His article appeared in *L'Illustration* on 20 July.
65 7 July 1875. See *The Letters of Algernon Charles Swinburne*, ed. E. Gosse and T. Wise, London, 1918, p. 226.
66 The first number was published in December 1875 and the review lasted only six months.
67 Mallarmé mentions in this context Chatto & Windus and Henry King, Payne's publisher.
68 Gosse, in his *French Profiles* (London, 1905), says he met Mallarmé in London and introduced him to Swinburne. Mallarmé and Swinburne did not in fact meet till some years later, in Paris. Gosse's memoirs were written in his old age and his memory may have played him false.
69 On his return to Paris from this visit, Mallarmé expressed his thanks to O'Shaughnessy for 'having made yourself known to me in such a charming way', but a letter dated 27 December 1875 reveals that the two men had met a few days earlier, for the first time ('enfin nous nous connaissons'). The explanation may be that O'Shaughnessy introduced himself briefly during one of Mallarmé's visits to the museum and before he himself left on his holiday.
70 Wright, op. cit., p. 45.
71 It has been alleged that O'Shaughnessy, after letting fall a number of fossilised fish skeletons, fitted the parts together as they came to hand, heads,

tails and bones, thus creating at least one entirely new species, which is perhaps on view in the Natural History Museum today.

72 Unpublished letter quoted by Marianna Ryan in *La Revue de Littérature comparée*, June–September 1958.

73 *Vathek* did not in fact appear till the following spring.

74 A. Fontainas, *Mes Souvenirs du Symbolisme*, Paris, 1928, p. 187.

75 The *National Observer* published, among others, 'Crise de vers' in March 1892 and 'Magie' in January 1893.

76 'Solennité' in 'Notes sur la théâtre', *National Observer*, May 1892.

77 *Ecrits divers sur Stéphane Mallarmé*, Paris, 1950, p. 9.

3 Verlaine's England

Unless otherwise stated, letters from Verlaine are quoted from *Correspondance de Paul Verlaine*, 3 vols, ed. Ad. van Bever, Paris, 1922–9. Verlaine's poems are quoted from *Verlaine: Oeuvres poétiques complètes*, ed. Y. Le Dantec and J. Borel, Bibliothèque de la Pléiade, Paris, 1968. Works by Rimbaud are quoted from *Arthur Rimbaud: Oeuvres complètes*, ed. Roland de Renéville and Jules Mouquet, Editions de Cluny, Paris, 1932.

1 Karl Marx, *Lettres à Kugelmann, 1862–1874*, Paris, 1930, p. 151.

2 See M. Vuillaume, 'Mes Cahiers rouges', no. IX, in *Cahiers de la Quinzaine*, Paris, 1914, p. 35.

3 'Laeti et errabundi' in *Parallèlement*.

4 A. Adam, *Paul Verlaine*, Paris, 1935, p. 8.

5 A. Rimbaud, 'Bonheur' in *Les Illuminations*.

6 In the famous 'Lettre du Voyant', addressed to Demeney on 15 May 1871, Rimbaud had proclaimed, 'Le poète se fait *voyant* par un long, immense et raisonné *dérèglement* de *tous les sens*. Toutes les formes d'amour, de souffrance, de folie; il cherche lui-même, il épuise en lui tous les poisons, pour n'en garder que les quintessences.' The idea was not especially original, but no one, perhaps, has sought the Absolute with more reckless passion than did Rimbaud.

7 'Vers pour être calomnié' in *Jadis et Naguère*.

8 'Laeti et errabundi'.

9 Ibid.

10 Letter to E. Lepelletier, 15 April 1873. *Correspondance*, vol. I.

11 Adolphe Retté, *Le Symbolisme*, Paris, 1903, pp. 102–10.

12 Marie Belloc Lowndes, *Where Love and Friendship Dwelt*, London, 1943, p. 156. The hope expressed by Verlaine was distinctly unrealistic, since Mathilde had in fact remarried several years previously.

13 'Ariettes oubliées II' in *Romances sans Paroles*.

14 A. Rimbaud, 'Vagabonds' in *Les Illuminations*.

15 F. Régamey, *Verlaine dessinateur*, Paris, 1896, p. 22.

16 This house was demolished in 1938. The numbers must have been changed in the interval, since the commemorative plaque, installed in 1922 by Paul Valéry in the presence of the French ambassador, was placed on the façade of no. 38.

17 A. Rimbaud, 'Délires I', in *Une Saison en Enfer*.

18 'Streets' in *Romances sans Paroles*.

19 Probably to Philomène Boudin, 27 November 1893. *Correspondance*, vol. II. (Lettres 'aux chères amies') Verlaine may have been referring to the syphilis from which he suffered so much towards the end of his life.

20 'Sonnet boiteux' in *Jadis et Naguère*.

21 'Fog' in *Chair*.

22 'There' in *Amour*. The manuscript is dated 1881 (Bibliothèque Doucet).

23 *Romances sans Paroles*. Most of the poems directly inspired by England are contained in the section entitled 'Aquarelles'.

24 A. Rimbaud, 'Mauvais sang' in *Une Saison en Enfer*.

25 Cazals and Verlaine first met several years later, so Cazals' sketches are done from imagination and from Verlaine's own descriptions.

26 Matuszewicz was an officer of the French Army who had joined the Communards. Verlaine and Rimbaud had hopes of him, but he seems to have faded quickly out of their lives.

27 In 'Premiers vers' collected in *Oeuvres poétiques complètes*.

28 Ford Madox Ford, *Mightier than the Sword*, London, 1938, p. 264.

29 This unknown poet may well have been John Payne, who often visited Madox Brown and was just beginning to make a name for himself.

30 See Sir Edmund Gosse, *French Profiles*, London, 1913, p. 314.

31 'Laeti et errabundi'.

32 This manuscript has never been recovered.

33 Camille Barrère had been educated at an English public school, but had run away to France to fight for the Commune. He had returned to London as an exile and later became French ambassador to London. The episode was recounted by him in his old age to Mr Vernon Underwood.

34 'Birds in the Night' in *Romances sans Paroles*.

35 *Rimbaud raconté par Paul Verlaine*, Paris, 1934, p. 60.

36 A. Rimbaud, 'Adieu' in *Une Saison en Enfer*.

37 A. Rimbaud, 'Mauvais sang' in ibid.

38 A. Rimbaud, 'Nuit de l'Enfer' in ibid.

39 G. Jean-Aubry, in his interesting account, 'Paul Verlaine et l'Angleterre', *La Revue de Paris*, October and December 1918, makes a great deal of this Kate and believes that 'Child-Wife' was addressed to her. This seems unlikely. Verlaine's letters, poems and reminiscences all stress this child-like aspect of Mathilde, but the poem may have had something of Kate too, for Verlaine speaks of her 'aigres cris poitrinaires, hélas!' There is no record that Mathilde was ever tubercular, whereas the description of Kate in 'A poor young Shepherd' suggests she may have been so.

40 'Ariettes oubliées V' in *Romances sans Paroles*.

41 'Green' in ibid.

42 'La neige à travers la brume' in *Bonheur*.

43 'Ariettes oubliées III' in *Romances sans Paroles*.

44 Cit. Delahaye, *Verlaine*, p. 164.

45 A. Rimbaud, 'Villes II' in *Les Illuminations*.

46 A. Rimbaud, 'Vagabonds' in ibid.

47 A. Rimbaud, 'Délires I' in *Une Saison en Enfer*.

48 Mr Vernon Underwood quotes this report, discovered by him in the Bibliothèque du Musée des Archives de la Police, in Paris. See *Verlaine et l'Angleterre*, Paris, 1956, p. 117.

49 Later Royal College Street.

50 See F. Lefèvre, *Entretiens avec Paul Valéry*, Paris, 1926, p. 14.
51 In *Hospital*, a series of poems describing Henley's own experience during his long illness, had been refused by practically every London editor because of its realistic tone and free-verse form.
52 Letter written from London, 12 December 1875, *Correspondance*, vol. III.
53 A. Rimbaud, 'Délires I' in *Une Saison en Enfer*.
54 E. Delahaye, *Verlaine*, Paris, 1919, p. 10.
55 'Sonnet boiteux' in *Jadis et Naguère*.
56 'L'immensité de l'humanité' in *Sagesse*.
57 'Un conte' in *Amour*.
58 'Myself as a French master', *Fortnightly Review*, July 1894.
59 Verlaine's account varies with that given later by Mrs Andrews to M. Jean-Aubry. See Aubry, op. cit.
60 Verlaine refers to her in his own account (see 'Myself as a French master') as Lily, but his memory was never reliable.
61 'Myself as a French master'.
62 Ibid.
63 'Londres' in *Poèmes divers*. See *Oeuvres poétiques complètes*.
64 Rimbaud, Delahaye and Lepelletier were all acting as temporary schoolmasters at about this time. 'Que de pions!' exclaimed Verlaine (Letter to Delahaye, 1 May 1875, *Correspondance*, vol. III).
65 'Myself as a French master'.
66 'At the beginning of his career', noted Félix Régamey (op. cit., p. 7), 'Verlaine had in him the stuff of a great draughtsman, but it remained unrecognised by the public and by himself.'
67 Mr Andrews never realised his ambition. He became very well-known locally as an ardent free-mason, a church-warden and a lay preacher, but the rest of his life was spent in Stickney, where he died at the age of forty-seven.
68 'Myself as a French master'.
69 See *Correspondance*, vol. III.
70 'J'ai naguère habité le meilleur des châteaux', *Amour*.
71 'J'avais peiné comme Sisyphe' in *Sagesse*.
72 'Paul Verlaine in Lincolnshire, by one who knew him', *TP's Weekly*, 2 December 1904.
73 'Un conte' in *Amour*.
74 Underwood has given an interesting analysis of the influence of the English hymnal on Verlaine's work, op. cit., pp. 220–31.
75 To G. Jean-Aubry, 27 July 1917. See Aubry, op. cit.
76 Annotations on the manuscripts in the Bibliothèque Doucet, Paris.
77 'L'échelonnement des haies' in *Sagesse*.
78 'Kaleidoscope' in *Jadis et Naguère*.
79 The poems of the Stickney period are scattered throughout the various volumes that appeared between 1881 and 1883, principally in *Sagesse* and *Amour*. Many of them show a return to the Parnassian conventions which Verlaine had abandoned under the influence of Rimbaud.
80 'A Germain Nouveau' in *Dédicaces*.
81 *Poésies d'Humilis* published anonymously, Paris, 1924, with a preface by E. Delahaye.
82 'Poèmes contemporains de *Sagesse*'.
83 Letter to Jean Richepin, 27 July 1875.

84 'Myself as a French master'.
85 Verlaine, whose recollections of this period became rather confused with the passage of time, says in 'Myself as a French master' that the owner of this grotto was his Italian friend, Signor Cella.
86 'Myself as a French master'.
87 'Bournemouth' in *Amour*.
88 'Myself as a French master'.
89 Westburn Terrace no longer exists and the site of the school is occupied by the Sandbourne Hotel in Poole Road.
90 *John Bull's Weekly*, 9 June 1906.
91 'Bournemouth' in *Amour*.
92 Ibid.
93 Ibid.
94 Lepelletier finally arranged for *Romances sans Paroles* to be printed in Sens, while Verlaine was in prison in Mons.
95 'Bournemouth' in *Amour*.
96 'Un veuf parle' in *Amour*.
97 'Ballade en rêve' in *Amour*.
98 This house is still known today as 'Remington'.
99 Mr Remington seems to have been referring to the actual period of Verlaine's engagement and did not mention the subsequent months spent as a holiday tutor.
100 'Lucien Létinois XV' in *Amour*.
101 'Vers pour être calomnié' in *Jadis et Naguère*.
102 For example, Garnier's portrait of Rimbaud, painted in 1872.
103 'Lucien Létinois XIII'.
104 'Myself as a French master'.
105 'Lucien Létinois XXIII'.
106 Ibid.
107 Letter from Miss Edith Grantley, quoted by Underwood, op. cit., p. 343.
108 'Lucien Létinois VI'.
109 Ibid., XV.
110 Ibid.
111 Ibid., VIII.

4 Lecturing in England: Mallarmé and Verlaine

Letters by Verlaine are quoted from *Correspondance de Paul Verlaine*, 3 vols, ed. Ad. van Bever, Paris, 1922–9. Poems by Verlaine are quoted from *Verlaine: Oeuvres poétiques complètes*, ed. Y. Le Dantec and J. Borel, Bibliothèque de la Pléiade, Paris, 1968. Letters from Mallarmé are quoted from *Stéphane Mallarmé: Correspondance*, vol. I, 1862–71; vol. II, 1871–85; vol. III, 1886–9, Gallimard, Paris, 1959–69.

1 Vermersch had died insane in 1878.
2 Letter to Arthur Symons, 2 October 1890. See *The Letters of Oscar Wilde*, ed. R. Hart-Davis, London, 1962, p. 276.
3 Obituary notice by Charles Whibley in *Blackwood's Magazine*, November 1898.
4 According to V. S. Pinto, of all the members of the Rhymers' Club who

considered themselves to be English Symbolists, only Symons and Yeats had really studied Mallarmé or had read Laforgue or Rimbaud. (See *Crisis in English Poetry, 1880–1940*, London, 1951, p. 15.)

5 26 March 1892. Henley edited the *National Observer* from 1889 to 1893. The journal was entitled *Scots Observer* for the first two years.

6 William Rothenstein, *Men and Memories*, London, 1931, vol. I, p. 127.

7 *La Revue encyclopédique*, 1 September 1895.

8 To R. de Montesquiou, 25 October 1893. *Correspondance*, vol. III.

9 'My visit to London', *Savoy*, April 1896.

10 'Fountain Court' in *Dédicaces*.

11 In 'My visit to London'.

12 Manuscript letter in the Bibliothèque Doucet, Paris.

13 See p. 50.

14 On 5 December 1893. See *Correspondance*, vol. III.

15 Stuart Merrill, *Prose et Vers*, Paris, 1929, p. 174.

16 'My visit to London'.

17 Michael Field, *Works and Days*, London, 1933, p. 189.

18 'Paul Verlaine's lecture at Barnard's Inn', 'Poèmes divers' in *Oeuvres poétiques complètes*.

19 This incident is reported by G. Jean-Aubry in 'Verlaine et l'Angleterre', *La Revue de Paris*, October and December 1918.

20 Arthur Symons, *The Symbolist Movement in Literature*, London, 1899, p. 35.

21 'My visit to London'.

22 Holbrook Jackson, *The Eighteen Nineties*, London, 1923, p. 35.

23 'Fountain Court' in *Dédicaces*.

24 Sir Charles Oman, *Memories of Victorian Oxford and of some Early Years*, London, 1941, p. 209.

25 Rothenstein, op. cit., vol. I, p. 138.

26 Oliver Elton, *Frederick York Powell*, Oxford, 1906, vol. II, p. 414.

27 Ibid., vol. I, appendix B, p. 455.

28 Ibid., p. 153.

29 'My visit to London'.

30 'Oxford' in 'Poèmes divers' in *Oeuvres poétiques complètes*.

31 'Non, il fut gallican, ce siècle, et janseniste!' in *Sagesse*.

32 Aubry, op. cit.

33 'My visit to London'.

34 Ibid.

35 'Souvenir de Manchester' in *Dédicaces*.

36 This lecture was printed in the *Fortnightly Review*, September 1894.

37 'Souvenir de Manchester'.

38 'My visit to London'.

39 See note on *La Musique et les Lettres* in *Stéphane Mallarmé, Oeuvres complètes*, p. 1601.

40 Charles Baudelaire, 'Correspondances' in *Les Fleurs du Mal*.

41 Paul Claudel in a letter to Mallarmé dated 25 March 1895, cit. Henri Mondor, *Vie de Mallarmé*, Paris, 1941, p. 710.

42 Paul Valéry, 'Au concert Lamoureux' in *Commerce*, 1930, no. xxvi.

43 Henry James, *English Hours*, London, 1905, p. 245.

44 Mariana Thompson, 'Mallarmé et ses amis britanniques', thesis, Paris, 1954 (in the Bibliothèque de la Sorbonne).

45 Obituary notice in *Blackwood's Magazine*, April 1930.
46 Thompson, op. cit.
47 Elton, op. cit., vol. I, p. 457.
48 Ibid., p. 158.
49 Mondor, op. cit.
50 Powell's translation of *La Musique et les Lettres* has unfortunately disappeared.
51 Introduction to *La Musique et les Lettres* (*Oeuvres complètes*, p. 642).
52 'Déplacement avantageux', a sort of introduction to the actual text of *La Musique et les Lettres*, appeared in part under the title of 'Le fonds littéraire' in *Le Figaro*, 17 August 1894, and in part in *La Revue Blanche*, April 1894.
53 'Déplacement avantageux'. Paul Bourget, who had visited Oxford a few years earlier, had returned with the same impression of the idyllic existence of a Fellow. See 'Sensations d'Oxford'.
54 Letter to Marie and Geneviève, 6 March 1894.
55 'Las de l'amer repos'.

5 Aestheticism and Imperialism: Paul Valéry in London

1 D. Brogan, *The Development of Modern France*, London, 1940, p. 183.
2 *La Revue des deux mondes*, 1 June 1892.
3 'Brada', *Notes sur Londres*, Paris, 1893.
4 L. Daudet, *Vingt-neuf mois d'exil*, Paris, 1927.
5 P. Bourget, *Etudes et Portraits*, Paris, 1895.
6 Preface to Marcel Schwob: *Oeuvres complètes*, vol. I, Paris, 1927.
7 Ibid.
8 He translated *Moll Flanders* in 1894.
9 M. Schwob, *Spicilège*, Paris, 1896, p. 124.
10 'Paul Valéry—Fauteuil xxxviii' in the series *Les Quarante* (Alcan, Paris, 1931).
11 'Réponse' in *Commerce*, 1932, no. xxix.
12 Ibid.
13 'My chief object has been to figure out as simply and clearly as possible exactly how I function as a whole: i.e., composed as I am of world, body, and thoughts.' 'Analecta XIX' in *Analects*, trans. Stuart Gilbert, *Collected Works of Paul Valéry*, vol. XIV, Routledge & Kegan Paul, London, 1970, p. 280.
14 'My early days in England', *Bookman's Journal*, December 1925.
15 Ibid.
16 André Gide–Paul Valéry: *Correspondance 1890–1942*, NRF, 1955, p. 205.
17 Ibid.
18 H. Marillier, cit. Holbrook Jackson, *The Eighteen-Nineties*, London, 1923, p. 117.
19 V. Larbaud, *Ce vice impuni, la lecture: domaine anglais*, Paris, 1925, p. 74.
20 R. L. Stevenson, *Memories and Portraits*, London, 1887, p. 158. Henley is portrayed under the name of 'Burly'.
21 Wilfrid Scawen Blunt, *My Diaries 1888–1914*, London, 1919, vol. II, p. 66.
22 F. Lefèvre, *Entretiens avec Paul Valéry*, Paris, 1926, p. 14.
23 André Gide–Paul Valéry, op. cit., p. 198.
24 'My early days in England'.
25 Ibid.

26 Ibid.
27 Ibid.
28 Ibid.
29 M. Schwob, *Spicilège*, p. 125.
30 *Lettres à Quelquesuns*, Paris, 1952, p. 51.
31 Manuscript entitled 'Ebauche autobiographique d'un cahier', reproduced in the catalogue of the Paul Valéry Centenary Exhibition at the Paris Bibliothèque Nationale, 1971.
32 Manuscript in the archives of Madame Agathe Valéry-Rouart.
33 See *Paul Valéry: Oeuvres*, vol. II., Bibliothèque de la Pléiade, 1960.
34 The manuscript of 'Le Yalou' in the Bibliothèque Doucet is dated 1895, but the date is uncertain and the tale was probably completed somewhat later.
35 'Témoignage d'amitié au peuple de la Grande Bretagne', *Le Figaro*, 5 July 1938.
36 W. E. Henley's preface to C. de Thierry, *Imperialism*, London, 1898.
37 Steevens became an outstanding war correspondent, wrote *With Kitchener to the Omdurman*, and was killed at the siege of Ladysmith.
38 W. E. Henley, 'To R.F.B.' in *Rhymes and Rhythms*, London, 1892.
39 'My early days in England'.
40 Letter to Pierre Louÿs, 12 October 1898. *Lettres à Quelquesuns*, p. 60.
41 'My early days in England'.
42 Introduction by Valéry to the English translation of *La Soirée avec Monsieur Teste*, trans. Merton Gould, London, 1936.
43 'My early days in England'.
44 'Although he was a pure Latin, he had something of the British type, preferably that of a statesman, with his regular features, the thick, vigorous moustache, the hair parted almost in the middle' (lecture by Agathe Valéry-Rouart in Oxford, 25 February 1969). However, Valéry's account of his visit to Meredith shows that he himself was very conscious of the 'foreignness' of his appearance.
45 It was not till 1923 that the Company paid its first dividends.
46 See *Le Temps*, 5 January 1896.
47 'An immense movement of solidarity is growing up between the descendants of the Dutch and French colonialists. They refuse to submit to the British yoke.' *La Patrie*, 21 April 1896.
48 Manuscript letter in the archives of Madame Agathe Valéry-Rouart.
49 'My early days in England'.
50 Lionel Decle, *Three Years in Savage Africa*, London, 1898, p. 563.
51 Ibid. (Preface).
52 'My early days in England'.
53 Sir D. Malcolm, *The British South Africa Company, Incorporated by Royal Charter*, privately printed, London, 1939, p. 29.
54 Cit. P. Champion, *Marcel Schwob et son temps*, Paris, 1927, p. 133.
55 André Gide–Paul Valéry, op. cit., p. 262.
56 Manuscript entitled 'Notes autobiographiques 1896' reproduced in the catalogue of the Paul Valéry Centenary Exhibition. Bibliothèque Nationale, Paris, 1971.
57 Manuscript in the archives of Madame Agathe Valéry-Rouart.
58 Introduction to the English translation of *La Soirée avec Monsieur Teste*.
59 Cit. Champion, op. cit., p. 131.

60 Cit. H. Massis, 'La nuit de Londres', *La Parisienne*, October 1954.
61 'Choses Tues', trans. Hilary Corke, *Collected Works of Paul Valéry*, vol. II, Routledge & Kegan Paul, London, 1970, pp. 155–6.
62 *Horizon*, May 1946.
63 *La Parisienne*.
64 Letter to Marcel Schwob, dated April 1896, cit. Champion, op. cit., p. 132.
65 Lefèvre, op. cit., p. 16.
66 'Avant-propos' to *Regards sur le monde actuel* in *Oeuvres*, vol. II.
67 Manuscript letter in the archives of Madame Agathe Valéry-Rouart.
68 André Gide–Paul Valéry, op. cit., p. 263.
69 V. Larbaud, 'Fauteuil xxxviii'.
70 Lecture delivered in Oxford, 25 February 1969.
71 *Les cahiers du Sud*, winter, 1946, special number, 'Hommage à Paul Valéry'.

6 Valery Larbaud and the 'Heart of England'

Unless otherwise stated, works by Valery Larbaud are quoted from *Valery Larbaud, Oeuvres*, ed. G. Jean-Aubry and Robert Mallet, Bibliothèque de la Pléiade, Paris, 1958.

1 W. S. Blunt, *My Diaries 1888–1914*, London, 1919, vol. II, p. 2.
2 J. de la Poulaine, *L'Anglomanie*, Paris, 1900.
3 Robert Mallet in *La Nouvelle Revue Française*, special number, 'Hommage à Valery Larbaud', February 1957.
4 *La complainte du vieux marin* (ed. Vanier), Paris, 1901.
5 Manuscript letter dated 5 September 1902 (Fonds Valery Larbaud, Vichy).
6 *Journal intime d'A. O. Barnabooth*. For the various avatars and editions of the Barnabooth journal, biography and poems, see Jacqueline Famerie, 'Essai de bibliographie chronologique de Valery Larbaud', appendix to the Pléiade edition, *Valery Larbaud: Oeuvres*.
7 *Beauté, mon beau souci*.
8 *Journal intime d'A. O. Barnabooth*.
9 'Voeux du poète' in *Poésies d'A. O. Barnabooth*.
10 Manuscript letter (Fonds Valery Larbaud, Vichy).
11 'Madame Tusseaud's' (sic), in *Poésies d'A. O. Barnabooth*.
12 'Londres' in *Poèmes par un riche amateur* (lines omitted from the definitive version published in 1913).
13 'Londres' in *Poésies d'A. O. Barnabooth*.
14 'Trafalgar Square la nuit' in ibid.
15 'Europe IX' in *Poèmes par un riche amateur*.
16 'Matin de novembre, près d'Abingdon' in *Poésies d'A. O. Barnabooth*.
17 'Europe II' in *Poèmes par un riche amateur*.
18 *Biographie d'A. O. Barnabooth*, preceding *Poèmes par un riche amateur*. This biography was replaced in the 1913 edition by Barnabooth's *Journal intime*.
19 'Ode' in *Poésies d'A. O. Barnabooth*.
20 *L'Oeuvre d'Art Internationale*, March–April, 1904.
21 'Coventry Patmore', *La Nouvelle Revue Française*, September–October 1911.
22 *Mon plus secret conseil*.
23 *Ce vice impuni, la lecture: domaine anglais*, Paris, 1925, p. 40.
24 'Le devoir avant tout' in *Poèmes par un riche amateur*. This poem, eliminated

from the later edition, is followed by a note: 'Written during a walk between the Albert Hall and the Mall, 25 May 1905', but there is no trace of a visit by Larbaud to London at this date, when he appears to have been in Italy with 'Isabelle', the heroine of *Mon plus secret conseil.*

25 Patrick MacCarthy, 'Valery Larbaud, critic of English literature', thesis, Oxford, 1968.

26 Undated manuscript letter in the Fonds Valery Larbaud, Vichy.

27 'Notes sur G. K. Chesterton', *La Phalange*, December 1908.

28 'Francis Thompson', *La Phalange*, June 1909 (with translations).

29 'Tono-Bungay by H. G. Wells', *La Phalange*, August 1909.

30 *Le coeur de l'Angleterre*, Paris, 1971, p. 109. During his lifetime, Larbaud opposed the publication of his notes in book form, feeling that many of them consisted of 'notes and impressions, not of travels, but of country walks. . . . Frankly, they would bore people who have not been in Warwickshire'.

31 *La Nouvelle Revue Française*, August 1910. Preface to Paul Claudel's translation of Chesterton's 'Christian Paradoxes', signed 'V.L.'.

32 'Notes sur Chesterton', *La Phalange* December 1908.

33 'Note on Sally Bishop by Temple Thurston', *La Phalange*, January 1909.

34 Note on Robert Ross, 'Aubrey Beardsley', *La Phalange*, March 1909.

35 'William Ernest Henley', *La Phalange*, July–August 1910.

36 'Le devoir avant tout' in *Poèmes par un riche amateur.*

37 *Journal d'A. O. Barnabooth.*

38 Ibid.

39 In *Enfantines.*

40 *Le coeur de l'Angleterre*, p. 84.

41 Ibid, p. 85.

42 Letter to H. Buriot-Darsiles, 21 June 1912, cit. G. Jean-Aubry, *Valery Larbaud, sa vie et son oeuvre*, Monaco, 1941, vol. I, p. 201.

43 *Beauté, mon beau souci.*

44 *Le coeur de l'Angleterre*, p. 115.

45 Ibid., p. 105.

46 'Douze villes ou paysages' in *Jaune Bleu Blanc.*

47 Marcel Arland, Preface to *Valery Larbaud, Oeuvres.*

48 Manuscript letter in the Fonds Valery Larbaud, Vichy.

49 Francis Jammes and Valery Larbaud: *Lettres inédites*, Paris, 1947. Letter dated 17 November 1911. Mrs Hardie, a friend of the Meynells, confirmed in an interview with Patrick MacCarthy, quoted in his thesis, 'that Larbaud had met Pound in Granville Place'.

50 'Coventry Patmore', *La Nouvelle Revue Française*, September–October 1911.

51 'Lettres anglaises', *La Nouvelle Revue Française*, August 1913.

52 'Weston-super-Mare', in *Poésies diverses.*

53 Manuscript letter to his mother, August 1909. Fonds Valery Larbaud, Vichy.

54 'Douze villes ou paysages' in *Jaune Bleu Blanc.*

55 *Le coeur de l'Angleterre*, p. 99.

56 Francis Jammes-Valery Larbaud, op. cit., July 1911.

57 Aubry, op. cit., says that Larbaud moved into Lawrence Mansions in 1909. However, a letter to Marcel Ray, dated 1910, is still headed with the Dover Street address.

58 *Beauté, mon beau souci.*

59 *La Nouvelle Revue Française*, October 1911.

60 *Beauté, mon beau souci.*
61 In a lecture on Samuel Butler, given by Valery Larbaud in Paris at Adrienne Monnier's bookshop on 3 November 1920, he compared Butler, 'not with the legenday Epicurus . . . of the erotic poems and the drinking songs, but the true Epicurus, the founder of one of the great sects of antiquity', and added, 'I often think that if Epicurus had lived today, he would have written many of the things Butler wrote.'
62 Ibid.
63 Manuscript letter to his mother, dated 1910, Fonds Valery Larbaud, Vichy.
64 *Lettres à André Gide*, Paris–Hague, 1948, 23 March 1912.
65 Letter to F. Jammes, 8 May 1900, cit. MacCarthy, op. cit.
66 *La Nouvelle Revue Française*, October 1911.
67 Letter to Paul Claudel, 14 July 1911, cit. Aubry, op. cit., p. 178.
68 Manuscript letter, undated, Fonds Valery Larbaud, Vichy.
69 Francis Jammes–Valery Larbaud, op. cit., 17 November 1911.
70 'You are one of the very rare people who are able to spiritualise their sensual emotions', Jacques Rivière wrote to him after reading *Beauté, mon beau souci.*
71 Francis Jammes–Valery Larbaud, op. cit., 17 November 1911.
72 Letter dated 21 May 1911 or 1912, cit. V. Milligan in his thesis 'Valery Larbaud anglicist', New York, Columbia University, 1953.
73 Cit. Aubry, op. cit., p. 165.
74 Ibid.
75 *La Nouvelle Revue Française*, August 1910. Preface to Paul Claudel's translation of Chesterton's 'Christian Paradoxes'.
76 22 June 1911, cit. Aubry, op. cit., p. 171.
77 William Rothenstein, *Men and Memories*, London, 1931, vol. II, p. 344.
78 Letter to Arthur Fontaine, dated 17 July 1911. See note by G. Jean-Aubry in Valery Larbaud, *Lettres à Andre Gide*, p. 154.
79 Francis Jammes–Valery Larbaud, op. cit., 22 June 1911.
80 Manuscript letter, dated 11 October 1911. Fonds Valery Larbaud, Vichy.
81 Manuscript letter, undated. Fonds Valery Larbaud, Vichy.
82 Symons says in his account that his visitors came on to him from Conrad's house, but his mental illness often blurred his recollections and Aubry, who had the story from Larbaud himself, is more reliable.
83 André Gide in the special number of *La Nouvelle Revue Française*, 'Hommage à Valery Larbaud', February 1957.
84 Quoted by G. Jean-Aubry in a letter to Valery Larbaud dated 25 August 1925. See G. Jean-Aubry–Valery Larbaud, *Correspondance 1920–1935*, Paris, 1971.
85 Aubry, op. cit., p. 176n.
86 Cit. Milligan, op. cit.
87 Valery Larbaud became ill in 1935 and remained paralysed for the rest of his life. The new edition of *Ce vice impuni, la lecture: domaine anglais* was among the many projects he was unable to realise.
88 Letter written from Edinburgh to H. Buriot-Darsiles, 7 July 1913, cit. Aubry, op. cit., p. 229.
89 'Europe IX' in *Poésies d'A. O. Barnabooth.*
90 Manuscript note, probably written in 1915, cit. Aubry, op. cit., p. 237.
91 See P. Mahillon in *La Nouvelle Revue Française*, February 1957.

7 Four Englands

1 Charles Baudelaire, 'Paysages, Salon 1845'. See *Baudelaire: Oeuvres complètes*, Bibliothèque de la Pléiade, Paris, 1961, p. 849.
2 Paul Valéry, *Ecrits divers sur Stéphane Mallarmé*, Paris, 1950, p. 11.
3 Mallarmé and Valéry, after being master and disciple, became close friends. Valéry's early style and most of his poetry, is unmistakably influenced by Mallarmé and there has always been a tendency to associate the two. The essential difference between the two men seems to me that Mallarmé had a strongly religious nature, although God was replaced in adolescence by Art, and then by what he called the Idea. Mallarmé's whole life, in fact, may be seen as a processus parallel to that of the saint towards complete holiness. Valéry's processus, on the contrary, was totally mental—a striving to possess the world through the operation of the intellect.
4 Valéry, op. cit.
5 For example, the opening line of the sonnet, 'Le vierge, le vivace et le bel aujourd'hui'.
6 'Magie'.
7 'Streets II' in *Romances sans Paroles*.
8 Manuscript article by Cazals, 'Pêle-mêle souvenirs', given by the author to Mr Cranmer-Byng in 1895, quoted by V. Underwood in *Verlaine et l'Angleterre*, Paris, 1956.
9 'Toute grace et toutes nuances', *La Bonne Chanson* II.
10 'Rhumbs', trans. Stuart Gilbert, in *Collected Works of Paul Valéry*, vol. XIV, Routledge & Kegan Paul, London, 1970.
11 Ibid.
12 R. Soulairol, *Paul Valéry*, Paris, 1952, p. 89.
13 'L'innommable' in *Poésies d'A. O. Barnabooth*.
14 *La Nouvelle Revue Française*, February 1957.
15 Preface to *Valery Larbaud: Oeuvres*, Bibliothèque de la Pléiade, Paris, 1958.
16 Larbaud's translation of *Ulysses* appeared in 1929.

Note

Since this book went to press, Chatelain's letters to Mallarmé have appeared in vol. IV of Mallarmé's *Correspondance*, Gallimard, Paris, 1974.

Index

Index

Index

Index

('L'Assaut'), 25; 'Les Fenêtres', 8, 25, 26–7; 'Hérodiade', 29, 36; 'Igitur', 29; 'Las de l'amer repos', 123; 'Plainte d'Automne', 24; 'Prose (pour Des Esseintes)', 14, 46; 'Pour votre chère morte, son ami', 34; 'Renouveau' ('Vere Novo'), 19; 'Sainte', 36; 'Soupir', 118; prose writings: *Autobiographie*, 8, 37; *Crise de vers*, 18, 27; *Déplacement avantageux*, 122, 203n; *Les Hérésies artistiques: l'art pour tous*, 11, 59; 'Magie', 32; *La Musique et les Lettres* (lecture), 117, 120, 121; preface to *Vathek*, 32, 42, 185; *Solennité*, 43; *Vers et musique en France*, 102; translations: 'The Raven' (Poe), 40; educational works: *Les Mots anglais*, 29, 40, 188; *Recueil de Nursery Rhymes*, 18, 196–7n

Mallet, Robert, 156, 157
Manchester, 113
Manet, Edouard, 39, 40, 41, 56
Manning, Cardinal, 90, 167
Mansfield, Katherine, 192
Marlowe, Christopher, 80
Marzials, Théo, 42
Marston, Dr, 36
Marsy, Eliane de (pseudonym of Kate and Ettie Yapp), 17
Marx, Eleanor, 46, 66
Marx, Karl, 44, 45, 46, 57, 66, 69
Maspero, Gaston, 32, 33, 34
Massis, Henri, 151, 152
Matuszewicz, Ludomir, 57, 200n
Maupassant, Guy de, 124
Mauté de Fleurville, Mathilde (Mme P. Verlaine), 48–9, 50, 59–61, 63, 65, 67, 68, 84, 86, 91–2, 104, 190
Maxwell, Dr, 77
Mendès, Catulle, 29, 30, 32, 35, 38, 40, 124
Mercure de France, La, 126, 193
Meredith, George, 3, 100, 104, 109, 127, 128, 133, 134–7, 138, 141, 142, 150, 154, 163–4, 167, 174, 176, 191
Merrill, Stuart, 106
Meynell, Alice, 133, 150, 166, 167, 168, 170, 174, 177, 178–9, 180, 183, 185
Meynell, Everard, 174

Meynell, Wilfrid, 166, 167, 168, 170, 174, 177, 185
Meyring, Karl, 45
Midsummer Night's Dream, 76
Mistral, Frédéric, 31, 32
Mondor, Dr Henri, 18, 118
Monmouth, 175
Montesquiou, Robert de, 103
Monticelli, Andrea, 53
Moore, George, 42, 74, 101
Morley, John, 30
Morris, William, 40, 109
Murchison, William, 96

Napoleon I, Emperor, 35, 136, 137, 138, 141, 150, 154, 191
Napoleon III, Emperor, 2, 5, 19, 30, 35
National, Le, 35
National Gallery, 53, 130
National Observer, 43, 102, 118, 131, 139
New Forest, 96
Newman, Cardinal, 167
New Review, 115, 131, 152, 153
New Weekly, 184
Nineteenth Century, 131
Noakes, Miss, 96
Norman, H. de V., 55
Notre-Dame-de-France, 5, 195n
Nouveau, Germain, 83–5, 86, 88, 95
Nouvelle revue française, 180
Nyasaland, 146

O'Connor, Daniel, 156, 166, 169, 170, 177, 180
O'Connor, Father Patrick, 96
Ogden, Mr, 24
Old Compton Street, 45
Oman, Sir Charles, 108
Orlestone, 183
Orpen, William, 174
O'Shaughnessy, 40, 41, 42, 58, 101, 120, 124, 198n
Oudet, Joseph-Emile, 46
Ouida, 193
Oxford, 111, 123, 141, 204n
Oxford Magazine, 111, 115, 117
Oxford Movement, 167

Pall Mall Gazette, 115, 118, 139, 140, 141, 146

Index

Schwob, Marcel, 70, 101, 118, 127, 128, 133, 134, 137, 140, 141, 147, 150, 163, 191, 193
Scott, Sir Walter, 125
Scratton, Rev. Mr, 77
Senate, 115
Sénonais, Le, 11
Shaw, G. B., 109, 133
Shakespeare, William, 18, 19, 57, 66, 76, 96, 113, 114, 124, 127, 172, 187, 191
Shannon, James, 126
Shelley, P. B., 31, 42
Shrewsbury, 173
Sickert, Walter, 134, 140
Siddal, 'Lizzie' (Mrs D. G. Rossetti), 6, 195n
Silvy, Alfred, 85
Smith, Dr, 85
Society for the Protection of the Morals of the French of Leicester Square, 6
Soho, 5–7, 44, 100, 107, 113, 123, 139, 156
Solent Collegiate School, 96
Solférino Restaurant, 139, 140, 148
Sommer, Mr de, 69
Sommerard, du, 28
Souden, John, 85, 88, 95
Southey, Robert, 31
Spectator, 3
Spread Eagle, 45
Stanley, Henry, 146
Steevens, George, 140, 146, 205n
Stendhal, 3
Stevenson, R. L., 109, 126, 127, 133
Stickney, 73, 74, 79, 80, 81, 82, 85, 86, 87, 90, 91, 95, 96, 97, 99, 114, 190
Stratford on Avon, 172
Studio, 132
Suppé, 128
Sussex Bell Inn, Haslemere, 119
Swinburne, A. C., 3, 6, 17, 30–1, 33, 37, 40, 41, 45, 58, 59, 71, 100, 124, 168, 174, 195n, 198n
Symbolists, 25, 27, 40, 101, 125, 127, 130, 135, 140, 183, 191
Symonds, Dr, 31
Symons, Arthur, 42, 101, 102–3, 104, 105, 106, 107, 112, 114, 121, 127, 131, 133, 183, 193

Taine, Hippolite, 2, 126, 168
Taylor Institute, Oxford, 110, 115, 117, 118, 120
Temps, Le, 144
Tennyson, Alfred, Lord, 3, 18, 37, 66, 77, 92, 96, 100, 124, 130, 166, 168, 195n
Thackeray, W. M., 18, 181
Thomas, Dylan, 192
Thompson, Francis, 167, 168, 174, 179, 180, 193
Thompson, 'Matabele', 140
Times, The, 2, 5, 139
Tintern Abbey, 175
Tobin, Agnes, 182, 183, 184, 185
Torio Koyata, Viscount, 138
Toulouse-Lautrec, Comte Henri de, 132
Tower of London, 53, 130
'Towers Subway', 53
Transvaal, 144, 146, 147
Treherne, Thomas, 168
Trench, Herbert, 185
Tristan, Flora, 66
Turner, Joseph, 53, 126, 134, 176
Tussaud's, Madame, 53, 128, 130, 159
Tynan, Katherine (Katherine Hinkson), 133, 167
Tyrrell, Father, SJ, 166, 174

Uganda, 146
Underwood, Vernon, 98, 189
L'Union démocratique, 45

Valéry, Paul, 1, 29, 116, 124–54, 190–2, 205n; in London as child, 128; second stay in London; 128–41; as employee of the 'Chartered Company', 141–54; and Decle, 144, 145–6, 191; and Gide, 128, 130, 134, 140, 142, 147, 190; and Gosse, 132; and Henley, 132, 133, 134, 139, 140, 142, 152; and Huysmans, 150; and Lord Kelvin, 137, 138; and Larbaud, 128 (quoted), 154; and Louÿs, 128, 141; and Mallarmé, 29, 43 (quoted), 116 (quoted), 128, 129, 188; and Meredith, 128, 134–7, 138, 141, 142, 150, 154; and Pennells, 132, 134, 138, 191; and Pollock, 136, 137, 138,

Index

Victor's Restaurant, 45
Vigfüssen, 109
Vigny, Alfred de, 57
Villiers de l'Ile Adam, J.–M., 29
Villon, François, 36, 127, 133
Vinci, Leonardo da, 143
Vuillaume, Maxime, 46
Vuillet's Restaurant, 84

Wagner, Richard, 36, 132
Wallace Collection, 53
Wallace, Richard, 47
Warren, Mrs, 171, 172
Warwick, 171, 172, 173, 192
Warwickshire, 172
Watts-Dunton, Theodore, 100
Wells, 175
Wells, H. G., 133, 185, 193
West, Tom, 75
Weston-super-Mare, 124, 192
Whale Inn, Boston, 87
Wheeler, Stephen, 174, 177, 185
Whibley, Charles, 101, 102, 117, 118, 122, 123, 131, 132, 138, 140, 144, 152
Whibley, Leonard, 117

Whistler, James McNeill, 42, 101, 118, 131, 132, 133, 134, 140, 146, 166, 176
Wilberforce, William, 58
Wilde, Oscar, 42, 101, 108, 126, 131, 149, 166, 176
Williams, Ernest, 140, 152
Windmill Street, 7, 21
Woolwich, 53
Wratislav, Theodore, 101
Wyse, William Bonaparte, 31–2, 35, 40, 41, 42, 197n, 198n

Yapp, George Wagstaff, 12, 18, 28, 32
Yapp, Martha (Mrs George), 12, 18, 28, 33
Yapp, Florence, 18, 28, 32
Yapp, Harriet (Ettie), 12, 13, 14, 17, 20, 22, 23, 28, 30, 32, 33, 34, 197n
Yapp, Isabelle, 18, 28, 32
Yapp, Kate, 12, 17, 20, 28
Yarningdale, 172
Yeats, William Butler, 101, 133
Yellow Book, 114, 149
York, 186

Zamoyski, General, 24
Zola, Emile, 38, 39, 101, 124, 128, 130